Knowledge
Relationship
Destiny
A Catechism of the Christian Faith

Analee B. Dunn

Patrick Visger

Bethesda
Christian Church

14000 Metropolitan Parkway • Sterling Heights, MI 48312
Phone (586) 264-2300 • Fax (586) 264-2751
E-mail: bcc@bethesdachristian.org
www.bethesdachristian.org

Knowledge Relationship Destiny *A Catechism of the Christian Faith*. Second Edition.

Unless otherwise indicated, scripture taken from *The Holy Bible, King James Version*

Scripture marked (NASB) taken from *New American Standard Bible ®*, copyright © 1960, 1962, 1963, 1968, 1971, 1972, 1973, 1975, 1977, 1995 by The Lockman Foundation. Used by permission.

Scripture marked (NCV) taken from *The Holy Bible, New Century Version*, copyright © 1987, 1988, 1991 by Word Publishing. Used by permission.

Scripture marked (NIV) taken from the *Holy Bible, New International Version ®*, copyright © 1973, 1978, 1984, by International Bible Society. Used by permission of Zondervan. All rights reserved.

Scripture marked (NKJV) taken from *The Holy Bible, New King James Version*, copyright © 1979, 1980, 1982 by Thomas Nelson, Inc. All rights reserved.

Scripture marked (NLT) taken from the *Holy Bible, New Living Translation*, copyright © 1996. Used by permission of Tyndale House Publishers, Inc., Wheaton, Illinois 60189. All rights reserved.

Cover photo: "Christian Cross 26" by Waiting For The Word,
https://www.flickr.com/photos/waitingfortheword/5602666438,
licensed under CC BY 4.0, http://creativecommons.org/licenses/by/4.0.
Cropped to fit page.

ISBN-10: 0996338101
ISBN-13: 978-0-9963381-0-3

● *5 6 3 1 1 5 0 4 2 0* ●

What is Catechism?

Catechism comes from the Greek *katecheo*, having to do with teaching. *Katecheo* is found in Galatians 6:6 where the Apostle Paul notes that he who is taught, or catechized, should share with him who is teaching, or catechizing. A catechism then is a teaching, and is often in the form of questions and answers.

Jesus frequently taught believers and skeptics alike by posing and taking questions. He was once asked "Lord, we don't know where you are going, so how can we know the way?" Jesus answered, "I am the way and the truth and the life. No one comes to the Father except through me. If you really knew Me, you would know my Father as well. From now on, you do know Him and have seen Him." In that brief question and answer is the meaning of catechism: a question is posed, and a clear concise answer gives revelation of God. *Knowledge Relationship Destiny—A Catechism of the Christian Faith* is a question/answer catechism written to address today's culture.

Effective Foundational Teaching

A catechism provides an effective way to answer the fundamental questions of Christianity. Using the technique of a question/answer catechism, students discover the truth of the Bible as they gain **knowledge** of the Word of God, encounter the life changing power of a **relationship** with Jesus Christ, and learn that they have a **destiny** in the Kingdom of God.

Conventions Used in This Text

The answers given to the questions within this text are complete yet concise. In most cases scripture referenced in an answer is given in the sidebar. When scripture is directly quoted within an answer, a reference and a Bible version are noted. In some cases a scripture is referenced which is not given in the text or the sidebar. These scriptures are prefaced with the word *see*, or *see also*, an indication that the scripture supports the answer and should be referenced in a Bible of choice.

All scripture in the text unless otherwise noted is taken from T*he Holy Bible, King James Version.*

Scripture marked NASB is taken from *New American Standard Bible.*

Scripture marked NCV is taken from *The Holy Bible, New Century Version.*

Scripture marked NIV is taken from the *Holy Bible, New International Version.*

Scripture marked NKJV is taken from *The Holy Bible, New King James Version.*

Scripture marked NLT is taken from the *Holy Bible, New Living Translation.*

Table of Contents

Lesson 1 - In the Beginning was the Word 1
1. What is the Bible? 2
2. Where did the Bible come from? 2
3. When was the Bible written? 2
4. Can I really believe what's in the Bible? 2
5. Isn't the Bible just stories—is there any proof that the stories in the Bible actually happened? 3
6. Can the Bible really be the inspired Word of God? ... 4
7. Why is the Bible organized the way that it is? 5
8. What is a testament? 6
9. What are the books of the Old Testament and how are they organized? 6
10. What are the books of the New Testament and how are they organized? 7
11. Who decided what should or should not be included in the Bible? 7
12. There are so many different Bibles, are they all the same? 10
13. What about all the different English language Bibles, are they all the same? 10
14. The Bible is so old; can it really apply to life today? 10

Lesson 2 - The Great I Am 13
1. Who is God? 14
2. Can the trinity of God be understood? 14
3. Can God be three in one? 15
4. How can I know that God exists? 16
5. Has anyone ever seen God? 16
6. In what forms did God reveal Himself? 16
7. Does God have a name? 17
8. Many names were ascribed to God, but did God ever tell mankind His name? 18
9. Doesn't everyone worship the same God? 18

Lesson 3 - The Existence of Evil 21
1. Is there more to our world than what our eyes can see? 22
2. What is the invisible realm? 22
3. What are angels? 22
4. What is the purpose of angels? 23
5. How do the angels carry out God's will? 23

6. What do angels look like? 24
7. Who was Lucifer? 24
8. How did Lucifer reject God? 24
9. What is sin? 24
10. What is iniquity? 25
11. How did evil come into the world? 25
12. Did the evil of Satan affect the world? 26
13. How can we deal with the influence of Satan and demons? 26

Lesson 4 - Seven Days of Creation 29
1. Who is the creator? 30
2. Why did God create? 30
3. When did God initiate creation? 30
4. How did God create everything? 31
5. How long did it take God to create everything? 31
6. In what order was everything created? 31
7. Is man different than the animals? 33
8. After woman was created, what was man's relationship to be with her? 33
9. What was man and woman's purpose after creation? 34
10. What does it mean that man was created in "the image" of God? 34

Lesson 5 - Sin Enters the World 39
1. What was life like when Adam and Eve were created? 40
2. What restriction did God place on Adam and Eve? 40
3. Did Adam and Eve obey God's instruction? ... 40
4. What happened? 40
5. How did God respond to the sin of Adam and Eve? 41
6. God said Adam and Eve would die, but they didn't, how could this be? 42
7. Is God unfair to punish everyone for the sin of Adam? 42
8. Did God make any provision to free man from the sin nature? 43
9. What is a covenant? 43
10. Did God punish Jesus for our sins? 44

Lesson 6 - The Flood and the Tower 47

1. What happened after Adam and Eve were driven out of the garden? 48
2. How great was the wickedness on the earth? 48
3. What did Noah do to be spared by God? 49
4. Why did God send the flood? 49
5. What's an ark? 49
6. How long did it take to build the ark and how big was it? 50
7. How many of each kind of animal was aboard the ark? 50
8. Was the flood global? 50
9. How long did the flood last? 50
10. What are some of the changes that occurred on earth as a result of the flood? 51
11. What was the covenant God made with Noah and his descendants? 51
12. What is the sign of this covenant? 51
13. After the flood, what did God command man to do, and what did man do? 51
14. What was the result? 52
15. What is the Tower of Babel's significance? 52

Lesson 7 - God's Covenant People 55

1. What were the aftereffects of God's confusing the languages at the Tower of Babel? 56
2. What were God's covenant promises to Abraham? 56
3. What was the sign of the Covenant God made with Abraham? 57
4. How did the nation promised through Abraham develop? 57
5. What did God instruct Moses to do? 58
6. What is the covenant God made through Moses? ... 58
7. How were Moses and the nation of Israel to keep their relationship with God? 58
8. What happened if someone broke the law? 59
9. What happened after Moses died? 59
10. What were God's covenant promises to David and the nation of Israel? 60
11. What happened to Israel? 60
12. If Israel fell as a nation, how could David's throne be eternal? 61

Lesson 8 - The Birth and Ministry of Jesus 65

1. Who is Jesus? 66
2. If Jesus is God, why was He born of a woman? 67

3. Why is the virgin birth so important? 67
4. Where was Jesus born? 67
5. What other unique occurrences are associated with the birth of Jesus? 68
6. Was Jesus raised differently because He was the Son of God? 68
7. How long was Jesus' ministry? 69
8. For what purpose did Jesus come to earth? 69
9. How did Jesus' life on earth come to an end? 69
10. Was Jesus the promised King from the line of David? 70

Lesson 9 - A Walk to the Cross 73

1. If Jesus never sinned, why did people seek to kill Him? 74
2. What happened that lead to Jesus' arrest? 74
3. What charges were brought against Jesus? 75
4. What happened after Jesus was sentenced to death? 78
5. Did Jesus go to hell? 79
6. Did Jesus really come back from the dead? 79
7. Why is the resurrection so important? 80

Lesson 10 - About Face 83

1. What happened after Jesus was resurrected? 84
2. Jesus is alive? 84
3. What was the significance of the life, death, and resurrection of Jesus? 85
4. How does one become a part of this New Covenant? 86
5. What is repentance? 86
6. Why is repentance necessary? 87
7. How can I repent? 88
8. How do I know my sins are forgiven? 89

Lesson 11 - Water Baptism 93

1. What follows repentance and forgiveness of sins? .. 94
2. What is a sacrament? 94
3. What is water baptism? 95
4. What is the outward sign in water baptism? 95
5. What is the inward work of the Holy Spirit in water baptism? 96
6. What is the "old man"? 96
7. What does circumcision have to do with water baptism? 96
8. Who should be baptized? 98

Lesson 12 - The Baptism of the Holy Spirit **101**

1. What happened after Jesus' ascension? 102
2. What did Jesus promise when He ascended? 103
3. Who is the Holy Spirit? 103
4. How did Jesus refer to the Holy Spirit? 103
5. How does the Bible record the coming of the Holy Spirit? 104
6. Does the Bible always refer to the coming of the Holy Spirit as the baptism of the Holy Spirit? 106
7. Does the baptism of the Holy Spirit occur today? . 107
8. What is the purpose of receiving the Holy Spirit? . 109

Lesson 13 - A Life of Worship **113**

1. Are the ten commandments relevant today? 114
2. What is worship? 114
3. Does God require worship? 115
4. What is the first commandment? 115
5. What is the purpose of the first commandment? ... 115
6. How should we keep the first commandment? 116
7. Is there a blessing in keeping the first commandment? 116
8. What is the second commandment? 116
9. What is the purpose of the second commandment? 116
10. What does God mean when He says He is jealous? 117
11. Does God forbid making images? 118
12. How should we keep the second commandment? 118
13. Is there a blessing in keeping the second commandment? 118
14. How do we worship God today? 118

Lesson 14 - Rest in Him **123**

1. What is a Christian? 124
2. What is the third commandment? 124
3. What is the purpose of the third commandment? . 124
4. How should we keep the third commandment? ... 125
5. Is it wrong to say, "I swear to God?" 125
6. Is there a blessing in keeping the third commandment? 126
7. What is the fourth commandment? 126
8. What is the purpose of the fourth commandment? 126

9. Is the sabbath day Saturday? 127
10. What is our day of rest? 128
11. What does belief in Christ have to do with rest? ... 128
12. Why do Christians worship on Sunday? 128
13. How should we keep the fourth commandment? 129
14. Is there a blessing in keeping the fourth commandment? 129

Lesson 15 - The Christian Family **133**

1. What is a Christian family? 134
2. What are the roles of husband and wife in a marriage? 134
3. What is the fifth commandment? 135
4. What is the purpose of the fifth commandment? .. 135
5. What does it mean to honor our father and mother? 136
6. Does honor extend to others in authority? 136
7. Must I obey my parents now that I am an adult? .. 137
8. Do parents have a responsibility in this commandment? 137
9. What is dedication of children? 138
10. How should we keep the fifth commandment? 138
11. Is there a blessing in keeping the fifth commandment? 138

Lesson 16 - Marriage and Divorce **141**

1. What is marriage? 142
2. What are the parameters of a Christian marriage? 142
3. Is sex before marriage a sin? 143
4. What is the seventh commandment? 144
5. What is the purpose of the seventh commandment? 144
6. What is adultery? 144
7. Isn't adultery and fornication the same thing? 145
8. How can lust be avoided? 146
9. Is adultery the only reason a Christian can be divorced? 146
10. How should we keep the seventh commandment? 146
11. Is there a blessing in keeping the seventh commandment? 146

Lesson 17 - Getting Along With Others 149
1. What is anger? 150
2. What is the sixth commandment? 150
3. What is the purpose of the sixth commandment? . 150
4. If I am angry with someone am I a murderer? 151
5. What does it mean to love my neighbor? 151
6. How should Christians reconcile their differences? 152
7. Doesn't the death penalty go against the sixth commandment? 153
8. What about abortion, is it murder? 153
9. How should we keep the sixth commandment? ... 154
10. Is there a blessing in keeping the sixth commandment? 154

Lesson 18 - Biblical Finance 157
1. What is a steward? 158
2. If we are stewards of what belongs to God, can we own property? 158
3. What is the eighth commandment? 158
4. What is the purpose of the eighth commandment? 159
5. What is stealing? 159
6. What is a tithe? 161
7. What is an offering? 161
8. What did Jesus teach about giving? 162
9. How should we keep the eighth commandment? 162
10. Is there a blessing in keeping the eighth commandment? 162

Lesson 19 - Living Honestly 165
1. Can my neighbor affect my goals and ambitions? 166
2. What is the ninth commandment? 166
3. What is the purpose of the ninth commandment? 166
4. What is bearing false witness? 167
5. Is it ever okay to lie? 168
6. How should we keep the ninth commandment? .. 168
7. Is there a blessing in keeping the ninth commandment? 168
8. What is the tenth commandment? 169
9. What is the purpose of the tenth commandment? 169
10. What does it mean to covet? 169
11. What are the results of coveting? 170
12. How should we keep the tenth commandment? .. 171
13. Is there a blessing in keeping the tenth commandment? 171

Lesson 20 - Leading and Serving 175
1. What is foot washing? 176
2. Is foot washing in the Bible? 176
3. What led to Jesus washing His disciples' feet? 177
4. What was the significance of Jesus washing feet? ..177
5. Is foot washing practiced today? 179
6. How is foot washing conducted? 179
7. Is there a blessing in foot washing? 179

Lesson 21 - Where Do I Go When I Die? 183
1. What happens when a Christian dies? 184
2. Where is a Christian's soul and spirit after death? 184
3. What happens when an unbeliever dies? 185
4. Is Sheol-Hades Hell? 185
5. Is there a resurrection of the dead? 186
6. Is there going to be a judgment? 186
7. What happens at the judgment? 186
8. Would a good God send people to Hell? 187
9. What are the rewards for the righteous? 187

Lesson 22 - Examine Yourself 191
1. What is the Lord's Supper? 192
2. What brought about the Lord's Supper? 192
3. How is Jesus our Passover? 192
4. What should we remember during the Lord's Supper? 193
5. How should we take the Lord's Supper? 194
6. What does it mean, a man must examine himself? 194
7. What does "not discerning the Lord's body" mean? 194
8. Are there blessings in taking the Lord's Supper? ...195

Lesson 23 - Prayer 199
1. What is prayer? 200
2. How should I pray? 200
3. Should I pray alone, or with others? 201
4. What is praying in the Holy Spirit? 201
5. When should I pray in tongues? 202
6. When I pray do I have to kneel? 202
7. Can I pray the same prayer more than one time? ..202
8. What if God doesn't answer my prayer? 203
9. I'm sick; whom should I ask to pray for me? 204
10. Why do the elders use oil? 204

Lesson 24 - The Importance of Belonging.............207

  1. What is the Church?.....................................208

  2. What is a local church?...............................209

  3. What is the purpose of a local church?.......209

  4. Who's in charge of a local church? 211

  5. How do pastors and elders get their authority?.....211

  6. What is the job of local church leaders? ...212

  7. What does it mean to submit to a local church?.....212

  8. I like my "TV church," must I belong to a local church?...213

  9. What does it mean to be confirmed in the faith?....213

10. Who should be confirmed? 213

11. When should one be confirmed? 214

12. How is confirmation administered? 214

Index...217

Index of Scripture 221

Lesson 1
In the Beginning was the Word

Scripture Reading

- Isaiah 55:3-4 and Jeremiah 31:31-34 (parallel prophecies)

- 2 Corinthians 3:6, 14 and Hebrews 9:15-18 (Old and New Covenant / Testament)

- Genesis 2:21; Isaiah 40:22 and Job 36:27-28 (knowledge in the Bible)

- Isaiah 40:8; Isaiah 55:11; Psalm 119:11; 2 Timothy 3:16; Hebrews 4:12 and 1 Peter 2:2 (the Word of God)

Introduction

In this lesson the Word of God, a standard and manual for life, is presented. People often question the validity of the Bible and its relevance for life application today. This lesson is organized to show that the Bible is indeed the Word of God, completely true and relevant today. The questions and answers given are progressive. They are first informative about the basics of the Bible, then building on one other, beginning with tangible evidence without requiring a passage or verse from the Bible. From this solid start, the lesson introduces scripture that agrees with documented history, and concludes with undeniable truth taken from the Word of God.

1. What is the Bible?

The Bible is a book of books, made up of a collection of 66 books. The word *bible* comes from the Greek word *Biblia*, meaning books. The Bible gives an account of man's time on earth and God's plan and purpose for the human race, and most importantly the way to salvation from sin and death through Jesus Christ.

2. Where did the Bible come from?

The Bible came from God. By the inspiration of His Spirit, more than 40 writers put His Word down in written format. Although many different literary styles were used, and even different languages, God inspired each writer to record His inerrant Word. Since that time the Word of God, inerrant in its original form, has been translated to many different languages.

3. When was the Bible written?

The Bible was written over a period of more than 1500 years, beginning about 1500 BC, as God inspired each writer to document His Word. The first part of the Bible, the Old Testament, was complete about 400 BC with 39 separate writings or books. God gave the second part of the Bible, the New Testament consisting of 27 books, in the latter part of the first century AD.

4. Can I really believe what's in the Bible?

The Bible is inspired and the original manuscripts are without error. There are well-documented transcription errors, particularly in passages that include numbers. However, the Bible is accurate, and without error represents the intents of the original inspired writers, so much so that we can confidently refer to it as the Word of God.

"For when any man of intelligence on the subject affirms the inerrancy of the Scriptures, he refers to these writings as they came from the hands of their authors, and not as they have come through the hands of uninspired copyists. In the Scriptures as thus defined, no man has yet successfully made out a single error in fact or in thought."[1]

---

[1] McGarvey, John W. *The Saturday Evening Post*, January 21, 1899

5. Isn't the Bible just stories—is there any proof that the stories in the Bible actually happened?

The Bible is the most investigated of all works of antiquity. The evidence that exists for the Bible and the events told in the Bible also exceeds that of any work of antiquity. Some examples:

Rosetta Stone

The Rosetta Stone was discovered in 1798 at Rosetta (Rashid) near the westernmost mouth of the Nile River, by an officer in Napoleon's Expedition to Egypt. The inscriptions helped in the understanding of ancient languages, thus greatly expanding the knowledge of biblical background and history.

Mesha Stele (Mesha or Moabite Stone)

The Mesha or Moabite stone is the first inscribed evidence of an event that took place in the Old Testament. Discovered in Palestine in 1886, the Stone parallels biblical history recorded in Second Kings, chapters 1 and 3. The stone is now displayed in the Louvre in France.[2]

Dead Sea Scrolls

One of the most dramatic discoveries of Biblical manuscript evidence dating back to 150 BC occurred within the past 100 years. In 1947, in a cave south of Jericho, a young shepherd discovered clay jars containing many leather scrolls of Hebrew and Aramaic writing, and fragmentary inscriptions. Following the initial discovery, further exploration of the area uncovered more clay jars containing scrolls and fragments. Fragments and sections of every book of the Old Testament, with the exception of the book of Esther, were identified, including an entire scroll of the book of Isaiah.

Balaam's Plaster Fragments

In 1967, pieces of plaster were discovered during excavations at Deir 'Alla in the Jordan River Valley that confirm the existence of Balaam and corroborate Numbers 22-24.[3]

---

[2] christianstudycenter.com
[3] Carnagey, Dr. Glenn. *Balaam: A Light to the Gentiles?*, CTS Journal, Volume 4, Number 4, October 1998: Chafer Theological Seminary

Isaiah 55:3-4
Incline your ear, and come unto me: hear, and your soul shall live; and I will make an everlasting covenant with you, even the sure mercies of David. Behold, I have given him for a witness to the people, a leader and commander to the people.

Jeremiah 31:31
Behold, the days come, saith the LORD, that I will make a new covenant with the house of Israel, and with the house of Judah.

Isaiah 40:22
It is he that sitteth upon the circle of the earth, and the inhabitants thereof are as grasshoppers; that stretcheth out the heavens as a curtain, and spreadeth them out as a tent to dwell in.

Job 36:27-28
[God] maketh small the drops of water: they pour down rain according to the vapour thereof: which the clouds do drop and distil upon man abundantly.

6. Can the Bible really be the inspired Word of God?

There is much in the Bible to verify that it is inspired of God and could not have possibly been contrived by man. The Old Testament prophets are but one example where God's revelations of events to unfold in the distant future were given to men. Also, it is nothing short of miraculous that men, born at different times and different places, never having met or given the opportunity to compare notes, would prophesy identical events.

Examples

- Isaiah 40:3, 5 and Malachi 3:1 prophesy that someone will precede and announce the coming of Jesus Christ.

- Isaiah 53:5; Zechariah 12:10 and Psalm 22:16 predict that the Messiah would be pierced.

- Isaiah 44:3 and Joel 2:28 foretell the sending of the Holy Spirit.

- Isaiah 55:3-4 and Jeremiah 31:31 prophesy the establishment of a new and everlasting covenant.

Moreover, the Bible is full of the wisdom of God, and has revealed truths and knowledge that man did not comprehend for hundreds of years.

Examples

- God told the prophet Isaiah that it was He that *sitteth upon the circle of the earth* (Isaiah 40:22). Hundreds of years before man theorized that the earth was a sphere, God had revealed it through His Word to the prophet. The word for circle here is translated from the Hebrew word *chug*, which, when in its masculine form as it is here, means "a circle, a sphere."[4]

- "Water evaporation was first used by the Phoenicians, Romans and Chinese to obtain salt from seawater. Large flats were filled with seawater and natural evaporation from the sun evaporated the water and left behind dry salt. The first boiling water evaporators in the US are traced back to the Onondaga Indians from the Syracuse, New York area in 1654."[5] But well before these times of the American Indians and the Phoenicians, Job spoke of evaporation cycles (Job 36: 27-28).

---

[4] Davidson, Benjamin. *The Analytical Hebrew and Chaldee Lexicon*, 1970: Zondervan
[5] Fink, Ronald G., *Environmental Science and Engineering*, May 2002, Wastewater Treatment By Evaporation

- Anesthesia was the most dramatic advancement in development of all medicine. Anesthetic dates to about A.D. 200, when Apuleius wrote, "If anyone is to have a member mutilated, burned or sawed let him drink half an ounce (mandrake root) with wine, and let him sleep till the member is cut away without any pain or sensation."[6] For some reason, the practice of drugging people before operating on them was discontinued during the Middle Ages. Anesthetic first came into modern medicine in the 19th century:

  - 1842 – First use of ether as anesthetic, Crawford Long (dentist)

  - 1845 – William Morton, a Massachusetts General Hospital doctor uses ether

  - 1846 – James Simpson uses chloroform

  Yet, the secret of operating on a person while they slept had been in the first book of the Bible all along (Genesis 2:21).

7. Why is the Bible organized the way that it is?

From the outside the Bible appears to be a large book that may take a long time to read. Although the Bible is bound as a single book, it is actually a collection of many books—66 in all. Some of the books are as short as one chapter, while others have many more—up to 150. Many books make it easier to read and study—it does not have to be read from cover to cover. The Bible is organized; consider it like a library where books are organized with a purpose in mind. The Bible is comprised of two main sections: the Old Testament and the New Testament, each with their own organization. The original Old Testament writings were primarily in the Hebrew language, and the majority of the New Testament was originally written in Greek.

Genesis 2:21
And the LORD God caused a deep sleep to fall upon Adam, and he slept: and he took one of his ribs, and closed up the flesh instead thereof;

---

[6] Walker, K. *The Story of Medicine*, 1954: London. Oxford Univ. Press.

2 Corinthians 3:6, 14
(God) hath made us able ministers of the new testament... But their minds were blinded: for until this day remaineth the same veil untaken away in the reading of the old testament; which veil is done away in Christ.

Hebrews 7:20
By so much was Jesus made a surety of a better testament.

Hebrews 9:15-18
And for this cause he is the mediator of the new testament, that by means of death, for the redemption of the transgressions that were under the first testament, they which are called might receive the promise of eternal inheritance. For where a testament is, there must also of necessity be the death of the testator. For a testament is of force after men are dead: otherwise it is of no strength at all while the testator liveth. Whereupon neither the first testament was dedicated without blood.

8. What is a testament?

A testament is a covenant (agreement) between God and man, as binding as a "last will and testament," which is an act whereby a person explicitly expresses their wishes to be carried out after death. The Old Testament and the New Testament are comprised of books pertaining to God's two main covenants with man (2 Corinthians 3:6, 14; Hebrews 7:20 and Hebrews 9:15-18).

9. What are the books of the Old Testament and how are they organized?

There are 39 books in the Old Testament, organized as follows:

- The Pentateuch (meaning five books), are the first five books of the Bible. They cover the beginnings (creation), the patriarchs of Israel, and the Laws given by God to Moses and the people of Israel.

  Genesis
  Exodus
  Leviticus
  Numbers
  Deuteronomy

- 12 History books, covering the rise, fall, and restoration of the nation of Israel.

  Joshua
  Judges
  Ruth
  1 and 2 Samuel
  1 and 2 Kings
  1 and 2 Chronicles
  Ezra
  Nehemiah
  Esther

- 5 poetry books.

  Job
  Psalms
  Proverbs
  Ecclesiastes
  Song of Solomon

- 17 prophetical books providing prophesies of a coming Savior, God's judgment of Israel and surrounding nations because of their sin, and of future events yet to be fulfilled. These are broken down into two divisions: 5 books of the Major Prophets and 12 books of the Minor Prophets.

Major:	Minor:
Isaiah	Hosea
Jeremiah	Joel
Lamentations	Amos
Ezekiel	Obadiah
Daniel	Jonah
	Micah
	Nahum
	Habakkuk
	Zephaniah
	Haggai
	Zechariah
	Malachi

10. What are the books of the New Testament and how are they organized?

There are 27 books that make up the New Testament and they are organized as follows:

• The four gospels—the life and ministry of Jesus Christ.	Matthew Mark Luke John
• One book of history of the beginnings of the New Testament Church.	Acts of the Apostles
• 21 epistles, or letters, to various people and churches. The letters set forth the doctrines of the New Testament Church.	Romans 1 and 2 Corinthians Galatians Ephesians Philippians Colossians 1 and 2 Thessalonians 1 and 2 Timothy Titus Philemon Hebrews James 1 and 2 Peter 1, 2, and 3 John Jude
• The final book of the New Testament is a letter, but it is better known as a prophetic book.	Revelation

11. Who decided what should or should not be included in the Bible?

The Bible was compiled over hundreds of years as each book or letter was inspired and came into existence. A canon (standard, or set of rules) was employed to ensure that only divinely inspired works were included.

- The Old Testament was well established before the coming of Jesus, primarily being compiled by the Israelite teacher and priest, Ezra, in the fifth century BC.

- The New Testament came together as writings were used authoritatively, followed by a formal process by early church leaders where books were authenticated by use of a canon.

One of the main standards of determining the authenticity is ensuring that a writing reveals Jesus Christ. Jesus is indeed shown in each of the 66 books of the Bible:[7]

Old Testament Book	Revelation of Jesus
Genesis:	The Seed of the Woman
Exodus:	The Passover Lamb—The Lamb of God
Leviticus:	The High Priest
Numbers:	The Star out of Jacob—The Morning Star
Deuteronomy:	The Prophet Like Moses
Joshua:	The Captain of Our Salvation
Judges:	The Messenger of Jehovah
Ruth:	Our Kinsman Redeemer
1 & 2 Samuel:	Lord and the seed of David
1 & 2 Kings & 1 & 2 Chronicles:	King of Kings, and Lord of Lords
Ezra and Nehemiah:	Lord of Heaven and Earth
Esther:	Our Heavenly Mordecai
Job:	The Living Redeemer
Psalms:	The Son of God
Proverbs & Ecclesiastes:	The Wisdom of God
The Song of Solomon:	The Chief Among Ten Thousand and Altogether Lovely
Isaiah:	Prophet of Grace and Glory
Jeremiah and Lamentations:	The Man of Sorrow
Ezekiel:	Our Great High Priest
Daniel:	Messiah Who is Cut Off, and the Stone that Fills the Earth
Hosea:	The Bridegroom Baring His Heart
Joel:	Jehovah Pouring out His Spirit
Amos:	The God of Israel
Obadiah:	Lord in His Kingdom
Jonah:	The Risen Prophet
Micah:	The Bethlehemite
Nahum:	The Bringer of Good Tidings
Habakkuk:	Lord in His Temple
Zephaniah:	Lord in the Midst of Israel
Haggai:	The Desire of All Nations
Zechariah:	The Lord of Glory
Malachi:	The Sun of Righteousness Rising

---

[7] Beall, M.D. *Christ in All the Scriptures* 1950: Bethesda Missionary Temple,

New Testament Book	Revelation of Jesus
Matthew:	King of the Jews
Mark:	Perfect Servant
Luke:	Perfect Man, The Virgin-Born Son of Man
John:	The Son of God
Acts:	The Ascended Lord
Romans:	The Lord of Righteousness
1 & 2 Corinthians:	The Firstfruits from Among the Dead
Galatians:	The Author of the Gospel
Ephesians:	Head and of the Church, His Bride
Philippians:	Our Ascended Lord
Colossians:	The Fullness of The Godhead
1 & 2 Thessalonians:	The Resurrection and the Life
1 & 2 Timothy:	Our Potentate
Titus:	God our Savior
Philemon:	Assumer of our Sin-Debt
Hebrews:	Our Great High Priest
James:	The Lord whose Coming Draws Nigh
1 & 2 Peter:	The Lamb of God and the Lord of Glory
1 & 2 & 3 John:	The Son of God
Jude:	The Coming Judge
Revelation:	The Lamb upon the Throne!

Dwight L. Moody penned a simple test of authenticity and a summary of why God gave us the Bible:

"The Bible sets forth two things—the cross and the throne.
The Old Testament points toward the cross (Jesus Christ).
The gospels tell the story of the cross.
The epistles point toward the throne (a resurrected Jesus in Heaven).
The revelation tells the story of the throne.
The Old Testament tells us what sin leads to, and ends with the words 'Lest I come and smite the earth with a curse.'(Malachi 4:6)
The New Testament shows us the way out of sin, and ends thus:
'The grace of our Lord Jesus be with you all.'
(Revelation 22:21)"

Isaiah 40:8
The grass withers and the flowers fall, but the Word of our God stands forever.

Isaiah 55:11
So shall my Word be that goeth forth out of my mouth: it shall not return unto me void, but it shall accomplish that which I please, and it shall prosper in the thing whereto I sent it.

Psalm 119:11
Thy Word have I hid in mine heart, that I might not sin against thee.

Matthew 4:4
But he answered and said, It is written, Man shall not live by bread alone, but by every Word that proceedeth out of the mouth of God.

Galatians 3:24
Wherefore the law was our schoolmaster to bring us unto Christ, that we might be justified by faith.

2 Timothy 3:16
All scripture is given by inspiration of God, and is profitable for doctrine, for reproof, for correction, for instruction in righteousness.

Hebrews 4:12
For the Word of God [is] quick, and powerful, and sharper than any two edged sword, piercing even to the dividing asunder of soul and spirit, and of the joints and marrow, and [is] a discerner of the thoughts and intents of the heart.

1 Peter 2:2
As newborn babes, desire the sincere milk of the Word, that ye may grow thereby:

12. There are so many different Bibles, are they all the same?

Some Bibles have more than 66 books and some have less. Bibles that have more than 66 books generally include additional books in the Old Testament called apocryphal books (from *apocryphus*, meaning secret). The apocryphal books were not considered authentic, and are not included in the Jewish Bible (confirmed by the discovery of the Dead Sea Scrolls). Hence the apocryphal books have been left out of most Christian Bibles.

A Bible that contains fewer than 66 books is likely a Jewish Bible (sometimes called Torah, Tanak, or Mikra) because it omits the New Testament.

13. What about all the different English language Bibles, are they all the same?

There are many variants of the Bible in the English language. It is good to use a Bible that has been proven over time and widely accepted. Such Bibles include the King James Version (KJV), the New American Standard Bible (NASB), and the New International Version (NIV). The KJV and the NASB are considered to be more literal in their translation from the languages of early manuscripts, where the NIV is more interpretive in its translation.

There are other English language Bibles that include much more interpretation (often termed paraphrases), rendering them easier to read but giving only a single perspective of the intent of the original writers. These Bibles include the Living Bible, the New Living Translation and the Message. Some versions have taken much liberty in their interpretations by removing the masculine references to God, the deity of Jesus, etc. and should be avoided.

14. The Bible is so old; can it really apply to life today?

The Bible has been around for a very long time, but God's Word is timeless and never grows old (Isaiah 40:8; Isaiah 55:11; Psalm 119:11; Matthew 4:4; Galatians 3:24; 2 Timothy 3:16; Hebrews 4:12 and 1 Peter 2:2).

Study Questions

1. Read Job 36:27-28 and Genesis 2:21. Do these passages that were written thousands of years ago help you to believe that the Bible is God's Word? Why or why not?_____

    _____

    _____

    _____

    _____

    _____

2. The Bible is not supported by history. Give some examples of why this statement is false._____

    _____

    _____

    _____

    _____

3. A friend tells you her Bible has more books in the Old Testament than your King James Version. Can you tell her why? _____

    _____

    _____

    _____

    _____

    _____

Lesson Journal

Use this section to record your thoughts on the topics in this lesson.

_____

_____

_____

_____

_____

_____

_____

_____

Lesson 2
The Great I Am

Scripture Reading

- Romans 1:18-23 (God seen in all creation)

- 1 Timothy 3:16 (mystery of the tri-unity of God)

- Jeremiah 10:10-11, 13:10 (one true God)

- John 1:1-14 (Jesus, God from the beginning)

- 1 John 5:7 (the Father, Son, and Holy Spirit are one)

- John 6:44 and Hebrews 11:6 (God draws people, they must believe)

- Exodus 3:14-15 and Proverbs 30:4 (the name of God)

- Psalm 115:4-8 (all other gods are man made)

Introduction

The concept of God may be familiar and comfortable to many, but the definition of who and what God is varies immensely among those who profess to believe in God, or a god. Debates abound regarding such things as God's supremacy, His will, His being, His oneness, and more. Though many volumes have been written, and many more are sure to come, this lesson focuses on describing the nature and character of God as succinctly as possible. Some of what is presented is merely an introduction that will be expanded further in later lessons, while the objective of this lesson is to establish the fundamental truths of God as presented in the Bible.

Colossians 2:9
For in him (Jesus) dwelleth all the fulness of the Godhead bodily.

Matthew 28:19
Go ye therefore, and teach all nations, baptizing them in the name of the Father, and of the Son, and of the Holy Ghost.

Jeremiah 10:10-11
But the LORD is the true God, he is the living God, and an everlasting king: at his wrath the earth shall tremble, and the nations shall not be able to abide his indignation. Thus shall ye say unto them, The gods that have not made the heavens and the earth, even they shall perish from the earth, and from under these heavens.

Jeremiah 13:10
This evil people, which refuse to hear my words, which walk in the imagination of their heart, and walk after other gods, to serve them, and to worship them...

Romans 1:21-23
Because that, when they knew God, they glorified *him* not as God, neither were thankful; but became vain in their imaginations, and their foolish heart was darkened. Professing themselves to be wise, they became fools, And changed the glory of the uncorruptible God into an image made like to corruptible man, and to birds, and fourfooted beasts, and creeping things.

1 Corinthians 8:4-6
We know that an idol is nothing in the world, and that there is none other God but one. For though there be that are called gods, whether in heaven or in earth, (as there be gods many, and lords many,) But to us there is but one God, the Father, of whom are all things, and we in him; and one Lord Jesus Christ, by whom are all things, and we by him.

1. Who is God?

God is the creator of all, with no beginning and no end, existing in three distinct persons, a trinity:

- The Father
- The Son
- The Holy Spirit

The Bible refers to these three as the "Godhead", for they are one (Colossians 2:9 and Matthew 28:19).

Any other god is man-made. False gods have been conjured up in man's imagination and manufactured by his hand to serve a purpose or fill a need at a convenient time. However, a true God, a living God, a triune God has always existed. God the Father, God the Son, and God the Holy Spirit are identified in scripture as separate and distinct persons, yet participants in all the attributes of God (Jeremiah 10:10-11, 13:10; Romans 1:21-23 and 1 Corinthians 8:4-6).

2. Can the trinity of God be understood?

God has revealed things about His nature and character that can be fully understood, but there are concepts of God that man will never fully comprehend. God has revealed His tri-unity, although it is a mystery:

> *1 Timothy 3:16*
> *And without controversy great is the mystery of godliness: God was manifest in the flesh, justified in the Spirit, seen of angels, preached unto the Gentiles, believed on in the world, received up into glory.*

While the human mind cannot comprehend God completely, some examples of the nature of a trinity can be used to gain insight into the concept of a three-in-one God.

Examples of Tri-unity

Everything that exists in the natural realm can be described in terms of three components: Matter, space and time, each of these also being examples of tri-unity.

- Matter exists in three states—solid, liquid, or gas.

- Space is three dimensional, where all things exist with a length, width, and height.

- Time is infinite, but existed in the past, is now present, and will exist in the future. It is a single continuum with three parts, past, present, and future.

3. Can God be three in one?

God the Father, God the Son, and God the Holy Spirit are identified in scripture as separate and distinct persons, yet the same in substance and equal in power and glory (1 John 5:7).

Many examples of the attributes of God given in the Bible are ascribed to God the Father, God the Son, and God the Holy Ghost. Some examples are given below.

1 John 5:7
For there are three that bear record in heaven, the Father, the Word, and the Holy Ghost: and these three are one.

Attributes:	God the Father	God the Son	God the Holy Spirit
The One True God	1 Chronicles 29:10 Matthew 6:9 Philippians 1:2 2 John 1:3	John 1:1 Colossians 2:9	1 John 5:7 Acts 5:3-4
God is Love	1 John 4:7-8, 16 Song of Solomon 2:4	Ephesians 5:25	Romans 15:30
God is Light	1 John 1:5	John 1:4-5 John 8:12	Daniel 5:14
God is Immutable (never changes)	Malachi 3:6	Hebrews 13:8	Isaiah 59:21
God is Omnipresent (everywhere)	Ephesians 4:6	Matthew 28:20	Psalm 139:7-10
God is Omnipotent (all powerful)	Genesis 17:1	Matthew 28:18	Romans 15:19
God is Omniscient (all knowing)	1 John 3:20	John 16:30	1 Corinthians 2:11
God is Eternal (no beginning, no end)	Psalm 90:2	Micah 5:1-2 Revelation 1:8	Isaiah 59:21 Galatians 6:8
God is the Creator	Isaiah 64:8 Malachi 2:10 Matthew 5:45	John 1:3 Colossians 1:16	Genesis 1:2 Job 33:4
God is our Savior	Psalm 89:26	Matthew 1:21 2 Timothy 2:10	Psalm 51:12 2 Thessalonians 2:13

Romans 1:20 NIV
For since the creation of the world God's invisible qualities--his eternal power and divine nature--have been clearly seen, being understood from what has been made, so that men are without excuse.

Psalm 19:1 NASB
The heavens are telling of the glory of God; And their expanse is declaring the work of His hands.

John 6:44
No man can come to me, except the Father which hath sent me draw him.

Hebrews 11:6 NASB
But without faith it is impossible to please Him, for he who comes to God must believe that He is, and that He is a rewarder of those who diligently seek Him.

2 Peter 3:9 NKJV
The Lord is not slack concerning His promise, as some count slackness, but is longsuffering toward us, not willing that any should perish but that all should come to repentance.

John 4:24
God is a Spirit: and they that worship him must worship him in spirit and in truth.

John 1:18
No man hath seen God at any time; the only begotten Son, which is in the bosom of the Father, he hath declared him.

1 Timothy 1:17
Now unto the King eternal, immortal, invisible, the only wise God, be honour and glory forever and ever. Amen.

Colossians 1:15
(Jesus) is the image of the invisible God, the firstborn of every creature.

Exodus 3:2
And the angel of the LORD appeared unto him in a flame of fire out of the midst of a bush: and he looked, and, behold, the bush burned with fire, and the bush was not consumed.

Hebrews 7:1 NIV
This Melchizedek was king of Salem and priest of God Most High.

Exodus 13:21
And the LORD went before them by day in a pillar of a cloud, to lead them the way; and by night in a pillar of fire, to give them light; to go by day and night:

4. How can I know that God exists?

God is clearly seen in all that He has created. His word declares that creation is a testimony to God, and that all who choose to ignore this undeniable display of His supremacy are without excuse (Romans 1:20 and Psalm 19:1).

God's creation declares His handiwork, and is part of a process He initiates to draw people to believe in Him and enter into a relationship with Him. God reveals Himself to those who respond to His drawing and diligently seek Him (John 6:44; Hebrews 11:6; and 2 Peter 3:9).

5. Has anyone ever seen God?

God is not a being that we can describe in our natural world, or comprehend with our natural senses. We cannot touch Him, smell Him or see Him. God is invisible. God's Word confirms that man has never seen Him, but He has presented an image in various forms for man to look upon (John 4:24; John 1:18; 1 Timothy 1:17 and Colossians 1:15).

6. In what forms did God reveal Himself?

God revealed Himself in various forms to men:

- **The Angel of the Lord**

  When the angel of the Lord is given attributes of God or exercises the prerogatives of God, this is a *theophany*, a self-manifestation of God (Exodus 3:2, see also Genesis 16:7-14, 21:17-21, 22:11-18, 31:11, 31:13; Judges 2:1-4, 5:23, 6:11-24, 13:3-22; 2 Samuel 24:16 and Zechariah 1:12, 3:1, 12:8). This angel of the Lord does not appear in the Bible after the incarnation of Jesus, and hence is taken to be a pre-incarnate appearance of Jesus Christ.

- **Melchizedek**

  Melchizedek was our High Priest, a representation of Jesus Christ, who appeared to Abraham (Hebrews 7:1).

- **In the burning bush**

  The Angel of the Lord appeared to Moses in the form of a bush on fire, but not being consumed (Exodus 3:2).

- **A pillar of cloud and a pillar of fire**

  God revealed Himself as a pillar of cloud and a pillar of fire to direct Moses and the nation of Israel (Exodus 13:21).

- **His Glory, a cloud**

    God revealed His Glory when He came to dwell in the tabernacle (the temple) (Exodus 40:34 and 1 Kings 8:11).

- **In the Flesh (Jesus Christ):**

    Jesus was God made flesh (John 1:14).

- **The Holy Spirit:**

    The Holy Spirit appeared as the form of a dove and as cloven tongues of fire (John 1:32 and Acts 2:3-4).

7. Does God have a name?

Knowing how to address God, what to call Him, has always been a question of interest. The verse below from the book of Proverbs shows that the question of how to address God is indeed a question of old. This verse from Proverbs is also prophetic, with a reference to God's Son. (Proverbs 30:4)

In the Bible, God was ascribed different names as He revealed His power and character. Each name reflected a divine attribute of God.

Name of God	Meaning
EL:	Strength, Mighty, Almighty, God
ELOHIM:	God the Creator and Preserver, Mighty and Strong (occurs over 2500 times in O.T.)
EL SHADDAI:	God Almighty, God all sufficient
EL ELYON:	Most High
ADONAI:	Lord (Capital 'L', lower case, 'ord') "Master" or "Lord"
JEHOVAH:	LORD (occurs over 6000 times in the Old Testament)
JEHOVAH-JIREH:	The Lord will provide
JEHOVAH-ROPHE:	The Lord who heals
JEHOVAH-NISSI:	The Lord our banner
JEHOVAH-M'KADDESH:	The Lord who sanctifies
JEHOVAH-SHALOM:	The Lord our peace
JEHOVAH-TSIDKENU:	The Lord our righteousness
JEHOVAH-ROHI:	The Lord our shepherd
JEHOVAH-SABAOTH:	The Lord of Hosts; The commander of the angelic host
KURIOS:	Supreme in authority, God, Lord, Master
CHRISTOS:	Anointed, Messiah
ABHIR:	Mighty One
THEOS:	God (Greek equivalent of Elohim)
THEOTES:	Godhead

Exodus 40:34
Then a cloud covered the tent of the congregation, and the glory of the LORD filled the tabernacle.

1 Kings 8:11
So that the priests could not stand to minister because of the cloud: for the glory of the LORD had filled the house of the LORD.

John 1:14
And the Word was made flesh, and dwelt among us, (and we beheld his glory, the glory as of the only begotten of the Father,) full of grace and truth.

John 1:32
And John bare record, saying, I saw the Spirit descending from heaven like a dove, and it abode upon him.

Acts 2:3-4
And there appeared unto them cloven tongues like as of fire, and it sat upon each of them. And they were all filled with the Holy Ghost, and began to speak with other tongues, as the Spirit gave them utterance.

Proverbs 30:4
Who hath ascended up into heaven, or descended? Who hath gathered the wind in his fists? Who hath bound the waters in a garment? Who hath established all the ends of the earth? What is his name, and what is his son's name, if thou canst tell?

8. Many names were ascribed to God, but did God ever tell mankind His name?

God revealed His name, and His Son Jesus Christ confirmed He was one with the Father by using the same name. Moses, an Old Testament leader of Israel, asked God His name and God gave this reply:

Exodus 3:14-15
*And God said unto Moses, I AM THAT I AM: and he said, Thus shalt thou say unto the children of Israel, **I AM** hath sent me unto you. And God said moreover unto Moses, Thus shalt thou say unto the children of Israel, The LORD God of your fathers, the God of Abraham, the God of Isaac, and the God of Jacob, hath sent me unto you: **this is my name for ever**, and this is my memorial unto all generations.*

The Hebrew word for "I am" transliterated in English is called the tetragrammaton, which is the four letter combination *JHVH* (sometimes rendered *YHWH*). The Hebrews' reverence for the name of God was such that they used this ineffable (unspeakable) combination of letters. Vowel points have since been added, and God's name is rendered Jehovah (or Yahweh). In English Bibles this name of God is generally translated as LORD (occurs over 6000 times in the Old Testament).

Exodus 6:2
And God spake unto Moses, and said unto him, I am the LORD (JHVH): And I appeared unto Abraham, unto Isaac, and unto Jacob, by the name of God Almighty (El Shaddai), but by my name JEHOVAH (JHVH) was I not known to them.

9. Doesn't everyone worship the same God?

There is one God only, the living and true God consisting of three persons in the Godhead, the Father, the Son, and the Holy Spirit; and these three are one true, eternal God, the same in substance, equal in power and glory. All other gods are manufactured by the imagination of man. (Deuteronomy 6:4; 1 Corinthians 8:4 and Psalm 115:4-8)

Deuteronomy 6:4
Hear, O Israel: The LORD our God is one LORD: And thou shalt love the LORD thy God with all thine heart, and with all thy soul, and with all thy might.

1 Corinthians 8:4
As concerning therefore the eating of those things that are offered in sacrifice unto idols, we know that an idol is nothing in the world, and that there is none other God but one.

Psalm 115:4-8
Their idols are silver and gold, the work of men's hands. They have mouths, but they speak not: eyes have they, but they see not: They have ears, but they hear not: noses have they, but they smell not: They have hands, but they handle not: feet have they, but they walk not: neither speak they through their throat. They that make them are like unto them; so is every one that trusteth in them.

Study Questions

1. Is there anything in this lesson that has helped you to understand, or better understand, the tri-unity of God? Explain. _____

   _____

   _____

   _____

   _____

   _____

2. Read 1 Corinthians 8:4 and Psalm 115:1-8. Knowing these scriptures, what would you say to someone who says we all worship the same god?_____

   _____

   _____

   _____

   _____

Lesson Journal

Use this section to record your thoughts on the topics in this lesson.

_____

_____

_____

_____

_____

_____

_____

_____

_____

_____

_____

_____

_____

Lesson 3
The Existence of Evil

Scripture Reading

- Colossians 1:15-16 (there are things created both visible and invisible)

- Hebrews 1:14 (angels are spirit beings)

- Daniel 10:6 (what one angel looks like)

- Psalm 103:20-21 (why God created angels)

- Isaiah 14:4,12-15 and Ezekiel 28:12-17 (the fall of Lucifer)

- 1 John 3:4 and James 4:17 (sin)

- Genesis 6:5, 12 (evil/iniquity of men); Joshua 22:17 (evil/iniquity of a city); and Psalm 85:2 (evil/iniquity of peoples/nations)

- 1 Peter 5:8 (Satan affecting our world)

- Ephesians 6:11,13-18 (the armor of God)

Introduction

Much is said in the Scriptures regarding things that cannot be seen by man. The universe is comprised of both things visible and invisible, all of which are creations of God. Man, the earth, and all the creatures of the earth are part of the dimension of the universe that can be seen. The invisible realm also includes beings and objects created by God. The Bible describes the beings in the unseen world as holy angels, and God created them innumerable.

The Bible teaches that angels existed prior to the creation of earth and man. At one point, an angel revolted against God and instigated a mutiny with other angels. These angels were cast out of the presence of God and down to the earth. The instigator had a name, Lucifer, also called Satan, and the angels that rebelled with him are called demons. It was Lucifer who introduced evil (iniquity) and sin in the invisible world, then in our world. The study in this lesson focuses on the holy angels, the fall of Lucifer from his initial position with God, and the introduction of evil and sin in God's creation.

Colossians 1:15-16
(Jesus) is the image of the invisible God, the firstborn of every creature: For by him were all things created, that are in heaven, and that are in earth, visible and invisible, whether they be thrones, or dominions, or principalities, or powers: all things were created by him, and for him.

Hebrews 1:14
Are not all angels ministering spirits sent to serve those who will inherit salvation?

Matthew 25:31
When the Son of man shall come in his glory, and all the holy angels with him, then shall he sit upon the throne of his glory.

Jude 1:6
And the angels which kept not their first estate, but left their own habitation, he hath reserved in everlasting chains under darkness unto the judgment of the great day.

Hebrews 2:6-7
What is man, that thou art mindful of him? or the son of man, that thou visitest him? Thou madest him a little lower than the angels;

Job 38:4-7
"Where were you when I laid the earth's foundation? Tell me, if you understand. Who marked off its dimensions? Surely you know! Who stretched a measuring line across it? On what were its footings set, or who laid its cornerstone while the morning stars sang together and all the angels shouted for joy?"

Jude 1:9
But Michael the archangel...

Luke 1:19
And the angel answering said unto him, I am Gabriel...

1 Peter 3:22
(Jesus Christ) is gone into heaven, and is on the right hand of God; angels and authorities and powers being made subject unto him.

Isaiah 6:2
Above it stood the seraphims: each one had six wings...

Ezekiel 10:20-21
...and I knew that they were the cherubims... and every one four wings...

1. Is there more to our world than what our eyes can see?

Our world and our universe have both a visible realm and an invisible realm.

2. What is the invisible realm?

The invisible realm exists outside of the visible, observable universe. This dimension includes the heavens (the place of God's dwelling), the unexplored universe, God, and His invisible creation—angels.

3. What are angels?

Angels (Hebrew *malak*, Greek *angelos*, literally, messenger) are beings created by God before the earth and mankind. God gave angels volition (capability to make choice) and multiple abilities superior to man. Scripture records the following information regarding angels:

- Invisible (Colossians 1:15-16)
- Spirit-beings (Hebrews 1:14)
- Holy (Matthew 25:31)
- Volitional (capable of making choice) (Jude 1:6)
- Abilities superior to man (Hebrews 2:6-7)
- Created by God before earth and mankind (Job 38:4-7)
- Angels have names (*Michael*: Jude 1:9, see also Daniel 10:13; *Gabriel*: Luke 1:19, see also Daniel 8:16; *Lucifer*: see Isaiah 14:4)

God created different orders and ranks of angels:

- Archangel (meaning chief) (Jude 1:9, see also 1 Thessalonians 4:16)
- Angels (Luke 1:19 and 1 Peter 3:22)
- Seraphim (Isaiah 6:2-7)
- Cherubim (Ezekiel 10:20-21, see also 1 Kings 6:23-27)
- Principalities (Colossians 1:16, see also Ephesians 1:21)
- Authorities (1 Peter 3:22)
- Thrones (Colossians 1:16)
- Powers (Colossians 1:16; 1 Peter 3:22, see also Ephesians 1:21)
- Mights (see Ephesians 1:21)
- Dominions (Colossians 1:16, see also Ephesians 1:21)

4. What is the purpose of angels?

God created angels to praise Him and carry out His will. The creation of angels established an order in the universe (Psalm 103:20-21; Psalm 148:2 and Hebrews 1:14).

Psalm 103:20-21
Praise the Lord, you his angels, you mighty ones who do his bidding, who obey his word. Praise the Lord, all his heavenly hosts, you his servants who do his will.

5. How do the angels carry out God's will?

Throughout the Old and New Testaments there are many examples of God's assignments for angels. Some examples:

- **Messengers**

  Angels delivered messages to those noted below and others:

  - Hagar (Genesis 16:7-12)
  - Gideon (Judges 6:11-22)
  - Jesus (Luke 22:39-43)

- **Assistants** (Daniel 6:22 and Matthew 2:13)

  Daniel 6:22
  My God sent his angel, and he shut the mouths of the lions. They have not hurt me, because I was found innocent in his sight.

- **Warriors** (Exodus 23:23; 2 Kings 19:35 and Revelation 14:19)

  Exodus 23:23
  My angel will go ahead of you and bring you into the land of the Amorites, Hittites, Perizzites, Canaanites, Hivites and Jebusites, and I will wipe them out.

- **Ministering spirits** (Matthew 4:11 and Matthew 18:10)

  Matthew 4:11
  Then the devil left him, and angels came and attended him.

- **Guards and coverings for God** (Genesis 3:24; see also Exodus 37 and Ezekiel 10)

  Genesis 3:24
  So he drove out the man; and he placed at the east of the garden of Eden Cherubims, and a flaming sword which turned every way, to keep the way of the tree of life.

Psalm 148:2
Praise him, all his angels, praise him, all his heavenly hosts.

Hebrews 1:14
Are not all angels ministering spirits sent to serve those who will inherit salvation?

Genesis 16:7
And the angel of the LORD found (Hagar) by a fountain of water in the wilderness...

Judges 6:11
Then the angel of the LORD came and sat under the oak that was in Ophrah, which belonged to Joash the Abiezrite as his son Gideon was beating out wheat in the wine press in order to save it from the Midianites.

Luke 22:43 NASB
Now an angel from heaven appeared to (Jesus), strengthening Him.

Matthew 2:13
When they had gone, an angel of the Lord appeared to Joseph in a dream. "Get up," he said, "take the child and his mother and escape to Egypt."

2 Kings 19:35
That night the angel of the Lord went out and put to death a hundred and eighty-five thousand men in the Assyrian camp.

Revelation 14:19
The angel swung his sickle on the earth, gathered its grapes and threw them into the great winepress of God's wrath.

Matthew 18:10
Take heed that ye despise not one of these little ones; for I say unto you, That in heaven their angels do always behold the face of my Father which is in heaven.

1 Kings 8:7
For the cherubims spread forth their two wings over the place of the ark, and the cherubims covered the ark and the staves thereof above.

Isaiah 6:2
Above it stood the seraphims: each one had six wings; with twain he covered his face, and with twain he covered his feet, and with twain he did fly.

Daniel 10:6
His body also was like the beryl, and his face as the appearance of lightning, and his eyes as lamps of fire, and his arms and his feet like in colour to polished brass, and the voice of his words like the voice of a multitude.

Matthew 28:3
And his appearance was like lightning, and his clothing as white as snow.

Ezekiel 28:12-17
Son of man, take up a lamentation upon the king of Tyrus,... Thou hast been in Eden the garden of God; every precious stone was thy covering, the sardius, topaz, and the diamond, the beryl, the onyx, and the jasper, the sapphire, the emerald, and the carbuncle, and gold: the workmanship of thy tabrets and of thy pipes was prepared in thee in the day that thou wast created. Thou art the anointed cherub that covereth... Thou wast perfect in thy ways from the day that thou wast created, till iniquity was found in thee. By the multitude of thy merchandise they have filled the midst of thee with violence, and thou hast sinned: therefore I will cast thee as profane out of the mountain of God: and I will destroy thee, O covering cherub, from the midst of the stones of fire. Thine heart was lifted up because of thy beauty, thou hast corrupted thy wisdom by reason of thy brightness: I will cast thee to the ground, I will lay thee before kings, that they may behold thee.

James 1:15
Then when lust hath conceived, it bringeth forth sin: and sin, when it is finished, bringeth forth death.

Romans 3:23
For all have sinned, and come short of the glory of God.

6. What do angels look like?

God created a variety of angels that have different forms. Angels have been described as having two, four, and six wings. At times angels have appeared in the form of a man, but the Bible also has given accounts of angels and their appearance in the invisible realm (1 Kings 8:7; Isaiah 6:2; Daniel 10:6; Matthew 28:3 and Ezekiel 28:13).

7. Who was Lucifer?

Lucifer was an angel beautifully created by God and anointed as a covering cherub to operate in God's presence (Ezekiel 28:13-15). Lucifer rebelled against God and was forever cast out of God's presence.

8. How did Lucifer reject God?

Lucifer became prideful and covetous, and set his heart on taking over the throne of God. He introduced sin and iniquity in heaven. God could not allow iniquity and sin in heaven, and cast Lucifer out of His presence.

Isaiah 14:12-15
How art thou fallen from heaven, O Lucifer, son of the morning! how art thou cut down to the ground, which didst weaken the nations! For thou hast said in thine heart, I will ascend into heaven, I will exalt my throne above the stars of God: I will sit also upon the mount of the congregation, in the sides of the north. I will ascend above the heights of the clouds; I will be like the most High. Yet thou shalt be brought down to hell, to the sides of the pit.

9. What is sin?

Sin is the willful disobedience or defiance (transgression) of any rule or law of God. The Hebrew and Greek words in the Bible connote a similar meaning, namely "to miss," or "to miss the mark" that has been set by God, which is to err or go astray (1 John 3:4; James 4:17; James 1:15 and Romans 3:23).

1 John 3:4
Whosoever committeth sin transgresseth also the law: for sin is the transgression of the law.

James 4:17 NIV
Anyone, then, who knows the good he ought to do and doesn't do it, sins.

10. What is iniquity?

Iniquity is evil: wickedness, unrighteousness, and lawlessness. Iniquity follows after a progression of sin, which in time produces evil. The Bible describes iniquity as the progressing of sin toward a lifestyle of evil and wickedness. Whereas sin is "missing the mark," iniquity can be characterized as a total disregard for the "mark," even a delighting in evil. The iniquity of Lucifer was a complete disregard for the position of God, but had no prior connection to anyone or anything (Ezekiel 28:15, 18 and Genesis 6:5, 12).

The Bible speaks of iniquity of:

- **Men** (Genesis 44:16, see also Job 34:32; Psalm 6:8; Psalm 18:23; Psalm 68:18; Isaiah 32:6 and Matthew 7:23)

- **Cities** (Joshua 22:17, see also Ezekiel 16:49)

- **People and nations** (Ezra 9:6, see also Psalm 85:2; Isaiah 1:4; Jeremiah 14:7; Ezekiel 44:12; Daniel 9:5 and Hosea 5:5, 13:12)

- **A family** (1 Samuel 3:14)

- **Priests** (Lamentations 4:13)

- **Angels** (Ezekiel 28:15, see also Ephesians 6:12)

11. How did evil come into the world?

The evil of Lucifer, who is also referred to as Satan, was brought to earth when Lucifer was cast out of God's presence after rebelling against God. He was cast out of heaven to earth, bringing evil with him (Isaiah 14:12 and Ezekiel 28:17).

Ezekiel 28:15, 18
Thou wast perfect in thy ways from the day that thou wast created, till iniquity was found in thee... Thou hast defiled thy sanctuaries by the multitude of thine iniquities, by the iniquity of thy traffic;

Genesis 6:5, 12
And God saw that the wickedness of man was great in the earth, and that every imagination of the thoughts of his heart was only evil continually... And God looked upon the earth, and, behold, it was corrupt; for all flesh had corrupted his way upon the earth.

Genesis 44:16 NASB
God has found out the iniquity of your servants

Joshua 22:17 NASB
Is not the iniquity of (the city of) Peor enough for us, from which we have not cleansed ourselves to this day...

Ezra 9:6
O my God, I am ashamed and blush to lift up my face to thee, my God: for our iniquities are increased over our head, and our trespass is grown up unto the heavens.

1 Samuel 3:14
...the iniquity of Eli's house shall not be purged with sacrifice nor offering for ever.

Lamentations 4:13
For the sins of (Israel's) prophets, and the iniquities of her priests...

Isaiah 14:12
How art thou fallen from heaven, O Lucifer, son of the morning! how art thou cut down to the ground, which didst weaken the nations!

Ezekiel 28:17 NASB
"Your heart was lifted up because of your beauty; You corrupted your wisdom by reason of your splendor. I cast you to the ground; I put you before kings, That they may see you.

Revelation 12:4, 9 NIV
His tail swept a third of the stars (angels) out of the sky and flung them to the earth... The great dragon was hurled down—that ancient serpent called the devil, or Satan, who leads the whole world astray. He was hurled to the earth, and his angels (stars) with him.

John 10:10
The thief cometh not, but for to steal, and to kill, and to destroy:

1 Peter 5:8 NIV
Be self-controlled and alert. Your enemy the devil prowls around like a roaring lion looking for someone to devour.

Ephesians 6:12
For we wrestle not against flesh and blood, but against principalities, against powers, against the rulers of the darkness of this world (demons), against spiritual wickedness in high places.

2 Corinthians 12:7 NIV
To keep me from becoming conceited because of these surpassingly great revelations, there was given me a thorn in the flesh, a messenger of Satan (a demon), to torment me.

Job 1:7, 2:2 NIV
The Lord said to Satan, "Where have you come from?" Satan answered the Lord, "From roaming through the earth and going back and forth in it."

Isaiah 14:12
How you have fallen from heaven, morning star, son of the dawn! You have been cast down to the earth, you who once laid low the nations!

James 4:7
Submit yourselves therefore to God. Resist the devil, and he will flee from you. Draw nigh to God, and he will draw nigh to you.

Psalm 119:11
Thy word have I hid in mine heart, that I might not sin against thee.

1 Corinthians 10:13-14 NIV
No temptation has seized you except what is common to man. And God is faithful; he will not let you be tempted beyond what you can bear. But when you are tempted, he will also provide a way out so that you can stand up under it. Therefore, my dear friends, flee from idolatry.

12. Did the evil of Satan affect the world?

Satan influenced a third of the angels to revolt against God. When Satan was cast down to earth, other mutinous angels referred to by the Bible as demons and devils were cast down with him. Satan and his fallen angels are enemies of mankind God. They seek the destruction of God's creation by deception, temptation, and affliction in order to keep mankind from having a relationship with God.

Satan is an adversary who seeks to lead all away from God; however he is not omnipotent, omnipresent, or omniscient, but is limited in his abilities by God. The Bible describes the fallen Lucifer as a ruler of the air (the unseen world), with his demonic forces set as princes and rulers in this unseen world forever in conflict with God (Revelation 12:4, 9; John 10:10; 1 Peter 5:8; Ephesians 6:12; 2 Corinthians 12:7; Job 1:7, 2:2 and Isaiah 14:12).

13. How can we deal with the influence of Satan and demons?

Though Satan is limited, God has allowed him to tempt and deceive people. The Bible describes Satan as a roaring lion seeking whom he may devour. We must deal with Satan's attempts to influence us. The Scriptures admonish us to:

- Submit to God and resist Satan (James 4:7)

- Flee from sin (1 Corinthians 10:14, see also 1 Corinthians 6:18; 1 Timothy 6:11 and 2 Timothy 2:22)

- Learn God's word to keep from sin (Psalm 119:11, see also Psalm 1)

- Put on the "whole armor of God" (Ephesians 6:11-18)

  Ephesians 6:11,13-18 NIV
  Put on the full armor of God so that you can take your stand against the devil's schemes... Therefore put on the full armor of God, so that when the day of evil comes, you may be able to stand your ground, and after you have done everything, to stand. Stand firm then, with the belt of truth buckled around your waist, with the breastplate of righteousness in place, and with your feet fitted with the readiness that comes from the gospel of peace. In addition to all this, take up the shield of faith, with which you can extinguish all the flaming arrows of the evil one. Take the helmet of salvation and the sword of the Spirit, which is the word of God. And pray in the Spirit on all occasions with all kinds of prayers and requests.

Study Questions

1. Read Colossians 1:16, Hebrews 1:14, 2:6-7, Matthew 25:31, Jude 1:6, and Isaiah 6:2-7. From these passages can you describe some of the angels God created?_____

    _____

    _____

    _____

    _____

    _____

    _____

2. Ezekiel 28:12-18 and Isaiah 14:4-15 describe Lucifer (Satan) using symbolism of earthly kings. What do you learn about Lucifer from these passages? Do you believe Lucifer exists? _____

    _____

    _____

    _____

    _____

    _____

    _____

Lesson Journal

Use this section to record your thoughts on the topics in this lesson.

_____

_____

_____

_____

_____

_____

_____

_____

_____

_____

Lesson 4
Seven Days of Creation

Scripture Reading

- Genesis chapters 1 and 2 (creation)

- Job 38:1-6 (creation)

- Exodus 20:11 (days of creation)

- Revelation 4:11 (purpose of creation)

Introduction

The topic of creation is one that can rouse much discussion and debate. The events of creation as discussed in the Bible raise many questions with believers and skeptics alike who attempt to conform Scripture to man's limited knowledge and understanding of our world. However, there is no need to invent Scriptural theories to conform the Bible to science. Objective science is not at odds with Scripture, but rather, when properly applied, proves the accuracy of God's unaltered Word.

As scientific knowledge increases, more and more of Scripture is proven absolutely accurate. From the first operation, where God put Adam to sleep to remove his rib (Genesis 2:21), to Job's statements about the earth hanging on nothing (Job 26:7), the accuracy of the Bible remains intact. Hence, in this lesson the objective is not to prove the accuracy of the Bible by way of scientific proof, as there is an abundance of material available on the subject. Instead, this lesson is presented from a strictly Biblical standpoint, using His Word alone to tell us of creation.

1 John 5:7
For there are three that bear record in heaven, the Father, the Word, and the Holy Ghost: and these three are one.

Isaiah 64:8
But now, O LORD, thou art our father; we are the clay, and thou our potter; and we all are the work of thy hand.

Malachi 2:10
Have we not all one father? hath not one God created us.

Matthew 5:45
That ye may be the children of your Father which is in heaven: for he maketh his sun to rise on the evil and on the good, and sendeth rain on the just and on the unjust.

Job 38:1, 4-7 NIV
Then the LORD answered Job out of the storm... He said: "Where were you when I laid the earth's foundation? Tell me, if you understand. Who marked off its dimensions? Surely you know! Who stretched a measuring line across it? On what were its footings set, or who laid its cornerstone while the morning stars sang together and all the angels shouted for joy?

John 1:3
All things were made by him (Jesus, the Word); and without him was not any thing made that was made.

Colossians 1:16
For by him (Jesus) were all things created, that are in heaven, and that are in earth, visible and invisible, whether they be thrones, or dominions, or principalities, or powers: all things were created by him, and for him:

Genesis 1:2
And the earth was without form, and void; and darkness was upon the face of the deep. And the Spirit of God moved upon the face of the waters.

Job 33:4
The Spirit of God hath made me, and the breath of the Almighty hath given me life.

1. Who is the creator?

The triune God is the creator of all things. God the Father, God the Son (Jesus), and God the Holy Spirit were active participants in the process of creation (1 John 5:7):

- **God the Father**

  (Isaiah 64:8; Malachi 2:10; Matthew 5:45 and Job 38:1, 4-7)

- **God the Son (Jesus)**

  (John 1:3 and Colossians 1:16)

- **God the Holy Spirit**

  (Genesis 1:2 and Job 33:4)

2. Why did God create?

God initiated the creation process by His will, because it pleased Him. The events of creation illustrate God's sovereignty, and He continues to operate in the lives of men for His good pleasure.

Revelation 4:11
Thou art worthy, O Lord, to receive glory and honour and power: for thou hast created all things, and for thy pleasure they are and were created.

Philippians 2:12-13
[W]ork out your own salvation with fear and trembling. For it is God which worketh in you both to will and to do of his good pleasure.

3. When did God initiate creation?

In the beginning.

Genesis 1:1
In the beginning God created the heaven and the earth.

John 1:1-3
In the beginning was the Word, and the Word was with God, and the Word was God. The same was in the beginning with God. All things were made by him; and without him was not any thing made that was made.

4. How did God create everything?

God spoke everything into existence. By His word He created:

Genesis 1:3
And God said, Let there be light…

Genesis 1:6
And God said, Let there be a firmament in the midst of the waters…

Genesis 1:9
And God said, Let the waters under the heaven be gathered together…

Genesis 1:11
And God said, Let the earth bring forth grass…

Genesis 1:20
And God said, Let the waters bring forth abundantly…

Genesis 1:24
And God said, Let the earth bring forth the living creature…

Genesis 1:26
And God said, Let us make man in our image…

Hebrews 11:3 NIV
By faith we understand that the universe was formed at God's command, so that what is seen was not made out of what was visible.

5. How long did it take God to create everything?

God created everything in six days, after which He rested for one day (Exodus 20:11).

Exodus 20:11
For in six days the LORD made heaven and earth, the sea, and all that in them is, and rested the seventh day.

6. In what order was everything created?

The sequence of God's creation is an excellent example of the orderliness of God. His creation followed an order whereupon each new addition added to, and relied upon, what had previously been created. God began with the basics, water and light, and followed with land, vegetation and animals, preparing an ideal environment for the culmination of His creation, man and woman.

The order of creation was:

- **Day One** (Genesis 1:1-3)
  - The heavens
  - A formless earth suspended in darkness and, other than water, completely empty (void). There were no other celestial bodies in the solar system (no stars, sun, moon, or other planets, just the earth)
  - Light
  - Separation of light from the darkness, a mechanism for the keeping of time, primarily the day and night cycle

Genesis 1:1-3
In the beginning God created the heaven and the earth. And the earth was without form, and void; and darkness was upon the face of the deep. And the Spirit of God moved upon the face of the waters. And God said, Let there be light: and there was light.

Genesis 1:7
And God made the firmament, and divided the waters which were under the firmament from the waters which were above the firmament: and it was so.

Genesis 1:9, 11
And God said, Let the waters under the heaven be gathered together unto one place, and let the dry *land* appear: and it was so.... And God said, Let the earth bring forth grass, the herb yielding seed, *and* the fruit tree yielding fruit after his kind, whose seed *is* in itself, upon the earth: and it was so.

Genesis 1:14, 16
And God said, Let there be lights in the firmament of the heaven to divide the day from the night; and let them be for signs, and for seasons, and for days, and years:... he made the stars also.

Genesis 1:20,22
And God said, Let the waters bring forth abundantly the moving creature that hath life, and fowl *that* may fly above the earth in the open firmament of heaven... And God blessed them, saying, Be fruitful, and multiply, and fill the waters in the seas, and let fowl multiply in the earth.

Genesis 1:24, 26-27
And God said, Let the earth bring forth the living creature after his kind, cattle, and creeping thing, and beast of the earth after his kind: and it was so... And God said, Let us make man in our image, after our likeness: and let them have dominion over the fish of the sea, and over the fowl of the air, and over the cattle, and over all the earth, and over every creeping thing that creepeth upon the earth. So God created man in his *own* image, in the image of God created he him; male and female created he them.

Genesis 2:2
And on the seventh day God ended his work which he had made; and he rested on the seventh day from all his work which he had made.

- **Day Two** (Genesis 1:7)

  Formation of Earth's atmosphere and hydrosphere, that is, the separation of water into two distinct parts:

  - Water on and beneath the earth

  - Atmospheric water, water above the earth

- **Day Three** (Genesis 1:9, 11)

  - Water separated by dry land

  - A method to moisturize the surface of the dry land using waters beneath the earth (springs)

  - Vegetation, seed-bearing plants, fruit bearing trees

- **Day Four** (Genesis 1:14, 16)

  - The sun and the moon, celestial bodies to track time in a detailed fashion, to mark day and night, months, seasons, and years

  - The completion of the solar system and universe with the addition of stars and other planets

- **Day Five** (Genesis 1:20, 22)

  - The fish of the sea and all the creatures that live in water

  - The fowl of the air, all of the birds

- **Day Six** (Genesis 1:24, 26-27)

  - All land animals (mammals, reptiles, and amphibians)

  - Man and woman in the image of God

  - God beheld His creation and it was "very good"

- **Day Seven** God rested (Genesis 2:2)

7. Is man different than the animals?

Man and woman were the last of the living creatures created by God. Genesis chapter one, gives an account of creation from the perspective of God, and states in verse 27 that *God created man in his own image, in the image of God created he him; male and female created he them.* God performed an operation on Adam, taking a rib and forming woman. Hence both Adam and Eve were formed in the image of God, created to have a relationship with God, with one another, and to fulfill their purpose of filling the earth and exercising dominion over it (Genesis 1:24-28, 2:15-17, 2:20-23).

Adam and Eve could speak, reason, make moral judgments, and they had a relationship with God (they worshiped God). This differentiated Adam and Eve from the other living creatures that God had created, and they were given dominion over the rest of creation.

So, man and woman were different from the animals. They had a relationship with God unlike any of the animals, and they were given authority over all the other living creatures.

8. After woman was created, what was man's relationship to be with her?

Adam loved the woman that God created. He immediately realized that the relationship between man and woman would be special, and that man and woman would be united together to become one flesh able to undertake God's directive to fill the earth.

Genesis 1:28 NASB
God blessed them; and God said to them, "Be fruitful and multiply, and fill the earth, and subdue it; and rule over the fish of the sea and over the birds of the sky and over every living thing that moves on the earth."

Genesis 2:23-24
And Adam said, This is now bone of my bones, and flesh of my flesh: she shall be called Woman, because she was taken out of Man. Therefore shall a man leave his father and his mother, and shall cleave unto his wife: and they shall be one flesh.

Genesis 3:20
And Adam called his wife's name Eve; because she was the mother of all living.

Genesis 1:24-28
And God said, Let the earth bring forth the living creature after his kind, cattle, and creeping thing, and beast of the earth after his kind: and it was so. And God made the beast of the earth after his kind, and cattle after their kind, and every thing that creepeth upon the earth after his kind: and God saw that it was good. And God said, Let us make man in our image, after our likeness: and let them have dominion over the fish of the sea, and over the fowl of the air, and over the cattle, and over all the earth, and over every creeping thing that creepeth upon the earth. So God created man in his own image, in the image of God created he him; male and female created he them. And God blessed them, and God said unto them, Be fruitful, and multiply, and replenish the earth, and subdue it: and have dominion over the fish of the sea, and over the fowl of the air, and over every living thing that moveth upon the earth.

Genesis 2:15-17
And the LORD God took the man, and put him into the garden of Eden to dress it and to keep it. And the LORD God commanded the man, saying, Of every tree of the garden thou mayest freely eat: But of the tree of the knowledge of good and evil, thou shalt not eat of it: for in the day that thou eatest thereof thou shalt surely die.

Genesis 2:20-23
And Adam gave names to all cattle, and to the fowl of the air, and to every beast of the field; but for Adam there was not found an help meet for him. And the LORD God caused a deep sleep to fall upon Adam, and he slept: and he took one of his ribs, and closed up the flesh instead thereof; And the rib, which the LORD God had taken from man, made he a woman, and brought her unto the man. And Adam said, This is now bone of my bones, and flesh of my flesh: she shall be called Woman, because she was taken out of Man.

9. What was man and woman's purpose after creation?

Adam and Eve were not to lead aimless lives. God gave them direction and purpose for their life on earth. After being created Adam was put in a garden to work it and to tend it. He was given a purpose, and his first task was the naming of all the animals. Woman was then created and God gave the couple authority over the entire earth and all living creatures. God instructed them to:

- Reproduce
- Fill the earth
- Subdue the earth
- Establish dominion over the entire earth

God's instruction to exercise dominion over the entire earth included dominion over:

- Self: Adam and Eve were instructed to exercise self-control by not eating of the tree of knowledge of good and evil (Genesis 2:16-17).

- Culture: Adam and Eve were instructed to reproduce and fill the earth and subdue it (Genesis 1:28). They would of necessity need to exercise dominion over the instructing of their children and the shaping of a culture.

- Every living creature: God gave Adam and Eve authority over every living thing, plant and animal, on the face of the earth (Genesis 1:28-29).

10. What does it mean that man was created in "the image" of God?

God is not a being that we can describe in our natural world, or comprehend with our natural senses. God is invisible. So, how is it that man was created in the image and likeness of God? The Bible declares that God is a spirit, and He created man with a spirit, the part that is in the image and likeness of God. When God created Adam, He made him different than the other creatures, having a body, a soul, and a spirit. It was the spirit that distinguished Adam as different, and it was the spirit given by God that gave Adam the image and likeness of God. (John 4:24 and 1 Thessalonians 5:23)

Man is a three-part being, a parallel to God's tri-unity. God formed man's body out of the dust of the ground, and then breathed life in him making him a living soul with a spirit. Each of these parts are unique:

Genesis 2:16-17 NIV
And the LORD God commanded the man, "You are free to eat from any tree in the garden; but you must not eat from the tree of the knowledge of good and evil, for when you eat of it you will surely die."

Genesis 1:28-29 NIV
God blessed them and said to them, "Be fruitful and increase in number; fill the earth and subdue it. Rule over the fish of the sea and the birds of the air and over every living creature that moves on the ground." Then God said, "I give you every seed-bearing plant on the face of the whole earth and every tree that has fruit with seed in it. They will be yours for food.

John 4:24
God is a Spirit: and they that worship him must worship him in spirit and in truth.

1 Thessalonians 5:23
And the very God of peace sanctify you wholly; and I pray God your whole spirit and soul and body be preserved blameless unto the coming of our Lord Jesus Christ.

- **The Body**

  The body is the physical portion of man that makes him conscious of the physical world via the five physical senses of seeing, hearing, smelling, tasting, and touching (Genesis 2:7 and 1 Corinthians 12:12). God's living creation: plants, animals, and man, all have a body.

- **The Soul**

  God said that He breathed into man, making him a "living soul." So, a soul makes one conscious of life. It is the personality of an individual, the inward part of a person that is reflected through the actions of the body; it is the soul that makes one self-conscious (Genesis 2:7). Animals and man have a soul.

- **The Spirit**

  The spirit of a man is that portion which was created in the image and likeness of God and distinguished man from God's other living creation. Having a spirit distinguished Adam from the animals in several ways:

  - God instilled Adam with a spirit (Job 32:8 and Zechariah 12:1).

  - Adam had wisdom and knowledge that the animals did not. He was able to rationalize, distinguish right from wrong, and possessed an ability for moral reasoning (Genesis 3:2-3; Exodus 31:3; Proverbs 17:27; Daniel 2:3; Daniel 5:12 and 1 Corinthians 2:11).

  - Adam was able to speak and communicate with God unlike the other creatures in the garden, his spirit making him God-conscious. Adam and Eve worshiped God.

    Genesis 3:8-10
    And they heard the voice of the LORD God walking in the garden in the cool of the day… And the LORD God called unto Adam, and said unto him, Where art thou? And he said, I heard thy voice in the garden…

    Numbers 11:17
    And I will come down and talk with thee there: and I will take of the spirit which is upon thee, and will put it upon them…

    Luke 1:47
    And my spirit hath rejoiced in God my Saviour.

    (See also Ezekiel 11:5; John 6:63; 2 Corinthians 4:13 and 1 Timothy 4:1)

Genesis 2:7
And the LORD God formed man *of* the dust of the ground, and breathed into his nostrils the breath of life; and man became a living soul.

1 Corinthians 12:12
For as the body is one, and hath many members, and all the members of that one body, being many, are one body: so also is Christ.

Job 32:8
But there is a spirit in man: and the inspiration of the Almighty giveth them understanding.

Zechariah 12:1
The burden of the word of the LORD for Israel, saith the LORD, which stretcheth forth the heavens, and layeth the foundation of the earth, and formeth the spirit of man within him.

Genesis 3:2-3
And the woman said unto the serpent, We may eat of the fruit of the trees of the garden: But of the fruit of the tree which is in the midst of the garden, God hath said, Ye shall not eat of it, neither shall ye touch it, lest ye die.

Exodus 31:3
And I have filled him with the spirit of God, in wisdom, and in understanding, and in knowledge, and in all manner of workmanship,

Proverbs 17:27
He that hath knowledge spareth his words: and a man of understanding is of an excellent spirit.

Daniel 2:3
And the king said unto them, I have dreamed a dream, and my spirit was troubled to know the dream.

Daniel 5:12
Forasmuch as an excellent spirit, and knowledge, and understanding, interpreting of dreams, and showing of hard sentences, and dissolving of doubts, were found in the same Daniel, whom the king named Belteshazzar:

1 Corinthians 2:11
For what man knoweth the things of a man, save the spirit of man which is in him?

Study Questions

1. Read Genesis chapters 1 and 2, and Exodus 20:11. Do you believe that God created the universe in six days? Why or why not? _____

_____

_____

_____

_____

_____

2. Your co-worker firmly believes that people are no different than animals, but have just developed further. What can you say from your reading of Genesis chapters 1 and 2 and other Scriptures given in the lesson about the differences between people and animals? _____

_____

_____

_____

_____

_____

_____

Lesson Journal

Use this section to record your thoughts on the topics in this lesson.

_____

_____

_____

_____

_____

_____

_____

_____

_____

_____

Lesson 5
Sin Enters the World

Scripture Reading

- Genesis 2 (creation)
- Genesis 3 (the fall of man)
- Romans 3:23; Romans 5:12-19 and Ephesians 2:1-3 (all have sinned, born in sin, death by sin)
- Matthew 8:22; John 3:3-7 and 1 Peter 4:6 (spiritual death and birth)
- Jeremiah 31:31-34 and Hebrews 10:16-18 (Old and New Covenant)
- Romans 5:6-8 and 1 John 3:16 (Jesus gave His life for us)

Introduction

God created the entire universe. He created man and woman and put them on the earth for His good pleasure, and gave them purpose for their lives. God loved Adam and Eve, and provided an environment for them to learn about all that He had created while they developed their relationships with Him through daily, personal fellowship. At the present time, believers have the universal Church of Jesus Christ established as their setting for growing in their relationships with Him.

God defined a relationship, or covenant, with His creation, placing one restriction on Adam and Eve. Being obedient to the single term, God set forth was all that was required. Unfortunately, Adam and Eve violated God's instruction and sinned against God. Their sin had consequences and the environment God had created for them was significantly altered, ushering in pain and suffering from childbirth to the ultimate death of the physical body. Man's life was also considerably altered with the initiation of weeds, thorns, thistles, and the daily toil of life. Moreover, all mankind shares in the consequences of this original sin, each person being born with the assurance that their physical body will one day die, and in need of a spiritual birth before that death occurs.

Study this lesson to see the consequences of sin, but take note of the immediate outpouring of God's love and His abundant grace; He promised to free mankind from the results of the first sin of Adam.

Genesis 1:27, 31
So God created man in his own image, in the image of God created he him; male and female created he them...And God saw every thing that he had made, and, behold, it was very good. And the evening and the morning were the sixth day.

Genesis 2:8-9
And the LORD God planted a garden eastward in Eden; and there he put the man whom he had formed. And out of the ground made the LORD God to grow every tree that is pleasant to the sight, and good for food; the tree of life also in the midst of the garden, and the tree of knowledge of good and evil.

Genesis 2:16-17
And the LORD God commanded the man, saying, Of every tree of the garden thou mayest freely eat: But of the tree of the knowledge of good and evil, thou shalt not eat of it: for in the day that thou eatest thereof thou shalt surely die.

Genesis 3:6
And when the woman saw that the tree was good for food, and that it was pleasant to the eyes, and a tree to be desired to make one wise, she took of the fruit thereof, and did eat, and gave also unto her husband with her; and he did eat.

Romans 5:12
Wherefore, as by one man sin entered into the world...

1 Timothy 2:14
And Adam was not deceived, but the woman...

Romans 4:15
...for where no law is, there is no transgression.

1 John 3:4
...for sin is the transgression of the law.

1. What was life like when Adam and Eve were created?

God loved the man and woman that He created. He prepared a garden, an ideal environment for them to learn and grow in their relationships with God, and a place where they could realize purpose for their lives. Adam and Eve had fellowship with God daily as He came to talk to them and teach them in the cool of the day. Their lives were focused on God's purpose and on worship to God by being obedient to Him.

God gave man dominion over the earth and all the creatures that He had created on land and in the sea. Food was provided for Adam and Eve by the vegetation and the trees bearing fruit in the garden. Adam was responsible for working the garden and tending it. He was also charged with naming the animals. The work Adam did required that he learn about all of the other things that God had created. This work gave Adam a purpose for his life, providing a fulfilling way to increase his mind and use his body (Genesis 1:27, 31 and Genesis 2:8).

2. What restriction did God place on Adam and Eve?

God gave Adam and Eve a single instruction regarding their behavior: He instructed them not to eat the fruit of a single tree in the garden, a tree called the *tree of the knowledge of good and evil*. God informed Adam and Eve that disobeying His instructions would result in serious consequences; they would surely die (Genesis 2:16-17).

3. Did Adam and Eve obey God's instruction?

Both Adam and Eve disobeyed God. (Genesis 3:6)

4. What happened?

Satan, disguised as a serpent, deceived Eve and convinced her to eat some of the fruit of the *tree of the knowledge of good and evil*. Adam, knowing full well what she had done, ate some of the fruit too after Eve offered it to him. Adam and Eve acted on their desire to become like God, wanting to live life their own way. They disregarded His commandment and decided that they could live independent of God. They allowed their desire for independence to cloud their judgment. By going against the command of God, Adam and Eve sinned (Romans 5:12; 1 Timothy 2:14; Romans 4:15 and 1 John 3:4).

After sinning Adam and Eve were ashamed and they felt guilt for the first time (Genesis 3:7). Their relationship with each other changed, and they made coverings for themselves because they were ashamed of their nakedness. Their relationship with God was forever altered. Because of their shame and guilt they did not know how to respond to God. They became fearful of God and hid themselves (Genesis 3:8-10). Adam and Eve then sought to excuse sin rather than confess it (Genesis 3:12-13).

5. How did God respond to the sin of Adam and Eve?

There were severe consequences for the sin of Adam and Eve, which altered the course of mankind. Adam pointed to Eve, Eve pointed to the serpent. God responded to all three:

- **The serpent, Satan: (Genesis 3:14-15 and Revelation 12:9)**

  - Cursed above all the livestock and all the wild animals

  - Must crawl on his belly and eat dust

  - Enmity (hostility) between him and the woman, and between their offspring (offspring of the serpent refers to sinners; offspring of the woman is a prophecy of Jesus Christ)

  - Jesus will crush his head, but Satan will strike His heel

- **The woman, Eve: (Genesis 3:16)**

  - The pain of childbirth would be multiplied

  - Her desire would be for her husband, and he would rule over her

  - Her body would one day die, like her husband's, and return to dust

- **The man, Adam: (Genesis 3:17-19)**

  - The ground was cursed so Adam would have to work hard all his life to derive food

  - His body would one day die and return to the dust from which he was made

Blood was shed for the first time to provide a covering because of sin. God killed animals in order to clothe Adam and Eve (Genesis 3:21). They were driven out of the Garden of Eden, cast out of the environment God had prepared, and they now had to focus on dealing with weeds and thistles. Adam's purpose for working changed, and he lost the fulfillment of learning and growing in the original setting God had prepared for him.

Genesis 3:7-19 NIV
Then the eyes of both of them were opened, and they realized they were naked; so they sewed fig leaves together and made coverings for themselves. Then the man and his wife heard the sound of the LORD God as he was walking in the garden in the cool of the day, and they hid from the LORD God among the trees of the garden. But the LORD God called to the man, "Where are you?" He answered, "I heard you in the garden, and I was afraid because I was naked; so I hid." And he said, "Who told you that you were naked? Have you eaten from the tree that I commanded you not to eat from?" The man said, "The woman you put here with me—she gave me some fruit from the tree, and I ate it." Then the LORD God said to the woman, "What is this you have done?" The woman said, "The serpent deceived me, and I ate." So the LORD God said to the serpent, "Because you have done this, "Cursed are you above all the livestock and all the wild animals! You will crawl on your belly and you will eat dust all the days of your life. And I will put enmity between you and the woman, and between your offspring and hers; he will crush your head, and you will strike his heel." To the woman he said, "I will greatly increase your pains in childbearing; with pain you will give birth to children. Your desire will be for your husband, and he will rule over you." To Adam he said, "Because you listened to your wife and ate from the tree about which I commanded you, 'you must not eat of it,' "Cursed is the ground because of you; through painful toil you will eat of it all the days of your life. It will produce thorns and thistles for you, and you will eat the plants of the field. By the sweat of your brow you will eat your food until you return to the ground, since from it you were taken; for dust you are and to dust you will return."

Revelation 12:9 NIV
He seized the dragon, that ancient serpent, who is the devil, or Satan...

Genesis 3:21 NIV
The LORD God made garments of skin for Adam and his wife and clothed them.

Romans 5:12, 15, 18-19
Wherefore, as by one man sin entered into the world, and death by sin; and so death passed upon all men, for that all have sinned: ...through the offence of one many be dead... Therefore as by the offence of one judgment came upon all men to condemnation... For as by one man's disobedience many were made sinners.

Titus 3:5
Not by works of righteousness which we have done, but according to his mercy he saved us, by the washing of regeneration, and renewing of the Holy Ghost.

Ephesians 2:1-3 NCV
In the past you were spiritually dead because of your sins and the things you did against God. Yes, in the past you lived the way the world lives, following the ruler of the evil powers that are above the earth. That same spirit is now working in those who refuse to obey God. In the past all of us lived like them, trying to please our sinful selves and doing all the things our bodies and minds wanted. We should have suffered God's anger because of the way we were. We were the same as all other people.

Romans 3:23
For all have sinned, and come short of the glory of God;

Deuteronomy 24:16
The fathers shall not be put to death for the children, neither shall the children be put to death for the fathers: every man shall be put to death for his own sin.

Ezekiel 18:20
The soul that sinneth, it shall die. The son shall not bear the iniquity of the father, neither shall the father bear the iniquity of the son: the righteousness of the righteous shall be upon him, and the wickedness of the wicked shall be upon him.

Jeremiah 31:29-30
In those days they shall say no more, The fathers have eaten a sour grape, and the children's teeth are set on edge. But every one shall die for his own iniquity: every man that eateth the sour grape, his teeth shall be set on edge.

6. God said Adam and Eve would die, but they didn't, how could this be?

Adam and Eve did die. The relationships that Adam and Eve had with God were forever changed. They were cast out of the Garden of Eden and the communion that they formerly enjoyed with God ended. The spirits of Adam and Eve, that part that completed them in the image and likeness of God and distinguished them from other living creatures, degenerated. Their spirits were now in need of regeneration. Hence, the death that they suffered "in that day" was spiritual. Physical death was also a consequence of their sin. God forbade them from partaking of the Tree of Life, which would have given them eternal life. Thus physical death was assured.

All mankind shares in the consequence of Adam's sin, receiving by birth the assurance of a physical death and the need of a spiritual regeneration. To this day mankind inherits the consequence of the first sin of Adam, which is often called the doctrine of original sin, or the sin nature (Romans 5:12, 15, 18-19; Titus 3:5 and Ephesians 2:1-3).

References to spiritual death and rebirth:

Matthew 8:22
And another of his disciples said unto him, Lord, suffer me first to go and bury my father. But Jesus said unto him, Follow me; and let the dead bury their dead.

John 3:3, 6-7
Jesus answered and said unto him, Verily, verily, I say unto thee, Except a man be born again, he cannot see the kingdom of God... That which is born of the flesh is flesh; and that which is born of the Spirit is spirit. Marvel not that I said unto thee, Ye must be born again.

1 Peter 4:6
For the gospel has for this purpose been preached even to those who are dead, that though they are judged in the flesh as men, they may live in the spirit according to the will of God.

7. Is God unfair to punish everyone for the sin of Adam?

All have inherited a sin nature from Adam and suffer consequences because of his sin (Romans 3:23). Adam's sin affected his descendents much the same as any father affects his lineage by the decisions, good or bad, which he makes in his lifetime. However, consequences are not the same as punishment. An individual is not punished for the sins of Adam, but for their own sins. God does not hold one accountable for another's sins (Deuteronomy 24:16; Ezekiel 18:20 and Jeremiah 31:29-30).

8. Did God make any provision to free man from the sin nature?

God said to Satan who had taken on the form of a serpent, *"I will put enmity between you and the woman, and between your seed and her seed; He shall bruise you on the head, and you shall bruise him on the heel,"* (Genesis 3:15). This verse speaks of God making a provision for Satan to be crushed. It is a prophetic reference to a savior, Jesus Christ, who would come through woman and defeat Satan completely.

This was the beginning of God's covenant with man to provide a way out of spiritual death through faith in Jesus Christ, and an example of God's grace. God made this provision for man, without man doing anything on his part to deserve salvation from death.

9. What is a covenant?

A covenant defines a relationship. A covenant includes conditions to be kept, and defines what will occur if the conditions are neglected by any involved in the covenant. When God initiates a covenant with man the terms are His and not negotiable; a unilateral covenant. In a unilateral covenant man's responsibility is to follow the conditions set by God.

By His grace God initiated His covenant by promising a way out of death by sin. He extended His covenant with mankind, freely offering life and salvation, requiring of sinners faith in Him, and the keeping of His covenant conditions. This covenant was administered differently from the time of Adam to the time of Jesus Christ. It was administered by promises, prophecies, sacrifices, and other types and ordinances delivered to the Jewish people, all pointing to Christ to come. It is referred to in the Old Testament as "the covenant" and in the New Testament as the "old covenant." Before Jesus, the old covenant was sufficient to instruct and provided a way for the covering of sins. Jesus ushered in a new and everlasting covenant, and it provides a way for any individual to have a personal relationship with Jesus Christ and obtain complete forgiveness of sins such that God remembers them no more (Jeremiah 31:31-34 and Hebrews 10:16-18).

Through one man, Adam, sin entered the world and death by sin. Through one man, Jesus Christ, salvation from sin and eternal life is available to all. Jesus, who was without sin, received the punishment for sin that rightly was due all sinners (Romans 5:15-17; Ephesians 2:1 and John 5:24).

Jeremiah 31:31-34
Behold, the days come, saith the LORD, that I will make a new covenant with the house of Israel, and with the house of Judah: Not according to the covenant that I made with their fathers in the day that I took them by the hand to bring them out of the land of Egypt; which my covenant they brake... After those days, saith the LORD, I will put my law in their inward parts, and write it in their hearts; and will be their God, and they shall be my people... for I will forgive their iniquity, and I will remember their sin no more.

Hebrews 10:16-18
This is the covenant that I will make with them after those days, saith the Lord, I will put my laws into their hearts, and in their minds will I write them; And their sins and iniquities will I remember no more. Now where remission of these is, there is no more offering for sin.

Romans 5:15-17 NCV
But God's free gift is not like Adam's sin. Many people died because of the sin of that one man. But the grace from God was much greater; many people received God's gift of life by the grace of the one man, Jesus Christ. After Adam sinned once, he was judged guilty. But the gift of God is different. God's free gift came after many sins, and it makes people right with God. One man sinned, and so death ruled all people because of that one man. But now those people who accept God's full grace and the great gift of being made right with him will surely have true life and rule through the one man, Jesus Christ.

Ephesians 2:1
And you hath he quickened, who were dead in trespasses and sins...

John 5:24
Verily, verily, I say unto you, He that heareth my word, and believeth on him that sent me, hath everlasting life, and shall not come into condemnation; but is passed from death unto life.

Matthew 20:28 and Mark 10:45
...the Son of Man did not come to be served, but to serve, and to give His life a ransom for many.

John 3:16
For God so loved the world, that he gave his only begotten Son, that whosoever believeth in him should not perish, but have everlasting life.

John 10:11 NASB
I am the good shepherd; the good shepherd lays down His life for the sheep.

Romans 5:6-8 NASB
For while we were still helpless, at the right time Christ died for the ungodly. For one will hardly die for a righteous man; though perhaps for the good man someone would dare even to die. But God demonstrates His own love toward us, in that while we were yet sinners, Christ died for us.

Philippians 2:7-8
But made himself of no reputation, and took upon him the form of a servant, and was made in the likeness of men: And being found in fashion as a man, he humbled himself, and became obedient unto death, even the death of the cross.

1 John 3:16 NASB
We know love by this, that He laid down His life for us.

10. Did God punish Jesus for our sins?

The Bible is clear that what Jesus did was of His own volition. Jesus was obedient to the will of God the Father, and He gave up His life of His own accord as a sacrifice for every person's sin. Jesus was not punished, but rather He freely accepted the punishment for sin that rightly was due all sinners. God, by His grace and love, did not leave men to die in their sins. He provided a means of salvation, through Jesus Christ, as a way in which all could come to Him and have life (Matthew 20:28; Mark 10:45; John 3:16; John 10:11; Romans 5:6-8; Philippians 2:7-8 and 1 John 3:16).

Study Questions

1. Read Genesis chapter 3. Describe Adam and Eve's sin. What was different about each of their sins?__

    _____

    _____

    _____

2. Read Jeremiah 31:31-34. God speaks of a broken covenant and a new covenant. What is a covenant?
    Describe the new covenant. _____

    _____

    _____

    _____

    _____

3. Read Romans 5:12-19. Is there anyone that is without sin? What does this passage say about the gift
    of God?_____

    _____

    _____

    _____

    _____

Lesson Journal

Use this section to record your thoughts on the topics in this lesson.

_____

_____

_____

_____

_____

_____

_____

_____

Lesson 6
The Flood and the Tower

Scripture Reading

- Read Genesis chapters 6 through 9 (the account of Noah and the flood)
- Genesis 11:1-9 (the tower of Babel)

Introduction

After Adam and Eve sinned, the sinful behavior of their descendents increased to great proportions. The sin of the human race was overwhelming and God was grieved that He had created man. God allowed mankind many years to turn to Him and follow His ways before He decided His only recourse was to destroy all life on the earth. He selected one man, Noah, and his family to spare in order to preserve life. God planned a worldwide flood to destroy every living creature on the face of the earth, and instructed Noah to build an ark, a huge boat. The ark would save Noah and his family, and representatives of all breathing creatures to repopulate the earth after the flood.

Noah believed God and followed His instructions, working about 100 years on the ark and preaching to the wicked before God sent the waters of the flood upon the face of the earth. When the floodwaters came, the entire earth was covered with water. After more than a year of waiting for the water to dry and recede, Noah and his family were able to exit the ark. God then made a covenant with Noah. God promised to never again destroy the people of the earth with a flood. This covenant was made with Noah and promised to all future generations.

God once again commanded mankind to be fruitful and fill the earth, but mankind's sinful behavior was soon evident. Instead of scattering over the earth, the population grew and settled in one location and built a shrine to man in the form of a tower. This act initiated idolatry and the worship of manmade objects instead of God. God intervened by confounding the language causing the population to disperse and scatter according to the languages that were spoken.

This lesson focuses on mankind's sinful behavior and rejection of God, and God's patience and grace as He gives ample time and opportunity for all to come to repentance.

1. What happened after Adam and Eve were driven out of the garden?

Adam and Eve had children, including two sons, Cain and Abel. Cain worked the ground and Abel tended flocks and both had knowledge of God and a relationship with God. Cain and Abel offered sacrifices to God, Cain made an offering from his harvest of the field and Abel offered to God the first and best of his flock. Abel had a genuine faith in God, for which he is commended in the New Testament book of Hebrews (11:4), and his offering was pleasing to God. Cain's attitude toward God was different than Abel's and his deeds were evil (1 John 3:11-12), so God had no regard for Cain's offering. God presented Cain the option of doing what was right, but instead Cain led his brother to a field where he killed him (Genesis 4:3-5, 8).

After Abel was murdered, Eve bore a son she named Seth. Eve considered Seth as the one to take the place of her righteous son Abel. It is through Seth that a line of people were established that "call upon the name of the Lord" (Genesis 4:26). Seth's offspring and descendants followed God, but as the population increased, sin escalated to a point where the "wickedness of man was great on the earth" (Genesis 6:5).

2. How great was the wickedness on the earth?

After killing his brother, Cain was punished by God and became a nomad. His descendants were wicked and more killings through his line are recorded in Genesis 4. As his descendants multiplied, their knowledge began to increase as they built cities and expanded their society. People became more self-centered and began to follow their own definitions of morality, their own ideas of right and wrong. The sin of Adam continued and escalated as society became increasingly violent and depraved (Genesis 6:5, 11-12). God decided to put an end to mankind allowing only the family of Noah, a descendent of Seth, to live. Noah preached but was ignored as people continued to live by their own rules right up until the time of destruction (Matthew 24:37-39 and 2 Peter 2:5).

3. What did Noah do to be spared by God?

Although Noah was a righteous man and "walked with God" (Genesis 6:9), he was not saved by God based on any works of his own, but rather God bestowed His favor upon Noah and saved him and his family. The word used in Genesis 6:8 is *grace*, a word derived from a Hebrew root meaning "to bend or stoop in kindness to an inferior; to favor,"[1] showing that God's grace was unmerited as He chose to condescend and "stoop in kindness" granting favor, or grace, to Noah.

God told Noah that He was going to destroy all life on the earth, and He commanded Noah to build an ark, promising Noah that He would establish a covenant with him. Noah believed all that God said to him, and Noah obeyed God by following His instructions to build an ark. Noah had faith in God, and he and his family were saved (Genesis 6:8, 22 and Hebrews 11:7).

4. Why did God send the flood?

Mankind multiplied on the earth and God allowed much time, over 1000 years, for the people to follow Him. But God became grieved over the wickedness of mankind, and He regretted that He created man. God purposed to eliminate mankind by sending a flood to cover the entire earth. But Noah found favor in the eyes of God, and God allowed Noah and his family to be saved in order to repopulate the earth. Even after declaring His will, God's patience endured as He allowed Noah time to build the ark to save his family and all the land animals, and preach God's righteousness to the wicked people (Genesis 6:6-7; 1 Peter 3:20 and 2 Peter 2:5).

5. What's an ark?

An ark is a great boat or ship, and in a more general sense, something that affords protection and safety. The ark that God commanded Noah to build served as his means of salvation from the flood.

Genesis 6:8-9, 22
But Noah found grace in the eyes of the LORD... Noah walked with God... Thus did Noah; according to all that God commanded him, so did he.

Hebrews 11:7
By faith Noah, being warned of God of things not seen as yet, moved with fear, prepared an ark to the saving of his house; by the which he condemned the world, and became heir of the righteousness which is by faith.

Genesis 6:6-7
The LORD was sorry that He had made man on the earth, and He was grieved in His heart. The LORD said, "I will blot out man whom I have created from the face of the land, from man to animals to creeping things and to birds of the sky; for I am sorry that I have made them."

1 Peter 3:20 NASB
When the patience of God kept waiting in the days of Noah, during the construction of the ark, in which a few, that is, eight persons, were brought safely through the water.

2 Peter 2:5
[God] did not spare the ancient world, but saved Noah, one of eight people, a preacher of righteousness, bringing in the flood on the world of the ungodly.

---

[1] Strong, James *Strong's Hebrew And Greek Dictionaries* World Bible Publishing; Updated edition, May 1, 1992

6. How long did it take to build the ark and how big was it?

It took Noah about 100 years to build the ark which was 450 feet long, 75 feet wide and 45 feet high. A vessel of this size, with three decks as God prescribed, would have more than

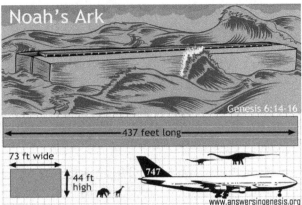

100,000 square feet of floor space, and over 1,500,000 cubic feet of volume (Genesis 6:15-16). During the time it took to build this great ship, Noah preached righteousness to the ungodly and had three sons to assist with the building (2 Peter 2:5).

7. How many of each kind of animal was aboard the ark?

Noah brought aboard the ark seven pairs of every clean animal and one pair of every unclean animal, and seven pairs of each fowl. The distinction regarding clean and unclean animals is not explicitly defined, but likely had to do with sacrificing clean animals. Noah was accustomed to making sacrifice to God, as were his ancestors (Genesis 4:4 and Genesis 8:20).

8. Was the flood global?

The flood was global; the waters covered the entire earth. This is what the Bible teaches and the record of the Bible cannot be dismissed as stories or myths that have been embellished. The waters "prevailed exceedingly" upon the face of the earth, the depth of the waters being so great that the highest mountain was about 22.5 feet below water. Water fell from above and sprang up from below the surface of the earth, separating the earth and causing great geographical changes (Genesis 7:18-20).

9. How long did the flood last?

Over a year elapsed by the time the waters had receded enough for Noah and his family to leave the ark. They had been in the ark 371 days. This long duration is another indication of the volume of water that covered the entire earth, dispelling any notion that the flood was only a local occurrence (Genesis 7:6, 8:13-16).

10. What are some of the changes that occurred on earth as a result of the flood?

The atmosphere changed altering the weather with rainfall, and the geography of land changed due to the initial violent springing of water from beneath the earth's surface and from the great pressure on the earth due to the abundance of water. God allowed meat to supplement man's diet, as the vegetation on the earth needed time to recover and produce fruit after the flood. God also defined capital punishment, declaring that life was in the blood and demanding one's life as the consequence for the taking of life (Genesis 7:11; Genesis 9:3 and Genesis 9:5-6).

11. What was the covenant God made with Noah and his descendants?

God promised man and all other living creatures that He would never again destroy the earth with a flood. God's grace was extended to all of Noah's descendants—all of mankind—and God even included all animals and birds (Genesis 9:8-11).

12. What is the sign of this covenant?

The rainbow.

> *Genesis 9:14-15*
> *It shall come about, when I bring a cloud over the earth, that the bow will be seen in the cloud, and I will remember My covenant, which is between Me and you and every living creature of all flesh; and never again shall the water become a flood to destroy all flesh.*

13. After the flood, what did God command man to do, and what did man do?

After the flood, God again commanded man to be fruitful, increase in number and fill the earth. However, as the population grew, mankind once again rebelled against God, gathering in one place specifically to keep from being scattered over the earth. They began to build a city, and set out to build a tower to honor man and make the people famous to future generations. The people spoke the same language, and were unified in their plans to make a tower to the heavens that would make their names great (Genesis 11:1-2, 4).

Genesis 7:11
...the fountains of the great deep were broken up, and the windows of heaven were opened.

Genesis 9:3 NKJV
Every moving thing that lives shall be food for you. I have given you all things, even as the green herbs.

Genesis 9:5-6 NASB
"Surely I will require your lifeblood; from every beast I will require it. And from every man, from every man's brother I will require the life of man. Whoever sheds man's blood, By man his blood shall be shed, For in the image of God He made man."

Genesis 9:8-11
And God spake unto Noah, and to his sons with him, saying, And I, behold, I establish my covenant with you, and with your seed after you; And with every living creature that is with you, of the fowl, of the cattle, and of every beast of the earth with you; from all that go out of the ark, to every beast of the earth. And I will establish my covenant with you; neither shall all flesh be cut off any more by the waters of a flood; neither shall there any more be a flood to destroy the earth.

Genesis 11:1-2, 4
Now the whole earth used the same language and the same words. It came about as they journeyed east, that they found a plain in the land of Shinar and settled there... They said, "Come, let us build for ourselves a city, and a tower whose top will reach into heaven, and let us make for ourselves a name.

Genesis 11:7-8
Come, let Us go down and there confuse their language, so that they will not understand one another's speech." So the LORD scattered them abroad from there over the face of the whole earth; and they stopped building the city.

Genesis 11:4
...and let us make for ourselves a name

14. What was the result?

God saw that mankind was unified, had built a tower, and had the resolve to accomplish their goals. So God intervened to confuse their efforts. God caused men to begin speaking different languages, thereby interrupting communication and breaking down the unity of mankind. As a result, people began to scatter across the face of the earth gathering together in groups that spoke the same language (Genesis 11:7-8).

15. What is the Tower of Babel's significance?

God's initiation of different languages resulted in the dispersion of the human race and the beginning of different nations. Even more significant was that this event represented the start of the practice of idolatry and the exaltation of man and manmade objects above the Almighty God. The intent of the tower and the city had been the exaltation of man above God (Genesis 11:4).

Study Questions

1. Genesis chapter 5 gives the many generations from Adam to Noah. Consider this as you read Genesis 6:5-22. Was God arbitrary or was God patient with man before He sent the flood?_____

    _____

    _____

    _____

2. Read Genesis 6:10-17. Do you believe the ark as described in this passage was large enough for Noah's cargo? _____

    _____

    _____

    _____

3. Read Genesis 8:20 – 9:17. How did God extend His grace after the flood? _____

    _____

    _____

    _____

4. Read Genesis 11:1-9. What are some reasons why God intervened at the Tower of Babel?_____

    _____

    _____

    _____

    _____

Lesson Journal

Use this section to record your thoughts on the topics in this lesson.

_____

_____

_____

_____

_____

_____

_____

_____

Lesson 7
God's Covenant People

Scripture Reading

- Genesis chapters 12 through 15 (the story of Abraham)
- Exodus chapters 1 through 4 (the story of Moses) and Exodus chapter 20 (God gives the law)
- Judges 2:10-19 (about judges)
- 1 Samuel 16 (the replacement of Saul by David) and 2 Samuel 7 (a covenant with David)
- Acts 2:25-36 (the everlasting throne of David)

Introduction

We see in this lesson the lives of three men, Abraham, Moses, and David, who were each chosen by God to be used for His divine purpose. God extended His covenant with each man, and included blessings that extend to all who believe in God. The Bible refers to this covenant as the first covenant.

After the incident of the Tower of Babel, people dispersed on the earth and began to settle in different areas. These people did not honor God, but instead worshiped idols. It was in an idol-worshiping family that Abraham was born, and from which God called him. God asked Abraham to do some difficult things, but Abraham had faith in God and exercised his faith by obeying what God told him. God initiated a covenant relationship with Abraham promising many blessings, and through Abraham, the nation of Israel was established in the land of Canaan, west of the Jordan River.

Due to famine, Israel relocated to Egypt and grew so great the Egyptians felt threatened and subjected them to slavery. Their suffering as slaves was great, and after nearly 400 years God chose Moses as a deliverer. Moses followed God's call, and by many miracles of God led the people out of Egypt. Their ultimate destination was the land of Canaan where Abraham originally settled. On their way, God revealed more of His character and established a covenant with the nation through Moses. God's covenant made a way for mankind to reestablish (restore) a relationship with God through belief in Him and obedience to His commandments. God wanted to be their leader, and told Moses if the people believed and obeyed, *"I will walk among you, and will be your God, and ye shall be my people,"* (Leviticus 26:12).

The people rejected God as their leader, and whined for a king like the other nations around them. God made it known that He had been rejected, yet granted their request establishing the monarchy of Israel beginning with King Saul. Saul's successor, King David, had a heart for God. God made a covenant with David, establishing his throne as an everlasting throne from which King Jesus would ultimately reign.

Joshua 24:2 NASB
Joshua said to all the people, "Thus says the LORD, the God of Israel, 'From ancient times your fathers lived beyond the River, namely, Terah, the father of Abraham and the father of Nahor, and they served other gods.

Genesis 15:9-10, 17-18
So (God) said to (Abram), "Bring Me a three year old heifer, and a three year old female goat, and a three year old ram, and a turtledove, and a young pigeon." Then he brought all these to Him and cut them in two, and laid each half opposite the other; but he did not cut the birds... It came about when the sun had set, that it was very dark, and behold, there appeared a smoking oven and a flaming torch which passed between these pieces. On that day the LORD made a covenant with Abram.

Genesis 12:1-3
Now the Lord had said unto Abram, Get thee out of thy country, and from thy kindred, and from thy father's house, unto a land that I will shew thee: And I will make of thee a great nation, and I will bless thee, and make thy name great; and thou shalt be a blessing: And I will bless them that bless thee, and curse him that curseth thee: and in thee shall all families of the earth be blessed.

Genesis 12:6-7
And Abram passed through the land unto the place of Sichem, unto the plain of Moreh. And the Canaanite was then in the land. And the Lord appeared unto Abram, and said, Unto thy seed will I give this land: and there builded he an altar unto the Lord, who appeared unto him.

Genesis 15:5 NASB
And (God) took (Abraham) outside and said, "Now look toward the heavens, and count the stars, if you are able to count them." And He said to him, "So shall your descendants be."

Genesis 17:5
Neither shall thy name any more be called Abram, but thy name shall be Abraham; for a father of many nations have I made thee.

1. What were the aftereffects of God's confusing the languages at the Tower of Babel?

The result was the beginning of nations. Over the course of many years, people scattered and those of like languages settled together and built cities. The idolatry that had begun with the building of the Tower of Babel escalated. The descendants of Noah's son Shem settled in the east and worshiped idols.

Yet God determined to have a people who would worship Him, and He chose a man named Abraham to be the father of this people. Abraham was a descendant of Shem (see Genesis 12-15). He was raised in a family that did not honor God, but worshiped idols (Joshua 24:2). His given name was Abram, meaning "exalted father," but God later changed his name to Abraham, meaning "father of a great multitude."

Abraham married his half sister Sarah, and moved with his father and nephew from his home in Ur to the city of Haran. In Haran God revealed Himself to Abraham and promised him many blessings. Abraham left Haran at the age of 75 and continued to grow in his relationship with God. God prospered Abraham and made a covenant with him, reiterating His many promises. Abraham believed God and was considered righteous because of his faith, and God determined to bless the world through Abraham.

2. What were God's covenant promises to Abraham?

God appeared to Abraham and initiated a covenant with him. To ratify His covenant, God required Abraham to shed the blood of animals (Genesis 15:9-10, 17-18). This was not unusual in Abraham's time, and Abraham would have understood that God intended to make, literally *cut*, a covenant with him (Genesis 15:9-10, 17-18).

God declared that Abraham would be blessed in many ways and Abraham believed God. God promised Abraham:

- His name would be great, and God would bless those that bless him and curse those that curse him
- All families of earth would be blessed through Abraham (Genesis 12:1-3, see also Genesis 22:17-18)
- The land of Canaan would be the legacy of Abraham's descendants (Genesis 12:6-7, see also Genesis 13:14-15)
- He would have innumerable descendants (Genesis 15:1-6)
- He would be the father of kings and great nations (Genesis 17:4-8)

3. What was the sign of the Covenant God made with Abraham?

God demanded a sign of the covenant between Abraham and Himself, requiring Abraham and all the males in his family and employ to be circumcised. Circumcision was to continue through each successive generation as a sign of God's blood covenant with Abraham (Genesis 17:10-14).

4. How did the nation promised through Abraham develop?

Abraham obeyed God, received the covenant promises, and became the father of a great nation (Hebrews 11:8-9 and Genesis 22:18).

Through Abraham's promised son, Isaac, his descendants began to multiply and grow. Isaac's son Jacob became known as Israel, and by God's divine leading, famine forced Israel's family to Egypt. Israel's family was just over 70 people when they first entered Egypt, but the people multiplied greatly to the point where the leaders of Egypt feared them. To control the large number of Israelites, Egypt enslaved the people. After over 400 years in Egypt, God brought Israel out of slavery through a leader He raised up, Moses. The Bible gives an excellent summary of the life of Moses in Acts 7:20-36.

The Start of the Nation of Israel

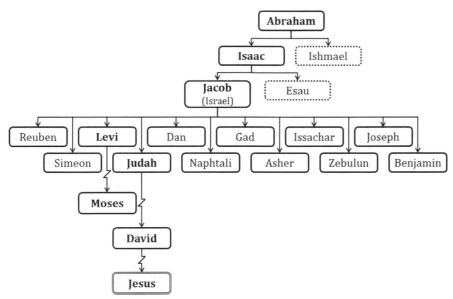

Genesis 17:10-14
"This is My covenant, which you shall keep, between Me and you and your descendants after you: every male among you shall be circumcised. And you shall be circumcised in the flesh of your foreskin, and it shall be the sign of the covenant between Me and you. And every male among you who is eight days old shall be circumcised throughout your generations, a servant who is born in the house or who is bought with money from any foreigner, who is not of your descendants. A servant who is born in your house or who is bought with your money shall surely be circumcised; thus shall My covenant be in your flesh for an everlasting covenant. But an uncircumcised male who is not circumcised in the flesh of his foreskin, that person shall be cut off from his people; he has broken My covenant."

Hebrews 11:8-9
By faith Abraham, when he was called, obeyed by going out to a place which he was to receive for an inheritance; and he went out, not knowing where he was going. By faith he lived as an alien in the land of promise, as in a foreign land, dwelling in tents with Isaac and Jacob, fellow heirs of the same promise;

Genesis 22:18 NCV
Through your descendants all the nations on the earth will be blessed, because you obeyed me.

Hebrews 11:27-29 NIV
By faith he left Egypt, not fearing the king's anger; he persevered because he saw him who is invisible. By faith he kept the Passover and the sprinkling of blood, so that the destroyer of the firstborn would not touch the firstborn of Israel. By faith the people passed through the Red Sea as on dry land; but when the Egyptians tried to do so, they were drowned.

Exodus 19:5-6 NASB
"'Now then, if you will indeed obey My voice and keep My covenant, then you shall be My own possession among all the peoples, for all the earth is Mine; 6and you shall be to Me a kingdom of priests and a holy nation.' These are the words that you (Moses) shall speak to the sons of Israel."

Leviticus 25:55, 26:3,12
For unto me the children of Israel are servants; they are my servants whom I brought forth out of the land of Egypt: I am the LORD your God... If ye walk in my statutes, and keep my commandments, and do them... I will walk among you, and will be your God, and ye shall be my people.

Numbers 14:11
The LORD said to Moses, "How long will this people spurn Me? And how long will they not believe in Me, despite all the signs which I have performed in their midst?"

Psalm 78:21-22
And anger also mounted against Israel, Because they did not believe in God And did not trust in His salvation.

Hebrews 3:16-19
For who provoked Him when they had heard? Indeed, did not all those who came out of Egypt led by Moses? And with whom was He angry for forty years? Was it not with those who sinned, whose bodies fell in the wilderness? And to whom did He swear that they would not enter His rest, but to those who were disobedient? So we see that they were not able to enter because of unbelief.

5. What did God instruct Moses to do?

God instructed Moses to return to Egypt to lead the people of Israel out of slavery into a land that would be their home. They were to return to the land where Abraham had settled. By many miracles of God, Moses secured the release of the people of Israel from their bondage in Egypt. He led them east of Egypt, across the Red Sea, to an area of wilderness where God met them and made a covenant through Moses with the nation of Israel (Hebrews 11:27-29).

6. What is the covenant God made through Moses?

God continued the covenant that He had established with Abraham, the first covenant, by giving more revelation to Moses concerning the relationship between God and His people. This covenant was extensive, but can be divided into four categories:

- The moral law (the ten commandments)
- Ceremonial law
- Civil law
- The plan for the tabernacle

On Mount Sinai God wrote His moral law in tablets of stone. God also promised that the people would be His possession and that He would continually lead them if they kept the covenant that He established (Exodus 19:5-6 and Leviticus 25:55, 26:3, 12).

7. How were Moses and the nation of Israel to keep their relationship with God?

They were to believe what God told them and by their faith obey all that God had commanded. Being obedient follows complete faith in God. Soon after receiving the covenant, many in the nation abandoned their faith and fell into unbelief, afraid to enter the land God had promised. God judged them because of their unbelief (Numbers 14:11; Psalm 78:21-22 and Hebrews 3:16-19).

8. What happened if someone broke the law?

God provided ways to deal with those that did not keep the law, those who sinned. God made it clear that through sacrifice, the shed blood of an animal, anyone who believed in God could make atonement for (cover) sin. Yet God knew that no man could keep the law perfectly, so He made His grace known by stating He *"forgives iniquity, transgression and sin,"* (Exodus 34:7 NASB).

Before Jesus Christ, God provided a way, through the law, to deal with sin for those who believed Him yet broke the law. Now, because of the sacrifice of Jesus Christ, there is no longer the need for other sacrifices, and for those who believe in Jesus Christ the *"righteousness of the law might be fulfilled in us,"* (Romans 8:4). Jesus Christ put an end to the necessity of animal sacrifice by freely giving His life as a sacrifice for sin (Hebrews 10:10-12 and Romans 3:20-24).

9. What happened after Moses died?

The people of Israel entered the land of Canaan that God had promised them, and began to establish the land as their own. God's law was supreme and the nation did well when the people obeyed and followed God, but fell under the subjugation of an enemy when they rejected God. When the bondage of the enemy grew too strong, the people cried out to God. He was faithful to rescue them by raising up a judge to lead the people to victory, and they would once again turn to God for a time. This cycle repeated for over 300 years until the people no longer relied on God at all, but on themselves. They rejected God as king, and did what they wanted to do, eventually demanding an earthly king to reign over them. In summary:

- God was to be the king of Israel (Judges 8:22-23)

- The people rejected God and demanded an earthly king (Judges 21:25 and 1 Samuel 8:5-7)

- God established the throne in Israel (1 Samuel 10:1)

After establishing the throne, God raised up a man named David from the tribe of Judah to be king over Israel. David, the second king of Israel, was a man that followed God, so much so that the prophet Samuel declared *"The LORD has sought out for Himself a man after His own heart, and the LORD has appointed him as ruler over His people,"* (1 Samuel 13:14 NASB). During his reign, God made a covenant with David, promising him that his throne would endure forever through his descendants.

Hebrews 10:10-12
By this will we have been sanctified through the offering of the body of Jesus Christ once for all. And every priest stands daily ministering and offering time after time the same sacrifices, which can never take away sins; but He, having offered one sacrifice for sins for all time, sat down at the right hand of God.

Romans 3:20-24
Therefore no one will be declared righteous in his sight by observing the law; rather, through the law we become conscious of sin. But now a righteousness from God, apart from law, has been made known, to which the Law and the Prophets testify. This righteousness from God comes through faith in Jesus Christ to all who believe. There is no difference, for all have sinned and fall short of the glory of God, and are justified freely by his grace through the redemption that came by Christ Jesus.

Judges 8:22-23 NLT
Then the Israelites said to Gideon, "Be our ruler! You and your son and your grandson will be our rulers, for you have rescued us from Midian." But Gideon replied, "I will not rule over you, nor will my son. The LORD will rule over you!"

Judges 21:25
In those days there was no king in Israel: every man did that which was right in his own eyes.

1 Samuel 8:5-7 NLT
"Look," they told (Samuel), "you are now old, and your sons are not like you. Give us a king like all the other nations have." Samuel was very upset with their request and went to the LORD for advice. "Do as they say," the LORD replied, "for it is me they are rejecting, not you. They don't want me to be their king any longer.

1 Samuel 10:1
Then Samuel took a flask of olive oil and poured it over Saul's head. He kissed Saul on the cheek and said, "I am doing this because the LORD has appointed you to be the leader of his people Israel.

10. What were God's covenant promises to David and the nation of Israel?

Through the prophet Nathan, God promised (1 Chronicles 17:7-15):

- He would make David's name great

- The nation of Israel would have a land to call their own, and they would receive rest from their enemies

- God said He would make David a house, not a house of brick and mortar, but a family and posterity such that it could be said of any descendant that they were *"of the house and lineage of David"*(Luke 4:4)

- David's descendants would reign on his throne

- The throne of David's son would be established forever, and the Lord would forever love him

- David's son would build a house (temple) for the Lord, and God would be his father, and he would be God's son

11. What happened to Israel?

The nation of Israel split only two generations after the death of king David. Two independent nations were established, one to the north called Israel (sometimes referred to as Ephraim or Samaria, the capital city), and one to the south called Judah (sometimes referred to as Jerusalem, the capital city). Each of these nations eventually fell into the hands of enemies and no longer existed as independent nations. Israel fell in 722 BC and Judah in 587 BC.

Although God allowed a time for the nation to be rebuilt, Israel never did regain independence during the periods of history covered in the Bible, and was continually subjected to the rule and authority of another empire. When Jesus Christ was born, the nation was under the rule of the Roman Empire. It wasn't until November 29, 1947, when the United Nations General Assembly passed Resolution 181, that Israel was officially recognized as a nation again.

12. If Israel fell as a nation, how could David's throne be eternal?

The covenant promise to David was that his throne would be eternal through his son. Although the dynasty was interrupted, one was eventually born that could fulfill the promise of taking the throne forever. That person is Jesus Christ, who is often referred to as "son of David" (Mary and Joseph, the earthly parents of Jesus, had ancestral roots that traced back to King David).

David and the prophets in the Old Testament spoke of one who would come to fulfill the promise of an eternal throne, and the New Testament confirms that Jesus was that fulfillment (Isaiah 9:6-7 and Acts 13:22-23).

The apostle Peter said the following about the eternal throne of David, preaching on the day of Pentecost:

Acts 2:25-36 NLT

"King David said this about (Jesus):

'I know the Lord is always with me. I will not be shaken, for he is right beside me. No wonder my heart is filled with joy, and my mouth shouts his praises! My body rests in hope. For you will not leave my soul among the dead or allow your Holy One to rot in the grave. You have shown me the way of life, and you will give me wonderful joy in your presence.'

Dear brothers, think about this! David wasn't referring to himself when he spoke these words I have quoted, for he died and was buried, and his tomb is still here among us. But he was a prophet, and he knew God had promised with an oath that one of David's own descendants would sit on David's throne as the Messiah... This prophecy was speaking of Jesus, whom God raised from the dead, and we all are witnesses of this. Now he sits on the throne of highest honor in heaven, at God's right hand... For David himself never ascended into heaven, yet he said,

'The LORD said to my Lord, Sit in honor at my right hand until I humble your enemies, making them a footstool under your feet.'

So let it be clearly known by everyone in Israel that God has made this Jesus whom you crucified to be both Lord and Messiah!"

Isaiah 9:6-7 NLT
For a child is born to us, a son is given to us. And the government will rest on his shoulders. These will be his royal titles: Wonderful Counselor, Mighty God, Everlasting Father, Prince of Peace. His ever expanding, peaceful government will never end. He will rule forever with fairness and justice from the throne of his ancestor David.

Acts 13:22-23 NASB
He raised up David to be their king, concerning whom He also testified and said, "I have found David the son of Jesse, a man after my heart, who will do all My will." From the descendants of this man, according to promise, God has brought to Israel a Savior, Jesus.

Study Questions

1. Read Genesis 17:10-14. Did God's covenant limit His grace to Abraham and his descendants only? ___

    _____

    _____

2. Read Hebrews 11:8-34. Abraham, Moses, and David are mentioned in this passage. How did these men respond to God's covenant? Now read Hebrews 11:6. Do you share that common ground with Abraham, Moses, and David? Why or why not? _____

    _____

    _____

    _____

3. God promised David his throne would be eternal. Can you explain this after reading Acts 2:25-36? ___

    _____

    _____

    _____

    _____

4. Do you think the eternal throne of David has anything to do with the government of the nation of Israel here on earth today? Why or why not? _____

    _____

    _____

    _____

Lesson Journal

Use this section to record your thoughts on the topics in this lesson.

_____

_____

_____

_____

_____

_____

_____

_____

_____

Lesson 8
The Birth and Ministry of Jesus

Scripture Reading

- John 1:1-14 (Jesus the Son of God)

- Luke 1:26-38 (angelic visit to Mary); Luke 2:1-20 (the birth of Jesus) and Luke 4:14-21 (Jesus announces His ministry)

Introduction

The previous lessons introduced God and His creation from the beginning, showed how sin entered the world through Adam, and highlighted the obvious grace of God as He revealed His plan to remedy the sin problem through a promised Savior. His grace and continued promises through Noah, Abraham, Moses, and David bring us to this lesson on the birth and ministry of Jesus, the promised Savior.

Jesus is God, the second person of the Trinity, who came to earth as a man by being born of a virgin. God's plan for man was to provide a final sacrifice for sin, a sacrifice that would not just cover sins, but eradicate them such that God could declare *"I will forgive their iniquity, and their sin I will remember no more,"* (Jeremiah 31:34, Hebrews 10:17). God executed His plan by causing a virgin, Mary, to conceive and deliver a child, Jesus. Jesus was fully God and fully man; He entered the world through the same natural process as every other man, but was miraculously conceived by God. He is both God and man, unlike cult leaders who claim to be a god.

Jesus was born in the city of Bethlehem, in the province of Judea, when the empire of Rome ruled over Israel. At the time of His birth Mary and His earthly father Joseph had traveled to a crowded Bethlehem, where no room was available for them. They took shelter where the animals were kept, and it was in this humble setting that Jesus entered the world and was laid in a manger. His miraculous birth was announced by angels and heralded by shepherds who came to honor Him.

Jesus was raised to learn the trade of Joseph, a carpenter. When He was about 30 years old He began to preach repentance and teach those who believed He was the Son of God. He also performed many miracles of healing. His preaching and teaching caused quite a stir, but many did not believe He was who He said He was. Some leaders worried He and His followers would cause an uprising and they sought to kill Jesus. Jesus allowed those who sought His life to accomplish their desire, as He willingly gave His life as a final sacrifice for sin. Jesus accomplished what previous sacrifices could not; as His sacrifice, once, for all, takes away sin.

John 1:10, 14
He was in the world, and the world was made by him, and the world knew him not... And the Word (Jesus) was made flesh, and dwelt among us, (and we beheld his glory, the glory as of the only begotten of the Father,) full of grace and truth.

Philippians 2:4-7 NLT
Your attitude should be the same that Christ Jesus had. Though he was God, he did not demand and cling to his rights as God. He made himself nothing; he took the humble position of a slave and appeared in human form.

1. Who is Jesus?

Jesus is God, the second person of the Trinity, who came to earth as a man by being born to a virgin. This union of divinity with humanity is called the incarnation (John 1:10, 14 and Philippians 2:4-7). The incarnation of Jesus fulfilled hundreds of prophecies written in the Old Testament.

The table below lists just 29 Old Testament prophecies of Jesus, these distinguished because they were fulfilled in a single day.

	Prophecy	Old Testament Reference	New Testament Fulfillment
1.	Betrayed by a friend	Psalm 41:9	Matthew 10:4
2.	Sold for 30 pieces of silver	Zechariah 11:12	Matthew 26:15
3.	Money to be thrown down in God's house	Zechariah 11:13	Matthew 27:5
4.	Price given for potter's field	Zechariah 11:13	Matthew 27:7
5.	Forsaken by His disciples	Zechariah 13:7	Mark 14:50
6.	Accused by false witnesses	Psalm 35:11	Matthew 26:59-61
7.	Mute before accusers	Isaiah 53:7	Matthew 27:12-19
8.	Wounded and bruised	Isaiah 53:5	Matthew 27:26
9.	Smitten and spit upon	Isaiah 50:6 Micah 5:1	Matthew 26:67
10.	Mocked	Psalm 22:7-8	Matthew 27:31
11.	Fell under the burden of the cross	Psalm 109:24	John 19:17 Luke 23:26
12.	Hands and feet pierced	Psalm 22:16	Luke 23:33
13.	Crucified with thieves	Isaiah 53:12	Matthew 27:38
14.	Made intercession for His persecutors	Isaiah 53:12	Luke 23:34
15.	Rejected by his own	Isaiah 53:3	John 7:5, 48
16.	Hated without a cause	Psalm 69:4	John 15:25
17.	Friends stood afar off	Psalm 38:11	Luke 23:49
18.	People shook their heads	Psalm 109:25	Matthew 27:39
19.	Stared upon	Psalm 22:17	Luke 23:35
20.	Garments divided and lots cast for garments	Psalm 22:18	John 19:23-24
21.	Suffered thirst	Psalm 69:21	John 19:28
22.	Gall and vinegar offered to Him	Psalm 69:21	Matthew 27:34
23.	His forsaken cry	Psalm 22:1	Matthew 27:46
24.	Committed Himself to God	Psalm 31:5	Luke 23:46
25.	His bones not broken	Psalm 34:20	John 19:33
26.	His heart broken	Psalm 22:14	John 19:34
27.	His side pierced	Zechariah 12:10	John 19:34
28.	Darkness over the land	Amos 8:9	Matthew 27:45
29.	Buried in a rich man's tomb	Isaiah 53:9	Matthew 27:57-60

2. If Jesus is God, why was He born of a woman?

God's plan for man was to provide a final sacrifice for sin, a sacrifice that would not just cover past sins, but eradicate them such that God could declare *"I will forgive their iniquity, and their sin I will remember no more,"* (Jeremiah 31:34 and Hebrews 10:17). God began to reveal His plan immediately after man sinned. After Adam and Eve sinned, God said of the serpent (Satan) *"I will put enmity between you and the woman, and between your seed and her Seed; He shall bruise your head, and you shall bruise His heel,"* (Genesis 3:15). The reference to the Seed of the woman is a reference to Jesus Christ, the one who would come to defeat the serpent (Satan).

The promise of a Savior was also given to Abraham, when God said, *"In your seed all the nations of the earth shall be blessed,"* (Genesis 22:18), which is explained in Galatians 3:16 where the apostle Paul states: *"Now to Abraham and his Seed were the promises made. He does not say, 'And to seeds,' as of many, but as of one, 'And to your Seed,' who is Christ."* God executed His plan by causing a virgin, Mary, to conceive a child, and that child was born Jesus (Genesis 3:14-15; Genesis 22:18; Galatians 3:16; Isaiah 7:14 and Luke 1:34-35).

3. Why is the virgin birth so important?

Jesus was fully God and fully man, and He entered the world through the same natural process as every other man, but was miraculously conceived by God. His virgin birth had been prophesied some 700 years prior to it actually taking place. If Jesus had both a natural father and a natural mother, He would not be unique, but like any other man. However, He was conceived by the Holy Ghost and born of the virgin Mary, coming into our world without inheriting the original sin of Adam. He is both God and man, distinguished from cult leaders who can only claim to be a god (Isaiah 7:14; Matthew 1:22; see also Luke 1:28, 31, 34-35 and Hebrews 4:15).

4. Where was Jesus born?

Jesus was born in the city of Bethlehem, in the province of Judea, when the empire of Rome ruled Israel. The circumstances of His birth were unusual. His mother, Mary, and his earthly father, Joseph, had traveled from the neighboring province of Galilee for a census, which required registration and the paying of taxes at one's city of birth. With many families gathered together for the census, there was no room in the inn for Mary and Joseph, so they took shelter where the animals were kept. Jesus was born in this humble abode of the animals, and his mother laid Him in a manger (Micah 5:2; Matthew 2:5-6; see also Luke 2:1-7).

Genesis 3:14-15
So the LORD God said to the serpent: "Because you have done this, You are cursed more than all cattle, and more than every beast of the field; On your belly you shall go, And you shall eat dust All the days of your life. And I will put enmity between you and the woman, and between your seed and her Seed; He shall bruise your head, and you shall bruise His heel."

Genesis 22:18
In your seed all the nations of the earth shall be blessed, because you have obeyed My voice.

Galatians 3:16
Now to Abraham and his Seed were the promises made. He does not say, "And to seeds," as of many, but as of one, "And to your Seed," who is Christ.

Isaiah 7:14
Therefore the Lord Himself will give you a sign: Behold, a virgin will be with child and bear a son, and she will call His name Immanuel.

Luke 1:34-35 NIV
"How will this be," Mary asked the angel, "since I am a virgin?" The angel answered, "The Holy Spirit will come upon you, and the power of the Most High will overshadow you. So the holy one to be born will be called the Son of God.

Matthew 1:22
Now all this took place to fulfill what was spoken by the Lord through the prophet: "Behold, the virgin shall be with child and shall bear a son, and they shall call his name Immanuel," which translated means, "God with us."

Micah 5:2 NIV
But you, Bethlehem Ephrathah, though you are small among the clans of Judah, out of you will come for me one who will be ruler over Israel, whose origins are from of old, from ancient times.

Matthew 2:5-6 TLB
O little town of Bethlehem, you are not just an unimportant Judean village, for a Governor shall rise from you to rule my people Israel.

Luke 1:26-27

And in the sixth month the angel Gabriel was sent from God unto a city of Galilee, named Nazareth, To a virgin espoused to a man whose name was Joseph, of the house of David; and the virgin's name was Mary.

Luke 2:10-14

And the angel said unto them, Fear not: for, behold, I bring you good tidings of great joy, which shall be to all people. For unto you is born this day in the city of David a Saviour, which is Christ the Lord... And suddenly there was with the angel a multitude of the heavenly host praising God...

Luke 2:28-30 NIV

Simeon took (Jesus) in his arms and praised God, saying: "Sovereign Lord, as you have promised, you now dismiss your servant in peace. For my eyes have seen your salvation, which you have prepared in the sight of all people..."

Matthew 2:1-2 NASB

Now after Jesus was born in Bethlehem of Judea in the days of Herod the king, magi from the east arrived in Jeru-salem, saying, "Where is He who has been born King of the Jews? For we saw His star in the east and have come to worship Him."

Matthew 2:16 NASB

Then when Herod saw that he had been tricked by the magi, he became very enraged, and sent and slew all the male children who were in Bethlehem and all its vicinity, from two years old and under...

Leviticus 12:7-8 NASB

This is the law for her who bears a child, whether a male or a female. But if she cannot afford a lamb, then she shall take two turtledoves or two young pigeons...

Luke 2:22, 24

And when the days of her purification according to the law of Moses were accomplished, they brought him to Jerusalem, to present him to the Lord... And to offer a sacrifice according to that which is said in the law of the Lord, A pair of turtledoves, or two young pigeons.

Matthew 13:55

Is not this the carpenter's son?

2 Corinthians 5:21

For He made Him who knew no sin to be sin for us,

5. What other unique occurrences are associated with the birth of Jesus?

- An angel announced His conception to Mary and Joseph (Luke 1:26-27; see also Matthew 1:20)

- An angel announced His birth to shepherds, and a multitude of angels praising God appeared to the shepherds (Luke 2:10-14)

- A prophet, Simeon, and a prophetess, Anna, recognized Him as Savior eight days after his birth when He was circumcised and presented in the temple (Luke 2:28-30; see also Luke 2:36, 38)

- A star appeared to wise men from the east and directed them to Bethlehem (Matthew 2:1-2)

- The presiding Jewish king under Roman rule, King Herod, heard of the birth of Jesus, believed Him to be the next King of the Jews, and attempted to have Him killed (Matthew 2:16-18)

6. Was Jesus raised differently because He was the Son of God?

Much of Jesus' life as a child and young adult is not documented. What is documented in the Bible of His young life is that He was born into a poor family (Leviticus 12:7-8 and Luke 2:22, 24), He was circumcised on His eighth day, dedicated in the temple in Jerusalem, He debated with teachers in the Jerusalem temple once when He was 12 years old, and He was trained as, and worked as, a carpenter. The people of His hometown of Nazareth recognized both Jesus and His earthly father, Joseph, as carpenters (Matthew 13:55; see also Mark 6:3).

He was likely raised as a normal Jewish boy, learning the word of God and the traditions of Judaism in the synagogue in Nazareth, while *"increasing in wisdom and stature"* (Luke 2:52). It seems that Jesus did not receive an advanced education, as his neighbors were astonished when He began to teach in the synagogue as an adult. The locals questioned His credentials, making note that He was merely a carpenter, implying that He was overstepping His station in life.

He left home to begin His ministry when He was about 30 years old, and due to the unbelief of the residents of Nazareth, Jesus adopted Capernaum, a fishing village at the northern end of the Sea of Galilee, as his hometown. Through all this time, Jesus remained sinless (2 Corinthians 5:21; see also Mark 6:1; 5-6 and Matthew 4:13).

7. How long was Jesus' ministry?

For three and a half years Jesus preached repentance and belief in the Savior, and taught disciples who would continue to preach and spread Christianity after He had left the earth. Jesus also performed many miraculous signs throughout Jerusalem and the surrounding areas. Jesus specifically taught that He was the Anointed One (the Messiah, the Savior) by claiming to be the One who fulfilled the prophecies of the Old Testament, most notably quoting (in Luke 4:18-19) a passage from Isaiah 61, stating *"The Spirit of the Lord GOD is upon Me, Because the Lord has anointed Me..."* (Mark 1:14-18; Matthew 28:19-20 and Luke 4:21; see also Isaiah 61:1-3).

8. For what purpose did Jesus come to earth?

Jesus came to earth to repair the breach between man and God that was caused by sin. A payment for sin had to be made. Sin separates man from God, and God required a payment for sin before man could restore his fellowship with God. Before Jesus, men made sacrifices to cover their sin; this was the payment that God required. Jesus willingly gave up His life, and made payment for sin once and for all. By doing so, Jesus redeemed (bought back) mankind (1 Peter 1:18-19; Titus 2:11, 13-14; see also Philippians 2:8; Galatians 2:20 and 1 Timothy 2:5-6).

9. How did Jesus' life on earth come to an end?

The preaching of Jesus was not received well by everyone, specifically the Jewish leaders. Many did not believe that Jesus was the Son of God. Some of the leaders felt threatened by Jesus' preaching and feared an uprising that would cause a Roman retaliation resulting in their loss of power. These Jews looked for ways to accuse Jesus of crimes. After Jesus had openly preached and taught for over three years, He was accused of blasphemy, being equal with God. This was a charge that Jesus refused to deny. Through several trials of false accusers and different authorities, the Jewish religious leaders persuaded the Roman authorities to execute Jesus by crucifixion. Through His trials, Jesus was mocked, beaten, flogged, and finally nailed to a cross. He died after hanging on the cross for several hours (Matthew 27:27-30; Mark 15:15; see also Luke 22:63-64; Luke 23:33 and Acts 2:36).

Mark 1:14-18 NIV
Jesus went into Galilee, proclaiming the good news of God. "The time has come," he said. "The kingdom of God is near. Repent and believe the good news!" As Jesus walked beside the Sea of Galilee, he saw Simon and his brother Andrew casting a net into the lake, for they were fishermen. "Come, follow me," Jesus said, "and I will make you fishers of men." At once they left their nets and followed him.

Matthew 28:19-20
(Jesus said), "Therefore go and make disciples of all nations, baptizing them in the name of the Father and of the Son and of the Holy Spirit, and teaching them to obey everything I have commanded you. And surely I am with you always, to the very end of the age."

Luke 4:21
"Today this Scripture is fulfilled in your hearing."

1 Peter 1:18-19 NIV
For you know that it was not with perishable things such as silver or gold that you were redeemed from the empty way of life handed down to you from your forefathers, but with the precious blood of Christ, a lamb without blemish or defect.

Titus 2:11, 13-14 NIV
For the grace of God that brings salvation has appeared to all men... our great God and Savior, Jesus Christ, who gave himself for us to redeem us from all wickedness and to purify for himself a people that are his very own, eager to do what is good.

Matthew 27:27-30 NIV
Then the governor's soldiers took Jesus into the Praetorium and gathered the whole company of soldiers around him. They stripped him and put a scarlet robe on him, and then twisted together a crown of thorns and set it on his head. They put a staff in his right hand and knelt in front of him and mocked him. "Hail, king of the Jews!" they said. They spit on him, and took the staff and struck him on the head again and again.

Mark 15:15 NIV
(Pilate) had Jesus flogged, and handed him over to be crucified.

Romans 1:3 NIV

(Jesus) as to his human nature was a descendant of David...

Isaiah 9:6-7 NLT

For a child is born to us, a son is given to us. And the government will rest on his shoulders... He will rule forever with fairness and justice from the throne of his ancestor David.

Acts 2:30 NLT

David was a prophet, and he knew God had promised with an oath that one of David's own descendants would sit on David's throne as the Messiah...

10. Was Jesus the promised King from the line of David?

Jesus in His human nature was a descendant of King David as was promised and prophesied in the Old Testament. His kingship was not of this world, as He declared, *"My kingdom is not of this world,"* (John 18:36). His throne is heavenly and it is where He resides today (Romans 1:3; Isaiah 9:6-7 and Acts 2:30).

Study Questions

1. Select and read several of the Old Testament prophecies and their New Testament fulfillments given in the table under question 1. Is there any doubt that Jesus was the One prophesied? What are your thoughts? _____

    _____

    _____

    _____

    _____

2. From studying this lesson, can you say why the virgin birth is so important to Christianity? _____

    _____

    _____

    _____

    _____

3. Read Luke 2:1-20 and give some insight into why the birth of Jesus was no ordinary birth._____

    _____

    _____

    _____

    _____

    _____

Lesson Journal

Use this section to record your thoughts on the topics in this lesson.

_____

_____

_____

_____

_____

_____

_____

_____

_____

Lesson 9
A Walk to the Cross

Scripture Reading

- Mark chapters 14 through 16 (the passion, or suffering, of Christ)

- Select one of the other gospels and read the account of Jesus' death and resurrection.

Introduction

For almost two thousand years the Christian Church has taught that Jesus was crucified, died, and was resurrected three days later. This has long been one of the church's foundational beliefs, along with the inerrancy of the Bible, the virgin birth, the future second coming of Jesus, etc.

Since the day Jesus was born there were those on the earth that sought to take His life. The presence of Jesus threatened secular leaders as well as the religious establishment, the former fearing He was a political leader and the latter because He taught against their hypocrisy with authority and gained many followers.

Jesus suffered for us and gave His life, and He continues the live and reign as He sits at the right hand of God. This lesson focuses on the last days of Jesus' life here on earth, and ends with a cornerstone of Christianity, the resurrection of Jesus.

Matthew 2:16 NIV
When Herod realized that he had been outwitted by the Magi, he was furious, and he gave orders to kill all the boys in Bethlehem and its vicinity who were two years old and under, in accordance with the time he had learned from the Magi.

Luke 4:28-30 NIV
All the people in the synagogue were furious when they heard this. They got up, drove him out of the town, and took him to the brow of the hill on which the town was built, in order to throw him down the cliff. But he walked right through the crowd and went on his way

John 8:58-59 NIV
"I tell you the truth," Jesus answered, "before Abraham was born, I am!" At this, they picked up stones to stone him, but Jesus hid himself, slipping away from the temple grounds.

Matthew 12:14 NASB
But the Pharisees went out and conspired against Him, as to how they might destroy Him.

John 11:41-48, 53
So they took away the stone. Then Jesus looked up and said, "Father, I thank you that you have heard me. I knew that you always hear me, but I said this for the benefit of the people standing here, that they may believe that you sent me." When he had said this, Jesus called in a loud voice, "Lazarus, come out!" The dead man came out, his hands and feet wrapped with strips of linen, and a cloth around his face. Jesus said to them, "Take off the grave clothes and let him go." Therefore many of the Jews who had come to visit Mary, and had seen what Jesus did, put their faith in him. But some of them went to the Pharisees and told them what Jesus had done. Then the chief priests and the Pharisees called a meeting of the Sanhedrin. "What are we accomplishing?" they asked. "Here is this man performing many miraculous signs. If we let him go on like this, everyone will believe in him, and then the Romans will come and take away both our place and our nation..." So from that day on they plotted to take his life.

1. If Jesus never sinned, why did people seek to kill Him?

From the day Jesus was born there were those who sought to take His life. Early on, King Herod, who ruled over the Roman province of Judea and the surrounding Jewish provinces, tried to kill Jesus. When Herod heard that there was one born *"King of the Jews"* (Matthew 2:2) he felt his throne threatened. In an attempt to kill Jesus, Herod ordered *"all the male children who were in Bethlehem and all its vicinity, from two years old and under"* (Matthew 2:16) to be killed. Jesus' earthly father Joseph was warned of this plot in a dream and fled to Egypt with his family.

When Jesus was about 30 years old He began a ministry of teaching, preaching, and healing. He taught that He was the Son of God, the One promised as a Savior. Many believed Jesus but many did not. On two occasions preceding His death by crucifixion, Jesus spoke very directly about who He was (Luke 4:16-30 and John 8:12-59). The people and leaders who heard what He said sought to kill Him on both occasions, and in both instances Jesus eluded His would-be killers.

His preaching and teaching continued to create panic in the Jewish religious leaders. Many did not believe that Jesus was the Son of God, and some of the leaders felt threatened by Jesus' preaching, fearing an uprising that would cause their loss of power if the Romans retaliated. The Jewish leaders looked for ways to accuse Jesus of crimes and ultimately were successful in arresting Jesus and inciting crowds of people to demand His death (Matthew 2:16; Luke 4:28-30; John 8:58-59 and Matthew 12:14).

2. What happened that lead to Jesus' arrest?

Jesus taught openly for three and a half years, as the Jewish leaders grew increasingly hostile toward Him. They made their decision to take His life after Jesus raised His friend Lazarus from the dead (John 11:53), a great miracle resulting in many new believers. When the leaders heard of this miracle they held a meeting, saying to each other, *"Here is a man performing many miraculous signs. If we let him go on like this, everyone will believe in him, and then the Romans will come and take away both our place and our nation,"* (John 11:47-48 NIV). The chief priest advised, *"It is better for you that one man die for the people than the whole nation perish,"* (John 11:50 NIV). When the meeting concluded, the chief priests had given orders that *"if anyone found out where Jesus was, he should report it so they might arrest him,"* (John 11:57 NIV) and they looked for an opportunity to seize Him.

After raising Lazarus, Jesus went to a secluded area, and then decided to go to Jerusalem to celebrate the Passover feast. Four days before Passover, Jesus' entrance into the city was anything but inconspicuous. Jesus mounted a colt to ride into the city, and when He had done so the crowd that followed Him began to spontaneously lay down their coats on the road or pulled palms from the trees and laid them in front of Jesus. The crowd also praised Him, saying *"Blessed is He who comes in the name of the Lord"* and *"Hosanna (an expression of enthusiastic praise[1]) in the highest,"*(Matthew 21:9).

When Jesus arrived at the temple, He found buyers and sellers exchanging merchandise and money. Jesus overturned the money-changers' tables and drove the merchants out saying, *"My house shall be a house of prayer, but you have made it a robbers' den,"* (Matthew 21:13).

The Jewish religious authorities were now incensed more than ever. They realized taking Jesus during the day would be difficult because of the crowds that followed Him. Their opportunity came in the form of Judas Iscariot, one of Jesus' own followers who betrayed Him. Jesus planned to celebrate the Passover in a private location, an upper room in one of the many buildings in the city, and Judas had agreed to disclose Jesus' location at night in exchange for 30 pieces of silver. He did so, and Jesus was arrested during the night while He prayed in a nearby garden (Matthew 21:6-13).

3. What charges were brought against Jesus?

Jesus was made to stand in six different hearings or trials. He was first charged with violating Jewish laws, specifically blasphemy, for claiming to be the Son of God, and then with breaking Roman laws. Jesus was arrested during the night and then beaten, mocked, spit upon, and flogged as He went through the following trials:

- **John 18:12-23, before Annas, the night of the arrest**

  After being arrested Jesus was immediately brought before Annas, one of the high priests, and father-in-law of Caiaphas, the presiding high priest. Jesus was questioned about His followers and teaching. He was bound and taken to Caiaphas.

---

[1] *Webster's Third New International Dictionary, Unabridged.* Merriam-Webster, 2002.

Matthew 21:6-13
The disciples went and did just as Jesus had instructed them, and brought the donkey and the colt, and laid their coats on them; and He sat on the coats. Most of the crowd spread their coats in the road, and others were cutting branches from the trees and spreading them in the road. The crowds going ahead of Him, and those who followed, were shouting, *"Hosanna to the Son of David; blessed is He who comes in the name of the Lord; Hosanna in the highest!"* When He had entered Jerusalem, all the city was stirred, saying, "Who is this?" And the crowds were saying, "This is the prophet Jesus, from Nazareth in Galilee." And Jesus entered the temple and drove out all those who were buying and selling in the temple, and overturned the tables of the moneychangers and the seats of those who were selling doves. And He said to them, "It is written, 'My house shall be called a house of prayer'; but you are making it a robbers' den."

John 18:12-14, 19-24 NIV
Then the detachment of soldiers with its commander and the Jewish officials arrested Jesus. They bound him and brought him first to Annas, who was the father-in-law of Caiaphas, the high priest that year. Caiaphas was the one who had advised the Jews that it would be good if one man died for the people... Meanwhile, the high priest questioned Jesus about his disciples and his teaching. "I have spoken openly to the world," Jesus replied. "I always taught in synagogues or at the temple, where all the Jews come together. I said nothing in secret. Why question me? Ask those who heard me. Surely they know what I said." When Jesus said this, one of the officials nearby struck him in the face. "Is this the way you answer the high priest?" he demanded. "If I said something wrong," Jesus replied, "testify as to what is wrong. But if I spoke the truth, why did you strike me?" Then Annas sent him, still bound, to Caiaphas the high priest.

Matthew 26:57, 59-61, 63-66 NIV

Those who had arrested Jesus took him to Caiaphas, the high priest, where the teachers of the law and the elders had assembled... The chief priests and the whole Sanhedrin were looking for false evidence against Jesus so that they could put him to death. But they did not find any, though many false witnesses came forward. Finally two came forward and declared, "This fellow said, 'I am able to destroy the temple of God and rebuild it in three days...' Jesus remained silent. The high priest said to him, "I charge you under oath by the living God: Tell us if you are the Christ, the Son of God." "Yes, it is as you say," Jesus replied. "But I say to all of you: In the future you will see the Son of Man sitting at the right hand of the Mighty One and coming on the clouds of heaven." Then the high priest tore his clothes and said, "He has spoken blasphemy! Why do we need any more witnesses? Look, now you have heard the blasphemy. What do you think?" "He is worthy of death," they answered.

Luke 22:66-71 NIV

At daybreak the council of the elders of the people, both the chief priests and teachers of the law, met together, and Jesus was led before them. "If you are the Christ," they said, "tell us." Jesus answered, "If I tell you, you will not believe me, and if I asked you, you would not answer. But from now on, the Son of Man will be seated at the right hand of the mighty God." They all asked, "Are you then the Son of God?" He replied, "You are right in saying I am." Then they said, "Why do we need any more testimony? We have heard it from his own lips.

Mark 15:1-5 NIV

Very early in the morning, the chief priests, with the elders, the teachers of the law and the whole Sanhedrin, reached a decision. They bound Jesus, led him away and handed him over to Pilate. "Are you the king of the Jews?" asked Pilate. "Yes, it is as you say," Jesus replied. The chief priests accused him of many things. So again Pilate asked him, "Aren't you going to answer? See how many things they are accusing you of." But Jesus still made no reply, and Pilate was amazed.

- **Matthew 26:57-68; see also Mark 14:53-65 and John 18:24, before Caiaphas, the night of the arrest**

After being taken from Annas, Jesus was brought before Caiaphas with scribes and elders gathered together. Caiaphas said, "*Tell us whether You are the Christ, the Son of God.*" Jesus answered, "*You have said it yourself,*" (Matthew 26:63-64). The crowd agreed that Jesus had blasphemed and deserved death. (Blasphemy was a capital crime under Jewish law, refer to Leviticus 24:16. "Leviticus 24:14-16 guides the Hebrew definition of blasphemy. The offense is designated as a capital crime,' and the offender is to be stoned by the community. Blasphemy involves the actual pronunciation of the name of God along with an attitude of disrespect."[2]) It was still night, and not lawful for the full Sanhedrin (the Jewish ruling council) to convene. Jesus would have to be kept and questioned again when the entire Sanhedrin had assembled in the morning.

- **Mark 15:1 and Luke 22:66-71; see also Matthew 27:1, before the Sanhedrin, the morning after the arrest**

Since the nighttime trial of Jesus was not legal, Caiaphas quickly had the Sanhedrin assemble in the morning and he repeated his question to Jesus, "*Are you the son of God?*" Jesus answered, "*Yes, I am,*" (Luke 22:70). The next step of the Jewish rulers was to secure permission to carry out the capital punishment, which required Roman approval. Jesus was brought before the Roman governor, Pilate.

- **Mark 15:1-5; see also Matthew 27:2, 11-14; Luke 23:1-5 and John 18:29-40, before Pilate, the morning after the arrest**

Jesus was now brought before Pilate, and it was here that the charges against Him were modified from strictly breaking Jewish religious laws to include crimes against Rome. As He stood before Pilate, the Jewish leaders said of Jesus, "*We found this man misleading our nation and forbidding to pay taxes to Caesar, and saying that He Himself is Christ, a King,*" (Luke 23:2 NASB). The leaders added the charge of inciting tax evasion and that He claimed to be a king to give Pilate a reason to side with them. Pilate did not find any reason to declare Jesus guilty of a capital crime, and when he heard that Jesus was from the province of Galilee, he sent Him to King Herod (Herod Antipas, son of Herod the Great who was king at the time of Jesus' birth).

[2] Butler, Trent C., et al., *Holman Bible Dictionary*, 1991: Nashville. Holman Bible Publishers.

- **Luke 23:6-12, before Herod, the day after the arrest**

  Jesus was brought before Herod who questioned Him *"at some length, but Jesus answered him nothing,"* (Luke 23:9). Herod and his soldiers then treated Jesus with contempt, dressing Him in a robe and mocking Him, and then sent Him back to Pilate.

- **Mark 15:6-14; see also Matthew 27:15-23; Luke 23:13-23 and John 19:1-16, before Pilate a second time, the day after the arrest**

  At His second appearance before Pilate, Jesus was questioned as the Jewish leaders pressed Pilate for the sanction to crucify. Pilate reiterated the innocence of Jesus, even stating that Herod found Him innocent and had sent Him back. To placate the accusers, Pilate had Jesus flogged, and his men twisted a crown of thorns and beat it into Jesus' head. Pilate presented Jesus to the Jews, perhaps hoping they would be satisfied with the punishment that He had received. They were not and further pressed Pilate to crucify Jesus for claiming to be the Son of God.

  Upon hearing that Jesus claimed to be the Son of God, Pilate made more efforts to release Him. But the Jewish leaders were shrewd and manipulated Pilate politically. They cried out, *"If you release this Man, you are no friend of Caesar; everyone who makes himself out to be a king opposes Caesar... We have no King but Caesar,"* (John 19:12, 15). After this, Pilate may have thought the Jews would appeal to Rome, an action that could affect his position, and he handed Jesus over to them to be crucified.

  Pilate had the authority to pass sentence on Jesus, and he also had the authority to document the crime. He had an inscription prepared and posted at the top of Jesus' cross. This inscription read *"Jesus of Nazareth, The King of the Jews,"* (John 19:19). To ensure that most anyone looking at the cross could read the sentence, Pilate had the inscription made in three languages: Latin, the official and legal language of Rome; Greek, the language of commerce and the most commonly spoken language; Hebrew, the language of the Jews.

  Oftentimes pictures of a crucifix are depicted with an inscription of INRI at the top, this inscription being the initials of the Latin words *Iesvs Nazarenvs Rex Ivdaeorvm* (Latin uses "I" instead of the English "J", and "V" instead of "U" i.e., Jesus Nazarenus Rex Judaeorum). The Jews protested this inscription and asked Pilate to change it to say, *"He said, 'I am the King of the Jews,"* but Pilate replied, *"What I have written I have written."* (John 19:1-3, 19-22)

Luke 23:6-12 NIV
On hearing this, Pilate asked if the man was a Galilean. When he learned that Jesus was under Herod's jurisdiction, he sent him to Herod, who was also in Jerusalem at that time. When Herod saw Jesus, he was greatly pleased, because for a long time he had been wanting to see him. From what he had heard about him, he hoped to see him perform some miracle. He plied him with many questions, but Jesus gave him no answer. The chief priests and the teachers of the law were standing there, vehemently accusing him. Then Herod and his soldiers ridiculed and mocked him. Dressing him in an elegant robe, they sent him back to Pilate. That day Herod and Pilate became friends—before this they had been enemies.

Mark 15:6-14
Now it was the custom at the festival to release a prisoner whom the people requested. A man called Barabbas was in prison with the insurrectionists who had committed murder in the uprising. The crowd came up and asked Pilate to do for them what he usually did. "Do you want me to release to you the king of the Jews?" asked Pilate, knowing it was out of self-interest that the chief priests had handed Jesus over to him. But the chief priests stirred up the crowd to have Pilate release Barabbas instead. "What shall I do, then, with the one you call the king of the Jews?" Pilate asked them. "Crucify him!" they shouted. "Why? What crime has he committed?" asked Pilate. But they shouted all the louder, "Crucify him!"

John 19:1-3, 19-22 NASB
Pilate then took Jesus and scourged Him. And the soldiers twisted together a crown of thorns and put it on His head, and put a purple robe on Him; and they began to come up to Him and say, "Hail, King of the Jews!" and to give Him slaps in the face... Pilate also wrote an inscription and put it on the cross. It was written, "Jesus The Nazarene, The King of The Jews." Therefore many of the Jews read this inscription, for the place where Jesus was crucified was near the city; and it was written in Hebrew, Latin and in Greek. So the chief priests of the Jews were saying to Pilate, "Do not write, 'The King of the Jews'; but that He said, 'I am King of the Jews.'" Pilate answered, "What I have written I have written."

4. What happened after Jesus was sentenced to death?

John 19:16-18 NIV
Finally Pilate handed him over to them to be crucified. So the soldiers took charge of Jesus. Carrying his own cross, he went out to the place of the Skull (which in Aramaic is called Golgotha). Here they crucified him, and with him two others—one on each side and Jesus in the middle.

Mark 15:33-39 NIV
At the sixth hour darkness came over the whole land until the ninth hour. And at the ninth hour Jesus cried out in a loud voice, "Eloi, Eloi, lama sabachthani?"—which means, "My God, my God, why have you forsaken me?" When some of those standing near heard this, they said, "Listen, he's calling Elijah." One man ran, filled a sponge with wine vinegar, put it on a stick, and offered it to Jesus to drink. "Now leave him alone. Let's see if Elijah comes to take him down," he said. With a loud cry, Jesus breathed his last. The curtain of the temple was torn in two from top to bottom. And when the centurion, who stood there in front of Jesus, heard his cry and saw how he died, he said, "Surely this man was the Son of God!"

John 19:38-42 NIV
Later, Joseph of Arimathea asked Pilate for the body of Jesus. Now Joseph was a disciple of Jesus, but secretly because he feared the Jews. With Pilate's permission, he came and took the body away. He was accompanied by Nicodemus, the man who earlier had visited Jesus at night. Nicodemus brought a mixture of myrrh and aloes, about seventy-five pounds. Taking Jesus' body, the two of them wrapped it, with the spices, in strips of linen. This was in accordance with Jewish burial customs. At the place where Jesus was crucified, there was a garden, and in the garden a new tomb, in which no one had ever been laid. Because it was the Jewish day of Preparation and since the tomb was nearby, they laid Jesus there.

- **The crucifixion of Jesus: John 19:16-18; see also Matthew 27:31-49; Mark 15:20-32 and Luke 23:26-44**

  Jesus was led from Pilate's Praetorium to a hill called Calvary (Hebrew *Golgatha*), meaning skull. On Calvary Jesus was crucified, a method of torturous death devised to be slow and painful, where the condemned had his hands and feet nailed to a cross. So painful was the death that the English word *excruciating* is derived from the word cross. Execution of criminals by crucifixion was not only meant to be painful but also humiliating. Crucifixion was conducted in public, during the daylight, so the condemned was displayed for all to see. The Romans commonly employed a cross that consisted of a vertical pole and a horizontal cross bar. Jesus was made to carry the cross that would be used in His execution.

- **The death of Jesus: Mark 15:33-41; see also Matthew 27:50-56; Luke 23:45-49 and John 19:30**

  After about six hours on the cross Jesus died, yielding His Spirit into the hands of His Father. The sky grew dark and there was an earthquake. The Romans that were watching Jesus were frightened, and their Centurian professed that He was truly the Son of God. As the earth shook, the veil in the temple that separated the "holy of holies" from the inner court was torn in two. This signified that the separation between man and God had been taken away, and that Jesus Christ had opened up a way for man to restore his relationship with God.

- **The burial of Jesus: John 19:38-42; see also Matthew 27:57-61; Mark 15:42-46 and Luke 23:50-56**

  Jesus' body was taken off the cross and two members of the Jewish ruling council, Nicodemus and Joseph of Arimathea, prepared Jesus' body for burial with spices and perfumes. The body of Jesus was put in a tomb hewn out of rock, and the tomb was covered with a large stone. Jesus' body was in the tomb, but Jesus' spirit had descended into Sheol-Hades (sometimes referred to as hell in various translations of the Bible). On the third day that His body was in the tomb, an angel rolled away the stone blocking the entrance, Jesus was resurrected, and He left the tomb.

5. Did Jesus go to hell?

The Apostle's Creed states that Jesus "descended into hell," (Ephesians 4:8-10). Actually, Jesus descended into Sheol-Hades, which is often translated Hell (the word *Sheol* (Hebrew) and *Hades* (Greek) mean "the place of departed souls"). There is a difference between Hades and Hell. Hell is a final abode not yet populated, and Sheol-Hades is a place that the Bible describes as located in the center of the earth where the wicked and righteous dead abode prior to the resurrection of Jesus. At that time Sheol-Hades was comprised of two distinct areas separated by an impassable chasm. One side was the abode of the wicked dead, and on the other was called paradise and housed the righteous dead (Refer to Luke 16:19-31).

6. Did Jesus really come back from the dead?

Jesus Christ arose from the dead. There is much in the way of tangible evidence that points to this conclusion:

- **The empty tomb**

    Three days after Jesus was placed in the tomb it was found empty. This occurred after a Roman guard detail had been set up to keep watch over the burial site, and the Jewish leaders had sealed the large stone in front of the tomb. The guards were stunned and fainted when the stone was rolled away and Jesus resurrected, and they reported all that happened to the chief priests. The guards were paid to lie about the incident, telling a story that while they slept at night the body of Jesus had been stolen (Matthew 27:65-66, 28:11-13 and Mark 16:4-6).

- **Eyewitnesses**

    After the resurrection, Jesus appeared to many eyewitnesses that documented the events. Each of the gospels record eyewitness encounters with Jesus, as does the book of Acts and Paul's first letter to the Corinthians. These were not isolated incidents. Jesus showed Himself many times to many people, and on one occasion to more than five hundred people (1 Corinthians 15:3-6).

    Following this, there was a sudden increase in the number of believers as His disciples preached the resurrection (Acts 2:24, 41). The apostle Paul was persecuted for being a Christian, and in defending himself stated he was on trial for preaching the resurrection. Paul also said, *"If Christ has not been raised, then our preaching is vain,"* (1 Corinthians 15:14).

Ephesians 4:8-10 NASB
Therefore it says, "When He ascended on high, He led captive a host of captives, And He gave gifts to men." (Now this expression, "He ascended," what does it mean except that He also had descended into the lower parts of the earth? He who descended is Himself also He who ascended far above all the heavens, so that He might fill all things.)

Matthew 27:65-66, 28:11-13
Pilate said unto them, Ye have a watch: go your way, make it as sure as ye can. So they went, and made the sepulchre sure, sealing the stone, and setting a watch... Now when they were going, behold, some of the watch came into the city, and showed unto the chief priests all the things that were done. And when they were assembled with the elders, and had taken counsel, they gave large money unto the soldiers, Saying, Say ye, His disciples came by night, and stole him away while we slept.

Mark 16:4-6 NASB
Looking up, they saw that the stone had been rolled away, although it was extremely large. Entering the tomb, they saw a young man sitting at the right, wearing a white robe; and they were amazed. And he said to them, "Do not be amazed; you are looking for Jesus the Nazarene, who has been crucified. He has risen; He is not here; behold, here is the place where they laid Him."

1 Corinthians 15:3-6 NASB
For I delivered to you as of first importance what I also received, that Christ died for our sins according to the Scriptures, and that He was buried, and that He was raised on the third day according to the Scriptures, and that He appeared to Cephas, then to the twelve. After that He appeared to more than five hundred brethren at one time, most of whom remain until now, but some have fallen asleep;

Acts 2:24, 41 NASB
(Peter said), "But God raised Him up again, putting an end to the agony of death, since it was impossible for Him to be held in its power..." So then, those who had received his word were baptized; and that day there were added about three thousand souls.

7. Why is the resurrection so important?

The resurrection of Jesus differentiates Him from false gods, prophets, and supposed saviors, none of which have been raised from the dead. As a Christian, believing in the resurrection is also important because:

- **The resurrection shows Jesus is the Son of God and the Christ (savior) our Lord**

Romans 1:3-4 NIV
(Jesus) as to his human nature was a descendant of David, and who through the Spirit of holiness was declared with power to be the Son of God by his resurrection from the dead: Jesus Christ our Lord.

- **The resurrection shows God has accepted the sacrifice of Jesus as atonement for sin**

Romans 4:22-25 NIV
This is why "it was credited to (Abraham) as righteousness." The words "it was credited to him" were written not for him alone, but also for us, to whom God will credit righteousness--for us who believe in him who raised Jesus our Lord from the dead. He was delivered over to death for our sins and was raised to life for our justification.

- **The resurrection provides hope for the future**

John 11:25-26 NASB
Jesus said to her, "I am the resurrection and the life; he who believes in Me will live even if he dies, and everyone who lives and believes in Me will never die. Do you believe this?"

1 Thessalonians 4:14 NIV
We believe that Jesus died and rose again and so we believe that God will bring with Jesus those who have fallen asleep in him. (See also, 1 Corinthians 15:12-55)

Philippians 3:10-11 NIV
I want to know Christ and the power of his resurrection and the fellowship of sharing in his sufferings, becoming like him in his death, and so, somehow, to attain to the resurrection from the dead.

Romans 6:4 NIV
Just as Christ was raised from the dead through the glory of the Father, we too may live a new life.

Romans 8:11 NIV
And if the Spirit of him who raised Jesus from the dead is living in you, he who raised Christ from the dead will also give life to your mortal bodies through his Spirit, who lives in you.

Study Questions

1. Read John chapter 11. What would you say to someone who asked, "If Jesus was such a wonderful miracle worker, why did people want to kill Him?" _____

    _____

    _____

    _____

    _____

2. Read Mark 14:43-15:47. List some of the sufferings Jesus endured for our sin._____

    _____

    _____

    _____

    _____

3. Read 1 Corinthians 15:12-55. What makes the resurrection of Jesus important to the Christian faith? __

    _____

    _____

    _____

    _____

Lesson Journal

Use this section to record your thoughts on the topics in this lesson.

_____

_____

_____

_____

_____

_____

_____

_____

Lesson 10
About Face

Scripture Reading

- Acts 1:1-9 (Jesus' appearance for 40 days and His ascension)

- Jeremiah 31:31-32 and Hebrews 8:6-11 (New Covenant)

- 2 Chronicles 7:14; Psalm chapter 51; Matthew 4:17 and Acts 2:36-41 (repentance)

- Romans 1:17, 3:28, 5:1-2 (justification)

Introduction

The life, ministry, death, resurrection, and ascension of Jesus brought forth the New Covenant that was promised in the Old Testament. By faith in Jesus Christ, any who repent of their sins will receive complete forgiveness, enter into the New Covenant, and experience a true relationship with God.

Jesus began His ministry preaching repentance, and His disciples and apostles continued to preach repentance after His resurrection. Repentance is much more than sorrow, as it affects the total person and his direction and purpose in life. It is necessary because of the breach between man and God, the breach of sin. Everyone has sinned and thus everyone must repent to gain right standing with God. True repentance is coupled with faith in Jesus Christ, the two working together to bring a sinner to submit to Jesus for forgiveness. This lesson explores repentance and how it affects the lives of those who by faith come to repent.

1. What happened after Jesus was resurrected?

Jesus spent 40 days with the disciples after the resurrection, fellow-shipping with them and instructing them.

The Bible does not give abundant detail about the time between Jesus' resurrection from the dead and His ascension into heaven, but each of the gospels record some of Jesus' appearances to His disciples after the resurrection. According to the gospel records, He appeared to Mary Magdalene first, then to the other women who testified of what they saw, then to two disciples as they walked to the town of Emmaus, and then He appeared to ten of His disciples who had not believed the women's testimony. At some point after this, Jesus appeared to over 500 believers who were gathered together (1 Corinthians 15:6). He also appeared to the disciples when Thomas was present, leading Thomas to believe and Jesus responding, *"Because you have seen Me, have you believed? Blessed are they who did not see, and yet believed."*

After forty days, the time came for Jesus to return to His Father in heaven. This event, referred to as His ascension, took place on the Mount of Olives, or Mount Olivet, a ridge to the east of Jerusalem. Jesus gathered together the eleven apostles and commanded them to return to Jerusalem and wait for the baptism of the Holy Spirit, *"not many days from now."* Jesus also told them that after the coming of the Holy Spirit the disciples would become powerful witnesses of Jesus Christ from their local towns to the remotest parts of the earth. Then, before their eyes, Jesus, alive and in the flesh, was raised up into a cloud as they stood looking until they could see Him no more (Acts 1:3-9).

2. Jesus is alive?

Jesus was alive when He ascended and remains alive today. He has taken up residence in Heaven at the right hand of God the Father. Jesus is alive to make intercession for those that offer their prayers and supplications in His name to His Father (Mark 16:19; John 16:23; Hebrews 7:25 and Revelation 1:18).

> ### Mark 16:19 NKJV
> *So then, after the Lord had spoken to them, He was received up into heaven, and sat down at the right hand of God.*

Acts 1:3-6, 8-9
To these (apostles) He also presented Himself alive after His suffering, by many convincing proofs, appearing to them over a period of forty days and speaking of the things concerning the kingdom of God. Gathering them together, He commanded them not to leave Jerusalem, but to wait for what the Father had promised, "Which," He said, "you heard of from Me; for John baptized with water, but you will be baptized with the Holy Spirit not many days from now...but you will receive power when the Holy Spirit has come upon you; and you shall be My witnesses both in Jerusalem, and in all Judea and Samaria, and even to the remotest part of the earth." And after He had said these things, He was lifted up while they were looking on, and a cloud received Him out of their sight.

1 Corinthians 15:6 NLT
After that he was seen by more than five hundred Christian brothers at one time, most of whom are still alive, though some have died by now.

John 16:23 NIV
In that day you will no longer ask me anything. I tell you the truth, my Father will give you whatever you ask in my name.

Hebrews 7:25
Therefore He (Jesus) is able also to save forever those who draw near to God through Him, since He always lives to make intercession for them.

Revelation 1:18 NKJ
I am He who lives, and was dead, and behold, I am alive forevermore.

3. What was the significance of the life, death, and resurrection of Jesus?

The coming of Jesus, His life, death, and resurrection, ushered in the New Covenant. At its core, the New Covenant is *Jesus Christ.* He embodies everything the New Covenant is. He is the Word of God and the Son of God, made flesh for us. He is the express image of God, made flesh for us to see and know and love. In Jesus Christ, God has given us a new basis for our relationship with God. God has given this covenant to allow us to reconcile our relationship with Him.

How can a person be a covenant? It is a biblical notion. In a prophecy about Christ, Isaiah 42:6 says that the Messiah, or Christ, would be made a covenant. The Bible calls Jesus a mediator, a go-between. A mediator's purpose is to get two parties to relate positively to each other. His work is what allows the barrier of sin to come down between man and God, and the relationship to bear positive fruit. Jesus is the mediator of the greatest covenant, or agreement, in human history. Jesus could do that because He was both God and human. He was not only able to *represent* both parties, He was able to *be* both parties.

The Old Testament prophesies a New Covenant and the New Testament confirms a New Covenant through Jesus Christ:

- **Old Testament Prophecies of a New Covenant**

  Isaiah 42:1, 6, 9; Isaiah 55:3; Ezekiel 16:59-60, and:

  Jeremiah 31:31-32
  Behold, the days come, saith the LORD, that I will make a new covenant with the house of Israel, and with the house of Judah: Not according to the covenant that I made with their fathers in the day that I took them by the hand to bring them out of the land of Egypt; which my covenant they brake, although I was an husband unto them, saith the LORD.

- **New Testament Confirmations of the New Covenant**

  Hebrews 9:12, 15-16; Hebrews 8:6, 10-11, and:

  1 Corinthians 11:25
  In the same way He took the cup also after supper, saying, "This cup is the new covenant in My blood; do this, as often as you drink it, in remembrance of Me."

Isaiah 42:1, 6, 9 NASB
Behold, My Servant, whom I uphold; My chosen one in whom My soul delights. I have put My Spirit upon Him... I will also hold you by the hand and watch over you, And I will appoint you as a covenant to the people, As a light to the nations,... Behold, the former things have come to pass, now I declare new things; before they spring forth I proclaim them to you.

Isaiah 55:3
Incline your ear, and come to Me. Hear, and your soul shall live; And I will make an everlasting covenant with you—The sure mercies of David.

Ezekiel 16:59-60
For thus says the Lord GOD, "I will also do with you as you have done, you who have despised the oath by breaking the covenant. Nevertheless, I will remember My covenant with you in the days of your youth, and I will establish an everlasting covenant with you."

Hebrews 9:12, 15-16 NASB
Not through the blood of goats and calves, but through His own blood, Jesus entered the holy place once for all, having obtained eternal redemption... For this reason He is the mediator of a new covenant, so that, since a death has taken place for the redemption of the transgressions ... For where a covenant is, there must of necessity be the death of the one who made it.

Hebrews 8:6, 10-11
But now Jesus has obtained a more excellent ministry, by as much as He is also the mediator of a better covenant, which has been enacted on better promises... For this is the covenant that I will make with the house of Israel after those days, says the Lord: I will put my laws into their minds, And I will write them on their hearts. And I will be their god, and they shall be my people. And they shall not teach everyone his fellow citizen, and everyone his brother, saying, 'know the lord,' for all will know me, from the least to the greatest of them. For I will be merciful to their iniquities, and I will remember their sins no more.

4. How does one become a part of this New Covenant?

On the day of Pentecost, after Peter had preached his first message, many who heard asked this same question. They put it this way, *"Brethren, what shall we do?"* (Acts 2:37). The apostle Peter gave them a very succinct answer. He said, *"Repent, and each of you be baptized in the name of Jesus Christ for the forgiveness of your sins,"* (Acts 2:38). Peter followed the example of Jesus, who preached repentance from the onset of His ministry (Matthew 4:17).

5. What is repentance?

Peter said, *"repent and be baptized."* Repentance first is a preparation and prerequisite for water baptism (discussed in the next lesson). Repentance couples faith in Jesus Christ with a want to turn from sin. It is the turning from sin toward God, and literally means to turn around. Repentance recognizes sin for what it is, an offense against God, and reacts to this recognition by turning away from sin to be reconciled with God.

Repentance is not something that can be earned through works or deeds, but requires a conscious and sincere desire to turn toward God. As a conscious effort, repentance is associated with a change of mind. Being a sincere desire it is associated with a change of heart. Recoiling from sin to be reconciled with God, repentance is a change of purpose. Repentance affects the total person:

- **Change of mind**

  Repentance requires a conscious effort to turn from sinful ways, a change in thinking, hence a change of mind. A conscious change of mind requires an acknowledgment that the current direction of life is not the right direction. Making such a change is humbling, and requires humility before God (2 Chronicles 7:14).

- **Change of heart**

  Repentance is also a matter of the heart. A change of heart requires accepting the sacrifice of Jesus Christ and being heartily sorry for sins. Not a simple "I'm sorry," but godly sorrow for willfully breaking the laws of God and sinning against God (Psalm 51:3-4 and Acts 2:37).

- **Change of purpose**

  A change of purpose means that one has committed to live for the Lord Jesus Christ and turn from his former way of life (Matthew 3:8). It is a result of the change of mind and heart. Repentance is a complete turn from self-reliance to submitting to God and relying on Him. God becomes the purpose for life.

6. Why is repentance necessary?

Repentance is necessary for forgiveness of sins because *"all have sinned and fall short of the glory of God,"* (Romans 3:23). Sin has broken our fellowship with God (1 John 3:4 and James 1:15), and we must repent and turn away from all forms of sin:

- **Sins of commission**

  Sin is the willful disobedience or defiance (transgression) of any rule or law of God. A sin of commission is a deliberate act of disobedience against God; it is knowingly doing what is wrong. These sins can be either outward or inward (mind, will, and emotions) and in practicality they are innumerable (Psalm 40:12). They include:

  Psalm 14:1
  The fool has said in his heart, "There is no God," They are corrupt, and have committed abominable injustice.

  1 John 3:15 NASB
  Everyone who hates his brother is a murderer; and you know that no murderer has eternal life abiding in him.

  Galatians 5:19-21 NIV
  The acts of the sinful nature are obvious: sexual immorality, impurity and debauchery; idolatry and witchcraft; hatred, discord, jealousy, fits of rage, selfish ambition, dissensions, factions and envy; drunkenness, orgies, and the like. I warn you, as I did before, that those who live like this will not inherit the kingdom of God.

  Hebrews 13:4 NASB
  Marriage is to be held in honor among all, and the marriage bed is to be undefiled; for fornicators and adulterers God will judge.

  Ephesians 5:3-5
  But among you there must not be even a hint of sexual immorality, or of any kind of impurity, or of greed, because these are improper for God's holy people. Nor should there be obscenity, foolish talk or coarse joking, which are out of place, but rather thanksgiving. For of this you can be sure: No immoral, impure or greedy person—such a man is an idolater—has any inheritance in the kingdom of Christ and of God.

  See also 1 Corinthians 6:9-11.

- **Sins of omission**

  Sin of omission is failing to do what you know to be right (James 4:17 and Matthew 25:44-45).

---

1 John 3:4
Whosoever committeth sin transgresseth also the law: for sin is the transgression of the law.

James 1:15
Then when lust hath conceived, it bringeth forth sin: and sin, when it is finished, bringeth forth death.

Psalm 40:12
For innumerable evils have compassed me about: mine iniquities have taken hold upon me, so that I am not able to look up; they are more than the hairs of mine head: therefore my heart faileth me.

James 4:17 NIV
Anyone, then, who knows the good he ought to do and doesn't do it, sins.

Matthew 25:44-45
"Then they also shall answer him, saying: Lord, when did we see thee hungry, or thirsty, or a stranger, or naked, or sick, or in prison, and did not minister to thee? Then he shall answer them, saying: Amen I say to you, as long as you did it not to one of these least, neither did you do it to me."

Romans 14:23 NLT
If you do anything you believe is not right, you are sinning.

Habakkuk 2:4
...but the just shall live by his faith.

Romans 1:17
For therein is the righteousness of God revealed from faith to faith: as it is written, The just shall live by faith.

Romans 3:28 NASB
For we maintain that a man is justified by faith apart from works of the Law.

Romans 5:1-2 NASB
Therefore, having been justified by faith, we have peace with God through our Lord Jesus Christ, through whom also we have obtained our introduction by faith into this grace in which we stand; and we exult in hope of the glory of God.

Galatians 3:11
But that no man is justified by the law in the sight of God, it is evident: for, The just shall live by faith.

Luke 19:8-10 NASB
Zaccheus stopped and said to the Lord, "Behold, Lord, half of my possessions I will give to the poor, and if I have defrauded anyone of anything, I will give back four times as much." 9And Jesus said to him, "Today salvation has come to this house, because he, too, is a son of Abraham. 10"For the Son of Man has come to seek and to save that which was lost."

Psalm 51:1-4, 10 NASB
Be gracious to me, O God, according to Your lovingkindness; According to the greatness of Your compassion blot out my transgressions. Wash me thoroughly from my iniquity And cleanse me from my sin. For I know my transgressions, And my sin is ever before me. Against You, You only, I have sinned And done what is evil in Your sight... Create in me a clean heart, O God, And renew a steadfast spirit within me. .

Luke 7: 44, 48, 50
"Do you see this woman? I entered your house; you gave Me no water for My feet, but she has wet My feet with her tears and wiped them with her hair...Then He said to her, "Your sins have been forgiven...Your faith has saved you; go in peace."

- **Sins of conscience**

Sins of conscience fall under the category of Christian liberty. Although an act may not be deliberate disobedience of God, if you consider something a sin and then commit the act, it is a sin. The apostle Paul used the example of eating meat that had been offered to idols. To some, to eat such meat was a sin, to others whose faith was unaffected by eating such meat, it was not a sin. Paul also used the example of honoring one day over another. The conclusion is to follow your conscience and avoid what you consider to be wrong (Romans 14:23).

Repentance, turning from sin toward God by faith, is required to be reconciled to God. After exercising faith in God by believing the Gospel of Jesus and repenting from sin, we are justified (Habakkuk 2:4; Romans 1:17; Romans 3:28; Romans 5:1-2 and Galatians 3:11). A simple way to remember what justified means is to think: *just as if I had* never sinned. By repenting and believing in Jesus, our sins are forgiven and we are able to approach God the Father because we are justified, cleansed from sin, just as if we had never sinned.

7. How can I repent?

The act of repentance includes confession of sin and the desire to change, based on faith in Jesus Christ. There is no particular formula to be followed. It is a conscious and genuine desire of the heart that can be manifested many ways by submitting to and confessing to Jesus Christ.

Job repented in dust and ashes (Job 42:1-6). David repented with great humility and remorse, confessing his sins, and begging mercy and cleansing from God (Psalm 51). Some have come to Jesus and repented with great joy (Zaccheus, Luke 19:1-10) and others with great remorse (unnamed woman, Luke 7:36-50). Jesus recognized both as being genuinely repentant, because He knows the heart. He knew in both cases there was sincere desire to turn around coupled with faith in Him. He acknowledged the authentic repentance by announcing both had come to salvation.

Job 42:1-6 NIV
Then Job replied to the LORD : "I know that you can do all things; no plan of yours can be thwarted. You asked, 'Who is this that obscures my counsel without knowledge?' Surely I spoke of things I did not understand, things too wonderful for me to know. "You said, 'Listen now, and I will speak; I will question you, and you shall answer me.' My ears had heard of you but now my eyes have seen you. Therefore I despise myself and repent in dust and ashes."

8. How do I know my sins are forgiven?

Whenever Jesus announced to a person that He had forgiven their sins, that person did not question His forgiveness. Jesus mentioned the faith of the forgiven (the paralytic, Matthew 9:2, the repentant woman, Luke 7:50), but it was those that had no faith in Jesus that questioned His forgiveness.

If by faith you have come to repentance, your faith is sufficient to believe that your sins are forgiven (1 John 1:9). The writer of Hebrews assures us of forgiveness when he describes the New Covenant, echoing an earlier prophecy from the book of Jeremiah, stating, *"For I will forgive their wickedness and will remember their sins no more,"* (Hebrews 8:12 NIV).

Matthew 9:2
Some men brought to him a paralytic, lying on a mat. When Jesus saw their faith, he said to the paralytic, "Take heart, son; your sins are forgiven."

Luke 7:50
Jesus said to the woman, "Your faith has saved you; go in peace."

1 John 1:9 NIV
If we confess our sins, he is faithful and just and will forgive us our sins and purify us from all unrighteousness.

Study Questions

1. Read Jeremiah 31:31-32, Hebrews 8:6-12, and Hebrews 9:11-15. Do you believe that Jesus Christ established the New Covenant that is talked about in these passages? How is the New Covenant better than the Old?_____

    _____

    _____

    _____

2. Read 1 Corinthians 6:9-11 and Galatians 5:19-21. List some of the sins mentioned in these passages that require repentance._____

    _____

    _____

    _____

3. Read Psalm 51. King David wrote this psalm of repentance after committing the sins of adultery and murder. His example of repentance is a model for all. In the New Covenant, by having faith in Jesus Christ we can repent and receive forgiveness. Have you come to repentance? Why or why not?_____

    _____

    _____

    _____

    _____

    _____

Lesson Journal

Use this section to record your thoughts on the topics in this lesson.

_____

_____

_____

_____

_____

_____

_____

Lesson 11
Water Baptism

Scripture Reading

- Acts 1 and 2 (the ascension of Jesus, day of Pentecost, baptism)

- Romans 6:1-8 and 1 Corinthians 12:12-14 (baptism) Colossians 2:11-12, 3:8-11 (circumcision of heart)

- Deuteronomy 10:12-16, 30:16 and Jeremiah 4:4 (Old Testament reference to circumcision of heart)

- Acts 19:1-7 (baptism of John's disciples)

Introduction

Entering a New Covenant relationship with Jesus requires repentance from sin and a profession of faith in Him as Lord and Savior. Repentance is an initial step of turning away from sin and toward a new life in Christ Jesus. What follows this initial step of repentance and faith is obedience to what Jesus taught, and that is for believers to be baptized in water.

Water baptism is a sacrament instituted by Jesus. John the Baptist, who proclaimed the coming of the Messiah, Jesus Christ, and baptized for repentance of sins, first taught baptism. Jesus submitted to the baptism of John, not because He needed to repent, but as an example for sinners and that He might obediently demonstrate what He was asking all people to do. The baptism of Jesus ended the ministry of John, as John directed his disciples to follow Jesus.

After Jesus spent 40 days appearing to His disciples after His resurrection, He ascended into heaven. Before Jesus ascended, He gave his apostles this charge: *"Go and make disciples of all nations, baptizing them in the name of the Father and of the Son and of the Holy Spirit, and teaching them to obey everything I have commanded you,"* (Matthew 28:19-20 NIV). When the feast of Pentecost was celebrated about a week after Jesus' ascension, there was a great stir in the city of Jerusalem with the manifestation of the Holy Spirit. On this day, the apostle Peter preached his first sermon and followed Jesus' charge telling repentant believers to be baptized. About 3000 were baptized that very day. The book of Acts documents many occurrences of believers being baptized, and the New Testament letter writers also taught the doctrine of baptism.

This lesson focuses on water baptism of repentant believers in Jesus Christ, and studies the parallels between Old Covenant circumcision and New Covenant baptism.

1. What follows repentance and forgiveness of sins?

On the day of Pentecost following the ascension of Jesus, as Peter preached his first message many who heard him asked this same question. They put it this way, *"Brethren, what shall we do?"* (Acts 2:37 NASB). Peter gave them a very succinct answer. He said, *"Repent, and each of you be baptized in the name of Jesus Christ for the forgiveness of your sins; and you will receive the gift of the Holy Spirit. For the promise is for you and your children and for all who are far off, as many as the Lord our God will call to Himself,"* (Acts 2:38-39 NASB).

Peter's response directed those who had come to believe in Jesus to repent (discussed in the previous lesson) and be water baptized— submit to the sacrament instituted by Jesus Christ. The response to Peter's instruction was great, as *"those who had received his word were baptized; and that day there were added about three thousand souls,"* (Acts 2:41 NASB).

2. What is a sacrament?

A sacrament is a sacred ordinance instituted by God. The word sacrament is not a biblical term, but is a word used to describe sacred rites ordained by God and observed by the New Covenant church. A sacrament consists of two parts: an outward visible sign and an inward spiritual work of grace performed by the Holy Spirit. It is the inward work that makes the ceremony of a sacrament a reality to the believer. "In the New Covenant rites become reality in Christ through the Holy Spirit who applies that reality to us."[1]

Different churches and denominations vary on what ordinances are considered to be a sacrament. Most Christian faiths define water baptism and the Lord's Supper as sacraments, others also include marriage, confirmation, anointing with oil, dedication of children, and footwashing.

---

[1] Beall, James Lee. *Laying the Foundation, Achieving Christian Maturity* 1976: Bridge Publishing Inc., Plainfield, NJ, pg. 157.

3. What is water baptism?

Water baptism is a sacrament instituted by Jesus Christ, having both an outward sign and an inward work of grace performed by the Holy Spirit. Water baptism is first introduced in the Bible with the baptism of John, who became known as John the Baptist. *"John's baptism was a baptism of repentance. He told the people to believe in the one coming after him, that is, in Jesus,"* (Acts 19:4 NIV).

John preached repentance, baptism, and faith in Jesus, the Lamb of God. John's instruction about repentance was plainly stated. He said that fruit, or evidence, must accompany repentance. Those listening to his message wanted to know what he meant by fruit of repentance and asked, *"What should we do?"* John explained the necessity of change using examples: share with others, don't cheat, don't extort, be content with what you have (Luke 3:7-14).

Jesus submitted to John's baptism and initiated New Covenant baptism. Jesus was *"tempted in all things as we are, yet without sin"* (Hebrews 4:15), so He did not need to repent. Yet He submitted to baptism. He did so as an example to sinners and to *"sympathize with our weaknesses,"* (Hebrews 4:15). Jesus also gave the command to His disciples to go out into the world and baptize believers (Matthew 28:18-20). The apostle Peter heeded these words and commanded believers to be baptized in the name of the Lord Jesus during his first sermon after Jesus' ascension (Acts 2:37-39).

4. What is the outward sign in water baptism?

In water baptism the outward sign is the washing by immersion in water of a repentant believer in the name of the Lord Jesus. Baptism is an outward announcement of repentance and faith in Jesus Christ as a believer submits to being baptized in His name. A believer being baptized is openly acknowledging repentance of sins and the former way of life. Peter said, *"repent and… be baptized in the name of the Lord Jesus for the remission of sins,"* (Acts 2:38). When he said "for the remission of sins," the meaning is "because of" the remission, or forgiveness of sins. To be baptized *because of* the forgiveness of sins means that faith in Jesus and repentance are prerequisites that must precede water baptism.

Through the outward means of water, a believer being baptized comes to relate to the death, burial and resurrection of Jesus by dying to self (repenting and shedding the old way of life), being buried in water and rising to walk in newness of life (Romans 6:3-8). As this outward action takes place, the Holy Spirit makes an inward change.

Matthew 28:18-20 NASB
And Jesus came up and spoke to them, saying, "All authority has been given to Me in heaven and on earth. Go therefore and make disciples of all the nations, baptizing them in the name of the Father and the Son and the Holy Spirit."

Acts 2:37-39 NKJV
Now when they heard this, they were cut to the heart, and said to Peter and the rest of the apostles, "Men and brethren, what shall we do?" Then Peter said to them, "Repent, and let every one of you be baptized in the name of Jesus Christ for the remission of sins; and you shall receive the gift of the Holy Spirit. For the promise is to you and to your children, and to all who are afar off, as many as the Lord our God will call."

Luke 3:7-8, 10-14 NIV
John said to the crowds coming out to be baptized by him, "You brood of vipers! Who warned you to flee from the coming wrath? Produce fruit in keeping with repentance…" "What should we do then?" the crowd asked. John answered, "The man with two tunics should share with him who has none, and the one who has food should do the same." Tax collectors also came to be baptized. "Teacher," they asked, "what should we do?" "Don't collect any more than you are required to," he told them. Then some soldiers asked him, "And what should we do?" He replied, "Don't extort money and don't accuse people falsely—be content with your pay."

Romans 6:3-8
Know ye not, that so many of us as were baptized into Jesus Christ were baptized into his death? Therefore we are buried with him by baptism into death: that like as Christ was raised up from the dead by the glory of the Father, even so we also should walk in newness of life. For if we have been planted together in the likeness of his death, we shall be also in the likeness of his resurrection: Knowing this, that our old man is crucified with him, that the body of sin might be destroyed, that henceforth we should not serve sin. For he that is dead is freed from sin. Now if we be dead with Christ, we believe that we shall also live with him.

Romans 6:1-8 NIV
What shall we say, then? Shall we go on sinning so that grace may increase? By no means! We died to sin; how can we live in it any longer? Or don't you know that all of us who were baptized into Christ Jesus were baptized into his death? We were therefore buried with him through baptism into death in order that, just as Christ was raised from the dead through the glory of the Father, we too may live a new life. If we have been united with him like this in his death, we will certainly also be united with him in his resurrection. For we know that our old self was crucified with him so that the body of sin might be done away with, that we should no longer be slaves to sin— because anyone who has died has been freed from sin. Now if we died with Christ, we believe that we will also live with him.

1 Corinthians 12:12-14 NIV
The body is a unit, though it is made up of many parts; and though all its parts are many, they form one body. So it is with Christ. For we were all baptized by one Spirit into one body—whether Jews or Greeks, slave or free—and we were all given the one Spirit to drink. Now the body is not made up of one part but of many.

Genesis 3:15 NIV
And I will put enmity between you and the woman, and between your offspring and hers; he will crush your head, and you will strike his heel.

Romans 8:7
Because the carnal mind is enmity against God: for it is not subject to the law of God, neither indeed can be.

James 4:4
know ye not that the friendship of the world is enmity with God? whosoever therefore will be a friend of the world is the enemy of God.

5. What is the inward work of the Holy Spirit in water baptism?

As a believer is baptized (immersed) into Christ and His death, burial, and resurrection through the external means of water, the Holy Spirit performs an inward washing, breaking the power of the sin nature inherited from Adam. The apostle Paul describes this inward spiritual work of the removal of the sin nature as burying the *"old man"* and as an operation performed without hands he refers to as the *"circumcision of heart."*

As the Spirit performs this work, the believer buried in water becomes dead to sin and is raised alive in Christ, (Romans 6:1-4). Paul teaches that as we are baptized into the death, burial, and resurrection of Jesus, we are baptized into the Body of Christ, and a spiritual bond is formed making us members of His Body in unity with other believers (1 Corinthians 12:12-14).

6. What is the "old man"?

Paul refers to the *"old man"* in Romans 6:3-8, which is a reference to the original sin nature that all inherit from Adam. Paul calls this sin nature *"the body of sin."* (See also Colossians 3:8-11 where Paul says you have put off the *"old man with his (wicked) deeds"* after speaking of baptism in Colossians chapter 2). The sin nature of the "old man" puts man in a position of hostility (the Bible uses the term *enmity*) toward God (Genesis 3:15; Romans 8:7 and James 4:4). All of mankind share in the consequences of the sin of Adam and baptism is the means of grace available to deal with this problem.

7. What does circumcision have to do with water baptism?

The Word of God refers to an operation that is performed without hands, an operation called the circumcision of heart. This circumcision is prefigured in the Old Testament by the circumcision of flesh, which followed soon after birth, and was commanded by God as a sign of all males who were in covenant relationship with Him. Likewise, under the New Covenant of Jesus Christ, baptism is an element of spiritual birth (being born again), a sign of the New Covenant, and commanded by God to follow repentance and faith in Jesus. For better understanding, read the scriptural comparison of the Old Covenant rite of circumcision and New Covenant baptism and circumcision of heart that follows.

- **New Covenant circumcision of heart was foreshadowed in the Old Testament**

  Although the Old Covenant rite of circumcision was defined as a sign in the flesh, God was interested in the attitude of the heart. He spoke of circumcision of heart, foreshadowing a time when Jesus Christ would come as a final sacrifice for sin and a spiritual reality could accompany the sign of the New Covenant, baptism. Deuteronomy 10:12-16; Deuteronomy 30:16, and:

  Jeremiah 4:4 NASB

  Circumcise yourselves to the LORD And remove the foreskins of your heart, Men of Judah and inhabitants of Jerusalem, Or else My wrath will go forth like fire And burn with none to quench it, Because of the evil of your deeds.

- **Old Covenant circumcision was a sign of the covenant**

  To be part of the Old Covenant God demanded a covenant sign, the cutting away of the flesh of the foreskin.

  Genesis 17:11

  And you shall be circumcised in the flesh of your foreskin, and it shall be the sign of the covenant between Me and you.

- **New Covenant baptism is a sign of the covenant**

  The New Covenant in Christ requires the sign of the covenant, water baptism. Jesus commanded it as did His apostles. By submitting to water baptism and the circumcision of heart a conscious declaration is made which is a sign before God and man of obedience to the command of Christ.

- **Old Covenant circumcision of flesh was commanded by God**

  Under the Old Covenant, God commanded circumcision of each newborn male child (Genesis 17:11-12; 21:4 and Acts 7:8).

- **New Covenant circumcision of heart is commanded by God**

  The teaching of the apostles is clear; baptism is required of repentant believers in Jesus Christ. Baptism follows repentance and faith in Jesus as an act of submission and obedience to God. Acts 2:37-38; Matthew 28:18-20; Colossians 3:8-11, and:

  Colossians 2:11-12

  And in (Christ) you were also circumcised with a circumcision made without hands, in the removal of the body of the flesh by the circumcision of Christ; having been buried with Him in baptism, in which you were also raised up with Him through faith in the working of God, who raised Him from the dead.

Deuteronomy 10:12-16 NASB
Now, Israel, what does the LORD your God require from you, but to fear the LORD your God, to walk in all His ways and love Him, and to serve the LORD your God with all your heart and with all your soul, and to keep the LORD'S commandments and His statutes which I am commanding you today for your good? Behold, to the LORD your God belong heaven and the highest heavens, the earth and all that is in it. Yet on your fathers did the LORD set His affection to love them, and He chose their descendants after them, even you above all peoples, as it is this day. So circumcise your heart, and stiffen your neck no longer.

Deuteronomy 30:16 NASB
Moreover the LORD your God will circumcise your heart and the heart of your descendants, to love the LORD your God with all your heart and with all your soul, so that you may live.

Genesis 17:11-12, 21:4
"And you shall be circumcised in the flesh of your foreskin, and it shall be the sign of the covenant between Me and you. And every male among you who is eight days old shall be circumcised throughout your generations..." Then Abraham circumcised his son Isaac when he was eight days old, as God had commanded him.

Acts 7:8
And He gave (Abraham) the covenant of circumcision; and so Abraham became the father of Isaac, and circumcised him on the eighth day

Colossians 3:8-11
But now ye also put off all these; anger, wrath, malice, blasphemy, filthy communication out of your mouth. Lie not one to another, seeing that ye have put off the old man with his deeds; And have put on the new man, which is renewed in knowledge after the image of him that created him: Where there is neither Greek nor Jew, circumcision nor uncircumcision, Barbarian, Scythian, bond nor free: but Christ is all, and in all.

Acts 19:1-7 NIV
While Apollos was at Corinth, Paul took the road through the interior and arrived at Ephesus. There he found some disciples and asked them, "Did you receive the Holy Spirit when you believed?" They answered, "No, we have not even heard that there is a Holy Spirit." So Paul asked, "Then what baptism did you receive?" "John's baptism," they replied. Paul said, "John's baptism was a baptism of repentance. He told the people to believe in the one coming after him, that is, in Jesus." On hearing this, they were baptized into the name of the Lord Jesus. When Paul placed his hands on them, the Holy Spirit came on them, and they spoke in tongues and prophesied. There were about twelve men in all.

8. Who should be baptized?

All who have repented of their sins and believe in Jesus must be obedient to Him and submit to being water baptized. In considering the Biblical record of water baptism, those who truly repented and exercised faith in Jesus Christ were given the instruction to be baptized. "Since water baptism is a meaningful response in obedience to the gospel, it must be done with understanding. We find no Scriptural record of the baptism of infants. Baptism was reserved for adults who confessed Jesus as Lord"[2] Even those who had been repentant and submitted to the baptism of John the Baptist, when they heard that Jesus had come and believed in Him, they were required to profess their faith in Jesus and be baptized in His name (Acts 19:1-6).

---

[2] Ibid, pg. 169

Study Questions

1. Read Romans 6:1-8 and 1 Corinthians 12:12-14. Describe how water baptism relates to the death, burial, and resurrection of Jesus. _____

_____

_____

_____

_____

_____

2. Read Colossians 2:6-15, Colossians 3:8-11. Describe the circumcision that occurs in water baptism. ___

_____

_____

_____

_____

_____

3. I would like to be water baptized. Why or why not. _____

_____

_____

_____

_____

_____

Lesson Journal

Use this section to record your thoughts on the topics in this lesson.

_____

_____

_____

_____

_____

_____

_____

_____

Lesson 12
The Baptism of the Holy Spirit

Scripture Reading

- Acts 2:1-4, 38-39 (the day of Pentecost, the first baptism of the Holy Spirit)
- Acts 8:14-19 (Samaritans receive the Holy Spirit)
- Acts 9:17-22 (Saul receives the Holy Spirit)
- Acts 10:44-48 (the household of Cornelius receives the Holy Spirit)
- Acts 18:8-11 through 1 Corinthians 1:7 2:4 (Corinthians receive the Holy Spirit)
- 1 Corinthians 12 and 14 (the gifts of the Holy Spirit)
- Acts 19:1-7 (baptism of John's disciples and the baptism of the Holy Spirit)

Introduction

The focus of this lesson is on what the Bible has to say about the Holy Spirit, beginning with the promise of Jesus to send the Holy Spirit. Jesus promised the coming of the Holy Spirit on the night He was arrested, and He reiterated His promise just before He ascended into heaven. Jesus described the Holy Spirit as a comforter, counselor, and helper for believers, and told His apostles to go and wait in the city of Jerusalem to be baptized in the Holy Spirit.

Less than a week after His ascension, the apostles and other believers were gathered in an upper room on the day of Pentecost, and received what Jesus had promised as they were baptized in the Holy Spirit. The baptism of the Holy Spirit was not limited to the day of Pentecost, but was experienced by Samaritans, Italians, Corinthians, and Ephesians. These points in Scripture show us that the outpouring of the Holy Spirit continued with new believers, and is equally relevant today. Yet, receiving the Spirit is not an end, but a beginning. It is by the Spirit of God that one matures in a relationship with Jesus Christ. The apostle Paul emphasized this in his letter to the believers in Galatia. He told the Galatians that life in the Spirit produces fruit that comes from a growing and maturing life with Christ. Paul said, *"But the fruit of the Spirit is love, joy, peace, patience, kindness, goodness, faithfulness, gentleness, self-control; against such things there is no law... If we live by the Spirit, let us also walk by the Spirit,"* (Galatians 5:22-23 NIV).

Study this lesson to learn about the baptism of the Holy Spirit, and about growing as a Christian by the Spirit of God.

1. What happened after Jesus' ascension?

Exodus 23:16 NIV
Celebrate the Feast of Harvest with the firstfruits of the crops you sow in your field. Celebrate the Feast of Ingathering at the end of the year, when you gather in your crops from the field.

Leviticus 23:15-16 NIV
From the day after the Sabbath, the day you brought the sheaf of the wave offering, count off seven full weeks. Count off fifty days up to the day after the seventh Sabbath, and then present an offering of new grain to the LORD.

Acts 2:1-4, 14-18 NASB
When the day of Pentecost had come, they were all together in one place. And suddenly there came from heaven a noise like a violent rushing wind, and it filled the whole house where they were sitting. And there appeared to them tongues as of fire distributing themselves, and they rested on each one of them. And they were all filled with the Holy Spirit and began to speak with other tongues, as the Spirit was giving them utterance... But Peter, taking his stand with the eleven, raised his voice and declared to them: "Men of Judea and all you who live in Jerusalem, let this be known to you and give heed to my words. "For these men are not drunk, as you suppose, for it is only the third hour of the day; but this is what was spoken of through the prophet Joel: 'And it shall be in the last days,' god says, that I will pour forth of my spirit on all mankind; and your sons and your daughters shall prophesy, and your young men shall see visions, and your old men shall dream dreams; even on my bondslaves, both men and women, I will in those days pour forth of my spirit and they shall prophesy.

Just prior to His ascension, Jesus gathered together the eleven apostles and commanded them to return to Jerusalem and wait for the baptism of the Holy Spirit, *"not many days from now."* After Jesus' ascension the apostles were obedient and returned to Jerusalem and assembled together with other believers, about 120 people, in the upper room of a building in the city. Here they waited as Jesus had requested, and were in unity devoting themselves to prayer.

Peter, in his prayer and Bible study, discovered that the book of Psalms prophesied the loss of one of the apostles, Judas Iscariot who had betrayed Jesus, and found a scripture that said, *"let another man take his office"* (Psalm 109:8). So, another believer who had been with them since their early ministry and had witnessed the death and resurrection of Jesus was selected to replace Judas.

About a week after the ascension of Jesus into heaven, another Jewish feast day was to be observed, the feast of Pentecost. Pentecost, meaning fiftieth, was celebrated to mark the end of the barley harvest, and the start of the wheat harvest, and was observed seven weeks and one day after Passover (Exodus 23:14-17 and Leviticus 23:15-22). On this day of Pentecost something unusual occurred. Those in the upper room heard the sound of a mighty rushing wind, and suddenly above their heads appeared cloven (split) tongues of fire, and they were filled with the Holy Spirit and began to speak as the Spirit enabled them.

This was the day that Jesus was referring to when He said prior to His ascension, *"not many days from now."* The 120 in the upper room that were filled with the Holy Spirit began to speak of the mighty deeds of God in languages that they had never been taught. Those in the city who heard the commotion were stunned. The apostle Peter stood up to preach and teach, explaining that what had taken place was prophesied by the prophets of old and part of the plan of God to pour out His Spirit on men and women, both young and old. This day that the Holy Spirit was made manifest marked the fulfillment of the promise Jesus made at His ascension, and the start of the New Covenant or New Testament Church (Acts 2:1-18).

2. What did Jesus promise when He ascended?

Jesus promised the coming of the Holy Spirit. All four gospels record the prophecy of John the Baptist, who said that one greater than he was coming who would baptize in the Holy Spirit. The one coming who was greater than John was Jesus Christ, and John acknowledged this stating, *"This is He on behalf of whom I said, 'After me comes a Man who has a higher rank than I, for He existed before me'… this is the One who baptizes in the Holy Spirit,"* (John 1:30, 33).

Jesus promised the coming of the Holy Spirit on the night that He was arrested (John 14:16), and He reiterated this promise just before He ascended into heaven, stating, *"you will be baptized with the Holy Spirit not many days from now… you will receive power when the Holy Spirit has come upon you; and you shall be My witnesses both in Jerusalem, and in all Judea and Samaria, and even to the remotest part of the earth,"* (Acts 1:5, 8).

3. Who is the Holy Spirit?

The Holy Spirit is God, the third person of the triune Godhead. He is a personal being who indwells believers in fulfillment of the prophecies of the prophets Joel and John the Baptist, and the promise of Jesus Christ.

The Holy Spirit is not an "active force" or an impersonal presence. Jesus referred to the Holy Spirit with personal pronouns, clearly identifying the person of the Holy Spirit. As a person of the Godhead, the Holy Spirit possesses all of the attributes of God. The Holy Spirit is omnipotent, omniscient, omnipresent, eternal, and is fully God having the complete nature and every other attribute of God. The Holy Spirit is personal, and He speaks, intercedes, comforts and teaches (Job 33:4; Isaiah 59:21; Acts 5:3, 4; John 14:26 and Galatians 6:8).

4. How did Jesus refer to the Holy Spirit?

The gospel of John records four instances (John 14:16, 14:26, 15:26, 16:7) where Jesus referred to the Holy Spirit, and He did so using the Greek word *parakletos. Parakletos* was a Greek term, meaning one who is called on to be an advocate, helper, or comforter of another, or one who would help plead a cause for another. The English versions of the Bible variously translate this word as "comforter" (KJV) "Helper" (NASB), "Counselor" (NIV), and "Advocate" (NRSV).

Jesus' descriptive term indicates that the Holy Spirit comes alongside believers, working on their behalf as a comforter, counselor, and helper.

Job 33:4
The Spirit of God hath made me, and the breath of the Almighty hath given me life.

Isaiah 59:21
My spirit that is upon thee, and my words which I have put in thy mouth, shall not depart out of thy mouth, nor out of the mouth of thy seed, nor out of the mouth of thy seed's seed, saith the LORD, from henceforth and for ever.

Acts 5:3-4
But Peter said, "Ananias, why hath Satan filled thine heart to lie to the Holy Ghost… thou hast not lied unto men, but unto God."

Galatians 6:8
…but he that soweth to the Spirit shall of the Spirit reap life everlasting.

John 14:16
And I will pray the Father, and he shall give you another Comforter, that he may abide with you for ever;

John 14:26
But the Comforter, which is the Holy Ghost, whom the Father will send in my name, he shall teach you all things, and bring all things to your remembrance, whatsoever I have said unto you.

John 15:26
But when the Comforter is come, whom I will send unto you from the Father, even the Spirit of truth, which proceedeth from the Father, he shall testify of me:

John 16:7
Nevertheless I tell you the truth; It is expedient for you that I go away: for if I go not away, the Comforter will not come unto you; but if I depart, I will send him unto you.

5. How does the Bible record the coming of the Holy Spirit?

On the day of Pentecost Peter said this *"promise is for you and your children and for all who are far off—for all whom the Lord our God will call,"* (Acts 2:39 NIV). The promise extends to believers today. The Bible gives testimony of believers who received the baptism of the Holy Spirit on, and after, the day of Pentecost.

Receiving the Holy Spirit

Scripture	Place	Received By	Sign or Result
Acts 2:1-4, 38	Jerusalem	120 disciples in upper room / 3000 believers	Wind, fire, tongues, and prophecy
Acts 8:14-18	Samaria	Samaritans	Visible/audible sign (v.18)
Acts 9:17-19	Damascus	Paul	Healing of eyes/ powerful preaching.
Acts 10:44-48	Caesarea	The house of Cornelius	Tongues and praising God
Acts 18:8-11 1 Cor. 1:7, 2:4	Corinth	Crispus and Corinthians	"not lacking in any gift" and "demonstration of the Spirit and of power"
Acts 19:1-7	Ephesus	Disciples baptized by John	Tongues and prophecy

- **120 apostles and disciples in Acts 2**

    Less than a week after His ascension, the apostles and other believers, about 120 people, received the promise of Jesus and were baptized in the Holy Spirit. The apostles and followers of Jesus waited for the baptism of the Holy Spirit as Jesus had instructed when He ascended. They gathered in an upper room and prayed, waiting for the promise. On the day of Pentecost, while they waited, praying and praising God, *"Suddenly a sound like the blowing of a violent wind came from heaven and filled the whole house where they were sitting. They saw what seemed to be tongues of fire that separated and came to rest on each of them. All of them were filled with the Holy Spirit and began to speak in other tongues as the Spirit enabled them,"* (Acts 2:3-4 NIV).

    Jews from many nations that had come to Jerusalem to observe Pentecost heard this sound and *"a crowd came together in bewilderment, because each one heard them speak in his own language,"* (Acts 2:6 NIV). The people began to ask questions, wondering what this was all about. Peter then stood and began to speak, *"This is what was spoken by the prophet Joel: 'In the last days,' God says, 'I will pour out My Spirit on all people. Your sons and daughters will prophesy, your young men will see visions and your old men will dream dreams. Even on my servants, both men and women, I will pour out My Spirit in those days, and they will prophesy,'"* (Acts 2:16-18 NIV).

- **The Samaritans in Acts 8**

Acts 8:14-17 says, *"When the apostles who were at Jerusalem heard that Samaria had received the word of God, they sent unto them Peter and John, who, when they were come down, prayed for them, that they might receive the Holy Spirit; for as yet he was fallen upon none of them; only they were baptized in the name of the Lord Jesus. Then laid they their hands on them, and they received the Holy Spirit."*

- **The conversion of Saul (Paul) in Acts 9**

Saul, a man who persecuted believers in Jesus, underwent a radical conversion as he traveled from Jerusalem north to Damascus. Saul was blinded and audibly heard Jesus speaking to him, as did others that were traveling with Saul. He went on to Damascus and fasted three days. Meanwhile, God spoke to a believer in Damascus named Ananias, and instructed him to visit and pray for Saul. *"So Ananias departed and entered the house, and after laying hands on him said, 'Brother Saul, the Lord Jesus, who appeared to you on the road by which you were coming, has sent me so that you may regain your sight and be filled with the Holy Spirit.' And immediately there fell from his eyes something like scales, and he regained his sight, and he got up and was baptized,"* (Acts 9:17-18). After this, Saul devoted his life to Jesus and became known by his Roman name, Paul.

- **The Gentiles in Acts 10**

In Acts 10, Peter visits a Gentile named Cornelius. While Peter was speaking to him and his family, *"the Holy Spirit fell on all them who heard the word. And they of the circumcision who believed were astonished, as many as came with Peter, because on the Gentiles also was poured out the gift of the Holy Spirit. For they heard them speak with tongues."* (Acts 10:44-46). The Jewish believers who were with Peter were astonished to see the Gentiles receive the Holy Spirit.

In Acts 11 Peter recounts to his fellow apostles the event of Acts 10: *"As I began to speak, the Holy Spirit fell on them, as on us at the beginning. Then remembered I the word of the Lord, how he said, John indeed baptized with water; but ye shall be baptized with the Holy Spirit. Forasmuch then, as God gave them the same gift as he did unto us, who believed on the Lord Jesus Christ, what was I, that I could withstand God?"* (Acts 11:15-17). That last statement shows there was no way to deny that the Gentiles had received the baptism of the Holy Spirit.

- **Crispus and Corinthians in Acts 18:8-11 and 1 Corinthians 1:7, 2:4**

  Acts 18 records some of the events of the second missionary journey of the apostle Paul. This was more than 10 years after the ascension of Jesus, when Paul was preaching to Greco-Roman cities. In the city of Corinth, Paul preached *"and many of the Corinthians when they heard were believing and being baptized,"* (Acts 18:8). In his first letter to the Corinthians, Paul reminds them that when he had preached to them, he had done so *"in demonstration of the Spirit and of power,"* (2:4 NASB) and that they were not *"lacking in any gift,"* (1:7 NASB). He also gave instruction regarding spiritual gifts, specifically the gifts of prophecy and tongues, saying such things as, *"do not forbid to speak in tongues,"* (1 Corinthians 14:39 NASB).

- **Believers in Ephesus in Acts 19**

  Acts 19:1-7 documents an event where 12 believers in Jesus received the Holy Spirit nearly 20 years after their conversion. This incident highlights the importance of water baptism as an accompaniment, ideally prior to, Holy Spirit baptism. Paul asked these believers if they had heard of the Holy Spirit, and when they replied "no," he inquired as to how they had been baptized. John the Baptist had baptized these believers over a decade earlier. Paul then instructed them to be baptized in the name of the Lord Jesus, and *"they were baptized in the name of the Lord Jesus. And when Paul had laid his hands upon them, the Holy Spirit came on them; and they spoke with tongues and prophesied,"* (Acts 19:5-6).

6. Does the Bible always refer to the coming of the Holy Spirit as the baptism of the Holy Spirit?

The Baptism of the Holy Spirit is spoken of in all four gospels, the book of Acts, and was taught by Jesus and His apostles.

In all four gospel accounts the promise is given that Jesus Himself will baptize with the Holy Spirit (Matthew 3:11; Mark 1:8; Luke 3:16 and John 1:33). This same promise was repeated by Jesus just prior to His ascension into Heaven: *"...Wait for the gift My Father promised, which you have heard Me speak about. For John baptized with water, but in a few days you will be baptized with Holy Spirit,"* (Acts 1:4-5 NIV).

The Bible variously refers to the baptism of the Holy Spirit as:

- **Receiving the Holy Spirit and the Holy Spirit falling upon believers** (Acts 8:14-16 and Acts 10:44)

- **Being filled with the Holy Spirit** (Acts 9:17-18)

- **The gift of the Holy Spirit poured out** (Acts 10:45-46; see also Romans 5:5)

- **The baptism with the Holy Spirit** (Acts 11:15-16)

- **The baptism in the Holy Spirit** (John 1:33)

7. Does the baptism of the Holy Spirit occur today?

The doctrine of baptisms (see Hebrews 6:2), which include water baptism, and baptism of the Holy Spirit, are separate from, and follow, salvation by repentance and faith in Jesus Christ. The baptism of the Holy Spirit was not just a one-time occurrence, but a promise made by God to all believers in Jesus Christ.

- **Peter taught: The Holy Spirit is promised to all**

  On the day of Pentecost, Peter explained the baptism of the Holy Spirit by quoting the prophet Joel, saying, *"This is what was spoken by the prophet Joel: 'In the last days,' God says, 'I will pour out My Spirit on all people. Your sons and daughters will prophesy, your young men will see visions and your old men will dream dreams. Even on my servants, both men and women, I will pour out My Spirit in those days, and they will prophesy,'"* (Acts 2:16-18 NIV).

  Peter explained that the baptism of the Holy Spirit that Jesus promised was being witnessed, and was available to *"all people,"* both *"men and women,"* and was a fulfillment of Old Testament prophecy. Peter also went on to say that the baptism of the Holy Spirit would be extended beyond the 120 men and women when he said, *"Repent and be baptized, every one of you, in the name of Jesus Christ for the forgiveness of your sins. And you will receive the gift of the Holy Spirit. The promise is for you and your children and for all who are far off–for all whom the Lord our God will call,"* (Acts 2:38-39 NIV).

Acts 8:14-16 NASB
Now when the apostles in Jerusalem heard that Samaria had received the word of God, they sent them Peter and John, who came down and prayed for them that they might **receive the Holy Spirit**. For He had not yet **fallen upon** any of them; they had simply been baptized in the name of the Lord Jesus.

Acts 10:44 NASB
While Peter was still speaking these words, **the Holy Spirit fell** upon all those who were listening to the message.

Acts 9:17-18 NASB
"Brother Saul, the Lord Jesus, who appeared to you on the road by which you were coming, has sent me so that you may regain your sight and be **filled with the Holy Spirit**." And immediately there fell from his eyes something like scales, and he regained his sight, and he got up and was baptized

Acts 10:45-46 NASB
All the circumcised believers who came with Peter were amazed, because the **gift of the Holy Spirit** had been **poured out on the Gentiles also**. For they were hearing them speaking with tongues and exalting God. Then Peter answered, "Surely no one can refuse the water for these to be baptized who have received the Holy Spirit just as we did (a reference to the baptism of the Holy Spirit on Pentecost), can he?"

Acts 11:15-16 NASB
"And as I began to speak, the Holy Spirit fell upon them just as He did upon us at the beginning. And I remembered the word of the Lord, how He used to say, 'John baptized with water, but you will be **baptized with the Holy Spirit**.'"

John 1:33
"I did not recognize Him, but He who sent me to baptize in water said to me, 'He upon whom you see the Spirit descending and remaining upon Him, this is the One who **baptizes in the Holy Spirit**.'"

Ephesians 6:18
Praying always with all prayer and supplication in the Spirit ...

1 Corinthians 14:2, 15 NIV
For anyone who speaks in a tongue does not speak to men but to God. Indeed, no one understands him; he utters mysteries with his spirit... So what shall I do? I will pray with my spirit, but I will also pray with my mind; I will sing with my spirit, but I will also sing with my mind.

Acts 9:17-18 NASB
"Brother Saul, the Lord Jesus, who appeared to you on the road by which you were coming, has sent me so that you may regain your sight and be **filled with the Holy Spirit**." And immediately there fell from his eyes something like scales, and he regained his sight, and he got up and was baptized.

Acts 8:14-16 NASB
Now when the apostles in Jerusalem heard that Samaria had received the word of God, they sent them Peter and John, who came down and prayed for them that they might **receive the Holy Spirit**. For He had not yet **fallen upon** any of them; they had simply been baptized in the name of the Lord Jesus.

Acts 19:1-5 NASB
It happened that while Apollos was at Corinth, Paul passed through the upper country and came to Ephesus, and found some disciples. He said to them, "Did you receive the Holy Spirit when you believed?" And they *said* to him, "No, we have not even heard whether there is a Holy Spirit." And he said, "Into what then were you baptized?" And they said, "Into John's baptism." Paul said, "John baptized with the baptism of repentance, telling the people to believe in Him who was coming after him, that is, in Jesus." When they heard this, they were baptized in the name of the Lord Jesus.

- **Jesus taught: The Father gives the Spirit**

Jesus too taught about the Holy Spirit. Once he said, *"If you then, being evil, know how to give good gifts to your children, how much more will your heavenly Father give the Holy Spirit to those who ask Him!"* (Luke 11:13).

- **Paul taught: Receive the Spirit and gifts of the Spirit**

The apostle Paul taught that believers receive gifts of the Spirit, but all do not receive the same gifts. He described the community of believers as a body, all having various gifts but working together as one. He said, *"To each one is given the manifestation of the Spirit for the common good,"* (1 Corinthians 12:7). He also reiterated that receiving the Holy Spirit was for all believers, and follows repentance and baptism, telling the Corinthians, *"For by one Spirit we were all baptized into one body, whether Jews or Greeks, whether slaves or free, and we were all made to drink of one Spirit,"* (1 Corinthians 12:13). Paul described receiving the Holy Spirit as a drink of one Spirit that follows baptism.

Paul also taught that the gift of the Holy Spirit was useful in prayer and worship (Ephesians 6:18 and 1 Corinthians 14:2, 15).

- **God fulfills His promises**

God fulfills His promises in a variety of ways, and no two human beings are alike in how they receive spiritual things. The New Testament shows that some believers received the baptism of the Holy Spirit by a sovereign act of God, such as the household of Cornelius (Acts 10). When this occurred, Peter commanded those who received the baptism of the Holy Spirit to be immediately water baptized. Others received the Spirit through the laying on of hands of a believer (Acts 9:17-18) or the laying on of hands of an apostle (Acts 8:14-16 and Acts 19:1–5) after they had been water baptized. These are the scriptural examples, and what believers should expect.

8. What is the purpose of receiving the Holy Spirit?

Upon giving His apostles instruction to preach to all nations and make them disciples, Jesus said, *"And behold, I am sending forth the promise of My Father upon you; but you are to stay in the city until you are clothed with power from on high,"* (Luke 24:49). Jesus added, *"You will receive power when the Holy Spirit has come upon you; and you shall be My witnesses both in Jerusalem, and in all Judea and Samaria, and even to the remotest part of the earth,"* (Acts 1:8 NIV).

Jesus let these disciples of His know that they would be empowered by the Holy Spirit to be effective witnesses after they had received the baptism of the Holy Spirit. This is a primary purpose of receiving the Holy Spirit.

In addition, it is by the Spirit of God that one matures in their relationship with Jesus Christ. The apostle Paul emphasized this in his letter to the believers in Galatia. These believers were being led astray by a false gospel, and Paul said *"Are you so foolish? Having begun by the Spirit, are you now being perfected by the flesh?"* (Galatians 3:3). When Paul mentions *"being perfected"* he is referring to being completed or becoming mature. In essence, he is asking if they are becoming mature Christians by the Spirit of God, or by works of the flesh. In his closing remarks to the Galatians he describes their growth as a journey, a walk, saying, *"But I say, walk by the Spirit, and you will not carry out the desire of the flesh,"* (Galatians 5:16). And he goes on to tell them that a life in the Spirit will begin to produce fruit, as he describes the fruit that comes with growing and maturing, *"But the fruit of the Spirit is love, joy, peace, patience, kindness, goodness, faithfulness, gentleness, self-control; against such things there is no law... If we live by the Spirit, let us also walk by the Spirit,"* (Galatians 5:22-23).

Study Questions

1. Read John 14:16-26. Use two different translations of the Bible if you have them available. How did Jesus describe the Holy Spirit? Who was sending the Holy Spirit? Do you see the Father, Son, and Holy Spirit throughout this passage? _____

    _____

    _____

    _____

    _____

2. Read Acts 2:16-18. Do you think this passage, taken along with Acts 8 (Samaritans receive the Spirit), Acts 10 (House of Cornelius receives the Spirit), Acts 18 and 1 Corinthians 2 (Corinthians receive the Spirit), Acts 19 (Ephesians receive the spirit nearly 20 years after Jesus' ascension), means that the promise of the baptism of the Holy Spirit extends to today? _____

    _____

    _____

    _____

    _____

3. Read Galatians 5:19-25. Do you think that "fruit of the Spirit" comes immediately after receiving the Holy Spirit? _____

    _____

    _____

    _____

    _____

Lesson Journal

Use this section to record your thoughts on the topics in this lesson.

_____

_____

_____

_____

_____

_____

_____

Lesson 13
A Life of Worship

Scripture Reading

- Exodus 20:1-7 (the first and second commandments)

- Deuteronomy 6:13-14 (honoring God alone)

- Matthew 5:17-18 (relevance of the law today)

- Psalm 51:17; Isaiah 28:13, 66:2 and Mark 12:30 (God considers the attitude of the heart)

- Habakkuk 2:18-29; Ephesians 5:5; Colossians 3:5 and Luke 16:13 (idolatry)

- Psalm 98:4-6, 100:1-5, 134:2, 150:1-6; John 4:23-24; 1 Corinthians 14:15; Ephesians 5:19 and Hebrews 10:25 (worship)

Introduction

Worship has to do with ascribing worth or value; regarding God it is honoring His worth. Worshiping God is not something that is done at a particular time on a certain day. Although there are times where individually or gathered together with other believers we honor and revere God's worthiness by offering Him praise and thanksgiving, worshiping God also involves honoring Him in all aspects of our life.

God commanded His people to worship Him alone. Throughout the Old Testament God continually requested complete devotion of His people. He made it clear when He gave Moses the Ten Commandments. Yet in spite of the commands, God desired, and continues to desire genuine worship from the heart of a believer, not based on compulsion.

This lesson focuses on the first two commandments which deal with man's relationship with God. These commandments share some common ground, emphasizing honoring our Lord with all aspects of our life. These commands are presented for the Christian today, and tie in worshiping God corporately with other believers, individually, and with one's entire life.

1. Are the Ten Commandments relevant today?

Before giving the first commandment, God gave a simple preface: *"And God spake all these words, saying, I am the LORD thy God, which have brought thee out of the land of Egypt, out of the house of bondage,"* (Exodus 20:1-2). This preface is an introduction to not just the first commandment, but to all of the law. In the first phrase, *"I am the LORD thy God,"* God reminded Israel of who He was—their God—the one and only true God. He then reiterated the nature of His relationship with the people: *"[I] have brought thee out of the land of Egypt, out of the house of bondage."* He alone saved them from slavery, and relationship with Him was therefore based on His undeserved grace. It is upon this foundation of saving grace, freely bestowed by Almighty God, that the law was given.

Likewise, we are saved by the grace of God through faith in Jesus, and following His moral law is fruit of our faith. So, following God's law does not earn His favor, but rather is a response to His grace received through faith in Jesus Christ, for *"the one who keeps His commandments abides in Him, and He in him,"* (1 John 3:24). Jesus Himself said, *"Do not think that I have come to abolish the Law or the Prophets; I have not come to abolish them but to fulfill them. I tell you the truth, until heaven and earth disappear, not the smallest letter, not the least stroke of a pen, will by any means disappear from the Law until everything is accomplished,"* (Matthew 5:17-18).

The law then does not serve as a means to salvation, but to define sin, and point to Christ, serving as a curb against sin and a guide for Christian lifestyle. God gave His commandments focusing first on those pertaining to relationship with Him, more simply put, commands having to do with worship.

2. What is worship?

Worship is an act of reverence, respect, admiration, or devotion. The word worship comes from the Old English *weorth* meaning worthy, and the suffix *-scipe* (-ship) meaning a state, condition, or quality.[1] The suffix adds deeper meaning, as in the words friendship (the state of being friends) and relationship (the state of being in relation). So worship is the state or quality of worth or worthiness. To worship God is to acknowledge His worth and worthiness by reverence, respect, admiration, and devotion, and is primary to being in relationship with God.

---

[1] *Webster's Third New International Dictionary, Unabridged.* Merriam-Webster, 2002.

3. Does God require worship?

From the beginning God required worship. Abel worshiped God with an acceptable sacrifice (see Genesis 4:4). Abraham worshiped God through sacrifice and giving (see Genesis 14:20). Throughout the Old Testament God required of man nothing less than a life devoted to Him (Micah 6:8). God promised blessings to those who obeyed Him and devoted themselves to Him (Deuteronomy 11:13-16). Although worship was commanded it was to be sincere in response to believing in God—it was and remains a matter of the heart (Psalm 51:17; Isaiah 29:13 and Isaiah 66:2).

God gave the law through Moses, and His law commanded worship, most prominently in the giving of the moral law—the Ten Commandments (see Exodus 20:1-17). In the Ten Commandments God gave His law in an orderly fashion, the first four commandments having to do with man's relationship with God, and the remaining six having to do with man's relationship with others. Although the element of worship can be found in the first four commandments, the first and second commands are explicit and emphatic regarding reverence to God.

4. What is the first commandment?

> *Exodus 20:3*
> *Thou shalt have no other gods before me.*

5. What is the purpose of the first commandment?

The first commandment is an emphatic command against all forms of idolatry. This commandment is a broad directive, speaking to a person's lifestyle and relationship with God. God indicates that in all areas of our life we must recognize Him first. God gave this commandment immediately after reminding the people of Israel that He was God and He alone had rescued them from slavery. God had done mighty miracles before the Pharaoh of Egypt, and God alone had brought them out of the land. His relationship to them was one of Savior and God, and they should never consider anything to be above God.

Our relationship with God through Jesus is likewise based on being saved by grace through faith. Nothing is to hinder that relationship. The Bible equates such things as covetousness, evil desires and greed with idolatry, hence anything in our life or lifestyle put before God is idolatry, and is therefore a false god (Isaiah 45:21; Ephesians 5:5 and Colossians 3:5).

Deuteronomy 11:13-16 NIV
So if you faithfully obey the commands I am giving you today—to love the LORD your God and to serve him with all your heart and with all your soul—then I will send rain on your land in its season, both autumn and spring rains, so that you may gather in your grain, new wine and oil. I will provide grass in the fields for your cattle, and you will eat and be satisfied. Be careful, or you will be enticed to turn away and worship other gods and bow down to them.

Micah 6:8 NIV
He has showed you, O man, what is good. And what does the LORD require of you? To act justly and to love mercy and to walk humbly with your God.

Psalm 51:17 NIV
The sacrifices of God are a broken spirit; a broken and contrite heart, O God, you will not despise.

Isaiah 29:13 NIV
The Lord says: "These people come near to me with their mouth and honor me with their lips, but their hearts are far from me. Their worship of me is made up only of rules taught by men."

Isaiah 66:2 NASB
I will look, To him who is humble and contrite of spirit, and who trembles at My word.

Isaiah 45:21
Look unto me, and be ye saved, all the ends of the earth: for I am God, and there is none else.

Ephesians 5:5 NASB
For this you know with certainty, that no immoral or impure person or covetous man, who is an idolater, has an inheritance in the kingdom of Christ and God.

Colossians 3:5 NIV
Put to death, therefore, whatever belongs to your earthly nature: sexual immorality, impurity, lust, evil desires and greed, which is idolatry.

Mark 12:30
And thou shalt love the Lord thy God with all thy heart, and with all thy soul, and with all thy mind, and with all thy strength: this is the first commandment.

Romans 4:20-21 NASB
(Abraham) did not waver in unbelief but grew strong in faith, giving glory to God, and being fully assured that what God had promised, He was able also to perform. Therefore it was also credited to him as righteousness.

6. How should we keep the first commandment?

The first commandment is kept first by believing in the triune God: The Father, the Son, and the Holy Spirit. When we have true faith in God, believing that He alone has given us life, our response will be worship: to love Him and desire an ongoing and deepening relationship with Him. Nothing of this world: family, work, school, homes, cars, possessions, etc. should take precedence over our relationship with God. He always comes first, and this is true worship.

7. Is there a blessing in keeping the first commandment?

The commandments are given to people of grace, people that have been saved from the slavery of sin by faith in Jesus Christ. The blessing in keeping the first commandment is the absolute assurance of salvation, reflected by our faith in, and an ever-deepening relationship with, Jesus Christ. Jesus said that we are to love the Lord our God with all of our heart, mind, soul, and strength (Mark 12:30). Love of God and Christ deepens as our relationship with Him endures and matures, and as we continue to keep Him first in our lives (Romans 4:20-21).

8. What is the second commandment?

Exodus 20:4
Thou shalt not make unto thee any graven image, or any likeness of any thing that is in heaven above, or that is in the earth beneath, or that is in the water under the earth: Thou shalt not bow down thyself to them, nor serve them: for I the LORD thy God am a jealous God, visiting the iniquity of the fathers upon the children unto the third and fourth generation of them that hate me; And showing mercy unto thousands of them that love me, and keep my commandments.

9. What is the purpose of the second commandment?

Whereas the first commandment forbids idolatry of all forms, the second commandment speaks to specific forms of idolatry having to do with the act of worship. God highlights the importance of worship in the second commandment by expressly forbidding the worship of any man-made idol. God's emphasis on worship is evident in His statement of detriments that result from idolatry, and of blessings that follow worshiping Him alone. Hence, the worship of God alone is the primary focus of the second commandment.

10. What does God mean when He says He is jealous?

The primary meaning of jealous is intolerance of unfaithfulness, which is the jealousy of God in the context of the second commandment. It is not synonymous with envy, the sense of desiring that which belongs to another, but rather God does not tolerate infidelity or the worship of anything that man has conjured up as a god, including:

- **Occult practices**

  Seeking psychics, palm readers, soothsayers, fortunetellers, tarot cards, Ouija boards, etc. is to seek knowledge from a source other than God. It is a form of idolatry that does not acknowledge God as one's sole source, and should not be practiced (Leviticus 19:26 and Deuteronomy 18:14). Some early Christians who had dealt in the occult serve as an example to us, as they burned their books of sorcery after coming to believe in Jesus (Acts 19:19).

- **Money / Possessions**

  King Solomon spent much time seeking fulfillment through the trappings of the world while neglecting his relationship with God. He had every imaginable worldly possession, yet concluded in the book of Ecclesiastes that they were all worthless and that God alone was worthy. Jesus summed up putting money before God in Luke 16:13 (see also Colossians 3:5).

- **Television / Internet / Sports / Hobbies / Entertainment**

  Things that are for entertainment and pleasure are not inherently evil, but can take priority over God. Anything that is made a priority over worshiping God is an idol. The apostle Paul warns to avoid people that deny God and love themselves, money and pleasure (2 Timothy 3:2-5, see also Ephesians 5:5).

Dishonoring God by idolatry results in *"visiting the iniquity of the fathers upon the children unto the third and fourth generation of them that hate me."* The Hebrew word for visit means to attend to, to visit, to lay upon as a charge, deposit.[2] Hence, the consequences of an iniquitous (wicked, unlawful) lifestyle also affect (attend to, visit) ones children and grandchildren.

Conversely, the affect on the children of those that choose to worship God alone is *mercy unto thousands of them that love me, and keep my commandments.* Here again this is indicative of one's lifestyle. A godly lifestyle results in blessings through generations.

Leviticus 19:26 NIV
Do not practice divination or sorcery

Deuteronomy 18:14 NIV
The nations you will dispossess listen to those who practice sorcery or divination. But as for you, the LORD your God has not permitted you to do so.

Acts 19:19 NIV
A number who had practiced sorcery brought their scrolls together and burned them publicly.

Luke 16:13 NIV
No servant can serve two masters. Either he will hate the one and love the other, or he will be devoted to the one and despise the other. You cannot serve both God and Money."

2 Timothy 3:2-5 NIV
People will be lovers of themselves, lovers of money, boastful, proud, abusive, disobedient to their parents, ungrateful, unholy, without love, unforgiving, slanderous, without self-control, brutal, not lovers of the good, treacherous, rash, conceited, lovers of pleasure rather than lovers of God—having a form of godliness but denying its power. Have nothing to do with them.

---

[2] *Brown-Driver-Briggs' Hebrew Definitions*, Institute for Creation Research, El Cajon, CA

Exodus 25:18
You shall make two cherubim of gold, make them of hammered work at the two ends of the mercy seat.

Exodus 26:31 NASB
You shall make a veil of blue and purple and scarlet material and fine twisted linen; it shall be made with cherubim, the work of a skillful workman.

1 Kings 6:21, 28 NASB
Also in the inner sanctuary he made two cherubim of olive wood, each ten cubits high. He also overlaid the cherubim with gold.

Exodus 31:3-5 NASB
I have filled him with the Spirit of God in wisdom, in understanding, in knowledge, and in all kinds of craftsmanship, to make artistic designs for work in gold, in silver, and in bronze, and in the cutting of stones for settings, and in the carving of wood, that he may work in all kinds of craftsmanship.

Deuteronomy 27:15
Cursed be the man that maketh any graven or molten image, an abomination unto the LORD, the work of the hands of the craftsman, and putteth it in a secret place.

Habakkuk 2:18-19
What profit is the idol when its maker has carved it, or an image, a teacher of falsehood? For its maker trusts in his own handiwork when he fashions speechless idols. Woe to him who says to a piece of wood, "Awake!" To a mute stone, "Arise!" And that is your teacher? Behold, it is overlaid with gold and silver, and there is no breath at all inside it.

Deuteronomy 6:13-14 NASB
You shall fear only the LORD your God; and you shall worship Him and swear by His name. You shall not follow other gods, any of the gods of the peoples who surround you.

Revelation 19:10
Worship God.

Revelation 22:9
Worship God.

11. Does God forbid making images?

God did not put a limit on man's creativity or artistic talents. The intent of the commandment is to keep man from raising an object to the level of adoration or worship. In fact, God authorized the creation of different images to be used in His temple, and provided talented craftsmen to accomplish the task. The making of images is not forbidden, but rather the making of an object or image to honor as a god.

- **Images commissioned by God**

  Exodus 25:18; Exodus 26:31 and 1 Kings 6:21, 28

- **Craftsmen given talent by God to create images**

  Exodus 31:3-5

- **Images forbidden to be used for worship**

  Deuteronomy 27:15 and Habakkuk 2:18-19

12. How should we keep the second commandment?

The second commandment is kept by reserving all of our worship for God alone, and never bowing down to or worshiping anyone or anything else (Deuteronomy 6:13-14; Revelation 19:10 and Revelation 22:9).

13. Is there a blessing in keeping the second commandment?

Keeping the second commandment results in the blessing of relationship and assurance associated with the first commandment. There is also the blessing of mercy and grace bestowed on children and family based on a lifestyle of honoring God and worshiping Him alone.

14. How do we worship God today?

God has not changed and does not change, and worshiping Him has not changed. It is a matter of the heart that is reflected in a life that completely honors Him. Worship was introduced in the Old Testament and reiterated in the New Testament. Worshiping Him is any act of reverence, respect, admiration, or devotion, including:

- **Gathering together to collectively worship God**

  Coming together with others to worship God collectively as a community of like-minded believers was established in the Old Testament and continued in the New. In the Old Testament the primary place of corporate worship was first the Tabernacle, then the permanent Temple in Jerusalem. These were the dwelling place of God. There were also times of community worship at different places (2 Chronicles 20:26).

  After the coming of Jesus and the Holy Spirit, God made His dwelling place within believers, the body became the temple of the Holy Ghost (1 Corinthians 6:19), and believers together also build a habitation for God (Ephesians 2:19-22). Coming together to worship God is still important and vital (Hebrews 10:25).

- **Praise and thanksgiving**

  The dwelling place of God is described as one surrounded by praise to Him. Isaiah the prophet described a vision where angels above the throne of God cried praise unto Him: *"Seraphim stood above Him, each having six wings: with two he covered his face, and with two he covered his feet, and with two he flew. And one called out to another and said, Holy, Holy, Holy, is the Lord of hosts, The whole earth is full of His glory,"* (Isaiah 6:2-3 NASB). We are instructed in the Psalms to approach God with praise and thanksgiving (Psalm 100:4) and that God is enthroned upon the praises of His people (Psalm 22:3).

  Animal sacrifices as a form of worship to God ceased with the coming of Jesus (John 4:23-24), and now, *"Through Jesus, therefore, let us continually offer to God a sacrifice of praise--the fruit of lips that confess his name,"* (Hebrews 13:15 NIV).

- **Lifting hands / Bowing before God**

  Raising hands, bowing and lying prostrate before God are signs of submission. Both the Old and New Testaments speak of humbly submitting to God through these various postures (Judges 7:15; 2 Chronicles 20:18; Psalms 134:2 and 1 Timothy 2:8).

---

2 Chronicles 20:26 NIV
On the fourth day they assembled in the Valley of Beracah, where they praised the LORD.

1 Corinthians 6:19 NASB
Or do you not know that your body is a temple of the Holy Spirit who is in you, whom you have from God, and that you are not your own?

Ephesians 2:19-22 NIV
Consequently, you are no longer foreigners and aliens, but fellow citizens with God's people and members of God's household, built on the foundation of the apostles and prophets, with Christ Jesus himself as the chief cornerstone. In him the whole building is joined together and rises to become a holy temple in the Lord. And in him you too are being built together to become a dwelling in which God lives by his Spirit.

Hebrews 10:25 NIV
Let us not give up meeting together, as some are in the habit of doing, but let us encourage one another—and all the more as you see the Day approaching.

Psalm 100:4
Enter into his gates with thanksgiving, and into his courts with praise: be thankful unto him, and bless his name

Psalm 22:3 NASB
Yet You are holy, O You who are enthroned upon the praises of Israel.

John 4:23-24 NASB
But an hour is coming, and now is, when the true worshipers will worship the Father in spirit and truth; for such people the Father seeks to be His worshipers. God is spirit, and those who worship Him must worship in spirit and truth.

Judges 7:15 NASB
When Gideon heard the account of the dream and its interpretation, he bowed in worship.

2 Chronicles 20:18 NIV
Jehoshaphat bowed with his face to the ground, and all the people of Judah and Jerusalem fell down in worship before the LORD.

Psalm 134:2
Lift up your hands in the sanctuary, and bless the Lord.

1 Timothy 2:8
I will therefore that men pray everywhere, lifting up holy hands, without wrath and doubting.

Psalm 150

Praise ye the LORD. Praise God in his sanctuary: praise him in the firmament of his power. Praise him for his mighty acts: praise him according to his excellent greatness. Praise him with the sound of the trumpet: praise him with the psaltery and harp. Praise him with the timbrel and dance: praise him with stringed instruments and organs. Praise him upon the loud cymbals: praise him upon the high sounding cymbals. Let every thing that hath breath praise the LORD. Praise ye the LORD.

Psalm 98:4-6

Make a joyful noise unto the LORD, all the earth: make a loud noise, and rejoice, and sing praise. Sing unto the LORD with the harp; with the harp, and the voice of a psalm. With trumpets and sound of cornet make a joyful noise before the LORD, the King.

1 Corinthians 14:15, 26 NASB

I will sing with the spirit and I will sing with the mind also... What then shall we say, brothers? When you come together, everyone has a hymn...

Ephesians 5:19 NASB

Speaking to yourselves in psalms and hymns and spiritual songs, singing and making melody in your heart to the lord

Colossians 3:16 NIV

...admonish one another with all wisdom, and as you sing psalms, hymns and spiritual songs with gratitude in your hearts to God.

Psalm 47:10

O clap your hands, all ye people; shout unto God with the voice of triumph.

Isaiah 55:12

For ye shall go out with joy, and be led forth with peace: the mountains and the hills shall break forth before you into singing, and all the trees of the field shall clap their hands.

Psalm 96:8-9 NIV

Ascribe to the LORD the glory due his name; bring an offering and come into his courts. Worship the LORD in the splendor of his holiness; tremble before him, all the earth.

Philippians 4:18 NIV

I have received full payment and even more; I am amply supplied, now that I have received from Epaphroditus the gifts you sent. They are a fragrant offering, an acceptable sacrifice, pleasing to God.

- **Music and singing**

  Psalms are songs accompanied by musical instruments. Many of the Psalms are songs of praise to God written by the musician King David. Psalm 150 and Psalm 98:4-6 give examples of songs and musical instruments used to worship God.

  In the New Testament, Jesus sang hymns with His disciples (see Matthew 26:30). Paul and Silas sang songs of praise while in prison (see Acts 16:25), and Paul wrote to the Corinthians, Ephesians, and Colossians about psalms and singing praise to God (1 Corinthians 14:15, 26; Ephesians 5:19 and Colossians 3:16).

- **Clapping hands**

  Clapping hands before the Lord is a way of joyfully honoring and thanking God with praise and thanksgiving (Psalms 47:10 and Isaiah 55:12).

- **Giving**

  Giving is an act of worship that acknowledges God as the one and only source of all things (Psalm 96:8-9 and Philippians 4:18).

- **A life devoted to God**

  Throughout the Old Testament God required those who believed in Him to devote their lives to Him. In the New Testament believers in Jesus are given the same charge: *"Therefore, I urge you, brothers, in view of God's mercy, to offer your bodies as living sacrifices, holy and pleasing to God—this is your spiritual act of worship,"* (Romans 12:1 NIV).

Study Questions

1. "I have been saved by grace and am no longer under the Law." Read Exodus 20:1-2 and Matthew 5:17-18. Do you think the previous statement is true or false? _____

   _____

   _____

   _____

   _____

2. Summarize the first commandment and state a blessing in keeping this commandment. _____

   _____

   _____

   _____

3. Summarize the second commandment and state a blessing in keeping this commandment. _____

   _____

   _____

   _____

4. Read Psalm 150, Hebrews 13:15, and Romans 12:1-2. What are some ways that you worship God with other believers and in your day-to-day life? _____

   _____

   _____

   _____

   _____

Lesson Journal

Use this section to record your thoughts on the topics in this lesson.

_____

_____

_____

_____

_____

_____

_____

Lesson 14
Rest in Him

Scripture Reading

- Exodus 20:7-11 and Deuteronomy 5:11-15 (the third and fourth commandment)

- 2 Timothy 2:19; Galatians 3:26-27; 2 Corinthians 5:20 and Revelation 3:8 (taking His name)

- Malachi 3:16-18 and Colossians 3:17 (honoring His name)

- Leviticus 23:3-16 (setting sabbath days)

- Matthew 11:28-30; Mark 2:27-28; Colossians 2:16-17; Hebrews 3:7-11 and Hebrews 4:1-11 (New Testament sabbath)

Introduction

A Christian has taken on the name of Christ and entered into a relationship with Him. The focus of this lesson is the third and the fourth commandments as guidelines for Christian living, which primarily apply to taking His name, and resting in a relationship with Him.

The third commandment has to do with honoring the name of God. To honor His name, to not take His name in vain, requires honoring His name in more than speech alone. To dishonor His name in speech certainly is taking His name in vain. However, the third commandment is directed to more than just speech. A Christian has literally taken the name of Christ, and His name must be revered in all aspects of life. To behave otherwise is to bring dishonor to His name.

In the fourth commandment God ordained a sabbath, or rest day. This rest established by God had no prior historic example other than the rest God took after His work of creation. Keeping this commandment required faith and trust in God the provider, as ceasing from labor had an economic impact. When Jesus Christ came to earth, He forever altered the way the fourth commandment was observed. Faith and trust are still required to keep the commandment, however rest is no longer found on a certain day, but rather in Christ. The book of Hebrews aptly states it this way: *"Now we who have believed enter that rest... There remains then a Sabbath rest for the people of God; for anyone who enters God's rest also rests from his own work, just as God did from His. Let us, therefore make every effort to enter that rest,"* (Hebrews 4:3,10-11). Hence, this command is kept by believing in Jesus Christ. It is only by belief in Him that one can obtain salvation, which is true rest. The consequences that God spoke in the original command still hold, as they are based on unbelief. Likewise, the blessings that God declared for those that follow His command still hold, and are acquired by faith in Jesus Christ.

2 Timothy 2:19 NASB
Nevertheless, the firm foundation of God stands, having this seal, "The Lord knows those who are His," and, "Everyone who names the name of the Lord is to abstain from wickedness."

Galatians 3:26-27 NKJV
For you are all sons of God through faith in Christ Jesus. For as many of you as were baptized into Christ have put on Christ.

Revelation 3:8 NIV
I know your deeds. See, I have placed before you an open door that no one can shut. I know that you have little strength, yet you have kept my word and have not denied my name.

2 Corinthians 5:20 NKJV
Now then, we are ambassadors for Christ, as though God were pleading through us: we implore *you* on Christ's behalf, be reconciled to God.

Matthew 15:3-9 NIV
Jesus replied, "And why do you break the command of God for the sake of your tradition? For God said, 'Honor your father and mother' and 'anyone who curses their father or mother is to be put to death.' But you say that if anyone declares that what might have been used to help their father or mother is 'devoted to God,' they are not to 'honor their father or mother' with it. Thus you nullify the word of God for the sake of your tradition. You hypocrites! Isaiah was right when he prophesied about you: "These people honor me with their lips, but their hearts are far from me. They worship me in vain; their teachings are merely human rules."

1. What is a Christian?

A Christian is a person who has entered into a relationship with Jesus Christ by repenting of sin and by faith believing that He is the Son of God. To say, "I am a Christian," is to acknowledge a relationship with Christ. The label "Christian" includes the name of Christ; hence anyone who claims to be a Christian has literally taken on the name of Christ (2 Timothy 2:19; Galatians 3:26-27 and Revelation 3:8).

Jesus exemplified reverence to the name of God in all that He did. Every Christian should strive to follow the example of Jesus, glorifying the name of God as an ambassador in His name (2 Corinthians 5:20). The third commandment emphasizes honoring His name.

2. What is the third commandment?

> *Exodus 20:7*
> *Thou shalt not take the name of the Lord thy God in vain; for the Lord will not hold him guiltless that taketh his name in vain.*

3. What is the purpose of the third commandment?

On the surface the third commandment may appear to be narrow in scope, pertaining specifically to speech regarding God. It is that and more, having to do with a believer's profession of faith in God and Christ and adherence to that faith. The third commandment emphasizes a life of honor to God through sincere belief in His name.

To illustrate: When a woman is married she customarily takes the name of her husband, and if she ever forsakes her husband she then has taken his name in vain. The word vain means having no real value, idle, worthless. Breaking a promise of fidelity indicates the promise itself was considered to have no real value, or was worthless.

The same holds for anyone that has professed the name of Jesus Christ, they have taken on His name and are identified as a Christian. To stray from their profession of Christ, to live a life that is contrary to the teaching of Christ, is denying God and taking His name in vain. Hence, the purpose of the third commandment is to preserve, through speech and through all aspects of life, the real value and worth, the honor and respect that is due the name of God.

God punctuates this command with a clause of judgment; *for the Lord will not hold him guiltless that taketh his name in vain*, the only one of the Ten Commandments with a promise of judgment to those who fail to keep it. This emphasizes the profoundness that God intends with this commandment (Matthew 15:3-9).

4. How should we keep the third commandment?

The third commandment is kept first by honoring God with all that we say. To take the name of God in vain while speaking is profane. Profane comes from the Latin *profanum*, meaning outside of the temple, or that which is outside of God. Profane talk is any talk that is outside or offensive to God, and includes:

- A false or broken promise, including false:

  - Swearing

  - Vow

  - Oath

- Vulgar speech

- Obscenity

Being profane also goes beyond speech, and includes thoughts and actions that are outside of God. The third commandment then is deeper than just profane speech. To keep it is to honor God in all aspects of life, endeavoring that thoughts, speech and actions, respect and revere God and our relationship with Jesus Christ. Our commitment to Jesus must be kept, and all we do should be done unto the Lord, considering our lives as worship to Him (Romans 12:1; 2 Timothy 2:19 and James 1:26-27).

5. Is it wrong to say, "I swear to God?"

Swearing, making an oath and taking a vow are all related. They have to do with invoking the name of God and making a promise, such as a promise to tell the truth or remain faithful to an obligation. In cases where a solemn promise is being made, such as a court of law, it is permissible to say, "So help me God," or "I swear to God." It is only when the promise or obligation is not kept that God's name in taken in vain, as it also is when using the name of God to express emotion such as, "it happened, I swear to God," or exclaiming "Jesus Christ!" in a moment of surprise. Jesus once quoted Leviticus 19:12 saying, *"You shall not swear falsely."* He was making the point that in ordinary conversation the name of God should not be invoked, but rather, *"Simply let your 'Yes' be 'Yes,' and your 'No,' 'No'"* (Matthew 5:37).

When Jesus taught His disciples to pray, He said, *"Our Father who is in heaven, Hallowed be Your name,"* (Matthew 6:9). Jesus began His model prayer with a short but perfect reference to God's supreme position in heaven. Hallowed means to respect greatly, and God's name is to be hallowed in all that is said and done (Deuteronomy 6:13-14).

Romans 12:1
Therefore I urge you, brethren, by the mercies of God, to present your bodies a living and holy sacrifice, acceptable to God, which is your spiritual service of worship.

2 Timothy 2:19 NASB
Nevertheless, the firm foundation of God stands, having this seal, "The Lord knows those who are His," and, "Everyone who names the name of the Lord is to abstain from wickedness."

James 1:26-27
If any man among you seem to be religious, and bridleth not his tongue, but deceiveth his own heart, this man's religion is vain. Pure religion and undefiled before God and the Father is this, To visit the fatherless and widows in their affliction, and to keep himself unspotted from the world.

Deuteronomy 6:13-14 NASB
You shall fear only the LORD your God; and you shall worship Him and swear by His name. You shall not follow other gods, any of the gods of the peoples who surround you.

Genesis 4:26 NASB
To Seth, to him also a son was born; and he called his name Enosh. Then men began to call upon the name of the LORD.

Malachi 3:16-18 NIV
Then those who feared the LORD talked with each other, and the LORD listened and heard. A scroll of remembrance was written in his presence concerning those who feared the LORD and honored his name. "They will be mine," says the LORD Almighty, "in the day when I make up my treasured possession. I will spare them, just as in compassion a man spares his son who serves him. And you will again see the distinction between the righteous and the wicked, between those who serve God and those who do not."

Colossians 3:17 NASB
Whatever you do in word or deed, do all in the name of the Lord Jesus, giving thanks through Him to God the Father.

6. Is there a blessing in keeping the third commandment?

When the serpent tempted Eve he said, *"You will be like God,"* (Genesis 3:5) and both Adam and Eve profaned the name of God by disobeying His command in an attempt to take His name and become like Him. God judged them and they were separated from God, because *"the Lord will not hold him guiltless that taketh his name in vain,"* (Exodus 20:7).

It was through the righteous line of Adam's son Seth that men *"began to call upon the name of the Lord."* (Genesis 4:26) Through Seth's line blessings came to Abraham, Moses, and to all mankind in the form of salvation from the curse of sin through faith in Jesus Christ. A life that honors Jesus Christ in all things is a life that follows the third commandment; out from under the curse it is a life under blessing (Genesis 4:26; Malachi 3:16-18 and Colossians 3:17).

7. What is the fourth commandment?

Exodus 20:8-11
Remember the sabbath day, to keep it holy. Six days shalt thou labour, and do all thy work: But the seventh day is the sabbath of the LORD thy God: in it thou shalt not do any work, thou, nor thy son, nor thy daughter, thy manservant, nor thy maidservant, nor thy cattle, nor thy stranger that is within thy gates: For in six days the LORD made heaven and earth, the sea, and all that in them is, and rested the seventh day: wherefore the LORD blessed the sabbath day, and hallowed it.

8. What is the purpose of the fourth commandment?

There are three significant elements in the fourth commandment: Remembrance, worship, and rest (sabbath, Hebrew *shabbath*, literally, rest) hence, *remember the Sabbath day, to keep it holy.*

• **Remembrance**

In the fourth commandment God intends remembrance, identifying a day of rest patterned after His creation rest. There was no prior pattern of a day of rest before the exodus of Israel from Egypt with the exception of creation. God instructs His people to remember the sabbath, and remember the example He set.

- **Worship**

  Second and closely tied with remembrance is worship. God not only commanded man to remember the sabbath, but also to remember *to keep it holy*. This remembrance then is an act of worship, a time to acknowledge the sovereignty, authority, and holiness of God with the cessation of work and other activities that distract from focus on Him alone.

- **Rest (sabbath)**

  The third and principal point is sabbath, i.e., rest. God established this rest for redemption and regeneration. Redemption is key. God commanded Israel to observe the first month of their year to remember their deliverance from bondage in Egypt. He did so by commanding the fifteenth day of the first month as a sabbath following the Passover, which celebrated Israel's liberation and redemption from Egypt. Regeneration is also important to the sabbath. With rest comes a time for regeneration for man. God also commanded a sabbath for the land every seven years, emphasizing the importance of regeneration for the land.

The purpose of the sabbath is therefore rest, as a time to remember and worship God who redeems and regenerates man (Deuteronomy 5:15 and Ezekiel 20:16).

9. Is the sabbath day Saturday?

Sabbath means rest, not *seventh day* or *Saturday*. God ordained specific periods of rest, namely: one day, two days, seven days, one year, and two years. Regarding the sabbath day, it was never a particular day of the week, but rather a day observed every seventh day. God prescribed that a sabbath should fall on the fifteenth day of the first month, with sabbath days to follow every seven days (Leviticus 23:3-7, 15-16). As a result, the day the sabbath was observed changed during the year.

Saturday, the seventh day of the week, was never intended to be *the* sabbath day, because the sabbath was not observed from the time of creation onward. The sabbath was started many years after creation, with God's creation rest serving as an example.

Deuteronomy 5:15 NIV
Remember that you were slaves in Egypt and that the LORD your God brought you out of there with a mighty hand and an outstretched arm. Therefore the LORD your God has commanded you to observe the Sabbath day.

Ezekiel 20:16
The children of Israel] despised my judgments, and walked not in my statutes, but polluted my sabbaths: for their heart went after their idols.

Leviticus 23:3-7
'For six days work may be done, but on the seventh day there is a sabbath of complete rest, a holy convocation. You shall not do any work; it is a sabbath to the LORD in all your dwellings. 'These are the appointed times of the LORD, holy convocations which you shall proclaim at the times appointed for them. 'In the first month, on the fourteenth day of the month at twilight is the LORD'S Passover. 'Then on the fifteenth day... you shall have a holy convocation; you shall not do any laborious work.

Colossians 2:16-17
Therefore do not let anyone judge you by what you eat or drink, or with regard to a religious festival, a New Moon celebration or a Sabbath day. These are a shadow of the things that were to come; the reality, however, is found in Christ.

Matthew 11:28-30
[Jesus said], "Come unto me, all ye that labour and are heavy laden, and I will give you rest. Take my yoke upon you, and learn of me; for I am meek and lowly in heart: and ye shall find rest unto your souls. For my yoke is easy, and my burden is light."

Hebrews 3:7-11 NASB
Therefore, just as the Holy Spirit says, "Today if you hear His voice, do not harden your hearts as when they provoked Me, as in the day of trial in the wilderness, where your fathers tried Me by testing Me, and saw My works for forty years. Therefore I was angry with this generation, and said, 'They always go astray in their heart, and they did not know My ways'; as I swore in My wrath, 'They shall not enter My rest.'"

Hebrews 3:13, 4:7 NASB
But encourage one another daily, as long as it is called Today... Therefore God again set a certain day, calling it Today

Hebrews 4:3,10-11
Now we who have believed enter that rest... There remains then a Sabbath rest for the people of God; for anyone who enters God's rest also rests from his own work, just as God did from His. Let us, therefore make every effort to enter that rest.

Mark 2:27-28
Then he said to them, "The Sabbath was made for man, not man for the Sabbath. So the Son of Man is Lord even of the Sabbath."

Acts 20:7
And upon the first day of the week, when the disciples came together to break bread, Paul preached unto them...

Hebrews 10:23-25
Let us hold fast the confession of our hope without wavering, for He who promised is faithful; and let us consider how to stimulate one another to love and good deeds, not forsaking our own assembling together, as is the habit of some, but encouraging one another; and all the more as you see the day drawing near.

10. What is our day of rest?

The resurrection of Jesus forever altered the commandment to rest. Rest is no longer to be observed on a prescribed day, but rest is to be observed in Christ, by a life devoted to Him. For a Christian, rest is not constrained to a particular day, a Christian's rest is in Christ. The commandment was given as a shadow of the rest Christians obtain through the redemption of Christ and regeneration of spirit (Colossians 2:16-17).

11. What does belief in Christ have to do with rest?

Jesus taught that those who come to Him find rest (Matthew 11:28-30). The book of Hebrews helps explain rest in Christ, pointing out that the original commandment was based on belief in God, and now it is belief in Jesus Christ that results in rest.

Psalm 95 describes how God did not let unbelievers into the Promised Land, He said, *"They will not enter My rest."* Hebrews reminds us of this by quoting Psalm 95. God saved the people of Israel from slavery in Egypt, and was going to allow them to enter into the Promised Land, what God described as *My rest*, but He was not going to allow unbelievers to enter His rest (Hebrews 3:7-11).

Hebrews goes on to say that a day has been ordained to enter the rest of Jesus Christ, and *today* is that day. In other words, Jesus avails Himself all day, every day, and all who believe in Him can enter His rest, the rest of salvation. Good works or benevolence cannot earn the rest offered in Jesus; it is only through faith in Him that we enter salvation rest. Jesus taught that the sabbath was made for man, and that He was Lord of the sabbath. By believing in Jesus Christ, the Lord of the sabbath, man can rest from his efforts to earn God's favor, and every day becomes a sabbath day (Hebrews 3:13, 4:7; Hebrews 4: 3,10-11 and Mark 2:27-28).

12. Why do Christians worship on Sunday?

Christians gather on Sunday to worship, not to keep a commandment but rather to follow the pattern established by the apostles and believers as described in the New Testament. Early Christians observed the first day of the week, Sunday, as a day to worship together and teach the Word of God. This highlights a clear change in the commandment, as the New Testament gives no indication that believers were violating God's law, but were keeping God's law by entering into the reality of rest found in Christ. Also, the Church was established for Christians to fellowship by gathering together with other believers to build each other up in faith, so a day of the week is set aside for this purpose (Acts 20:7 and Hebrews 10:23-25).

13. How should we keep the fourth commandment?

The fourth commandment is kept by believing in Jesus Christ. It is only by belief in Him that one can obtain salvation, which is the true rest that comes from His redemption and regeneration. Unbelief results in being kept from His rest, in this life and in eternity. The seriousness of this is foreshadowed by the severity of the punishment that was meted out to those that did not keep this commandment before the coming of Christ. The fourth commandment was the one most often mentioned in the Old Testament as being neglected, and breaking this commandment was a capital crime. This exemplifies two extremes: a life of rest in Christ for those that believe and death to them that do not believe (Exodus 35:2; Romans 8:4-6 and Romans 6:23).

14. Is there a blessing in keeping the fourth commandment?

The commandments are given to people of grace, people that have been saved from the slavery of sin by faith in Jesus Christ. As in the first commandment, the blessing in keeping the fourth commandment is the absolute assurance of salvation, reflected by our faith in, and ever deepening relationship with, Jesus Christ (Colossians 2:16-17). The assurance of our rest in Him is now, as it will be in eternity as prophesied by Isaiah, when he said, *"For as the new heavens and the new earth, which I will make, shall remain before me, saith the LORD, so shall your seed and your name remain. And it shall come to pass, that from one new moon to another, and from one sabbath to another, shall all flesh come to worship before me, saith the LORD,"* (Isaiah 66:22-23).

Exodus 35:2
Six days shall work be done, but on the seventh day there shall be to you an holy day, a sabbath of rest to the LORD: whosoever doeth work therein shall be put to death.

Romans 8:4-6
...The righteousness of the law might be fulfilled in us, who walk not after the flesh, but after the Spirit. For they that are after the flesh do mind the things of the flesh; but they that are after the Spirit the things of the Spirit. For to be carnally minded is death; but to be spiritually minded is life and peace.

Romans 6:23
For the wages of sin is death; but the gift of God is eternal life through Jesus Christ our Lord.

Colossians 2:16-17
Therefore do not let anyone judge you by... a Sabbath day... the reality, however, is found in Christ.

Study Questions

1. Read Exodus 20:7, 2 Timothy 2:19, and Revelation 3:8. Explain how the third commandment has more to do with lifestyle than just speech. _____

_____

_____

_____

2. Read Hebrews 4:1-11. Can you explain what it means to take rest in Jesus Christ? _____

_____

_____

_____

_____

_____

3. Summarize the third commandment and state a blessing in keeping this commandment. _____

_____

_____

_____

4. Summarize the fourth commandment and state a blessing in keeping this commandment. _____

_____

_____

_____

Lesson Journal

Use this section to record your thoughts on the topics in this lesson.

_____

_____

_____

_____

_____

_____

_____

Lesson 15
The Christian Family

Scripture Reading

- Exodus 20:12 and Deuteronomy 5:16 (the fifth commandment)

- Deuteronomy 5:29-33 (obedience and the promise of long life)

- Ephesians 6:1-4 and Colossians 3:20 (children obey parents)

- Deuteronomy 11:18-21, 32:46-47 and Proverbs 22:6 (teaching children)

- Romans 13:1-7 (all authority comes from God)

- Deuteronomy 5:33; Matthew 19:17 and John 3:36 (obedience and life/eternal life)

Introduction

The fifth commandment is the first that varies from a focus on God and His authority and sovereignty, and shifts to man and authority of man with respect to others. The focus is on the godly family and authority that begins with and emanates from the family leaders, namely, parents. God's command is to honor parents, but includes a promise of extended life. The promise here is to a people, not necessarily an individual, a promise ensuring longevity of generations to those who honor and respect their elders. Though honor is commanded to be bestowed on parents, it is incumbent upon parents to raise their children according to the Word of God, as Paul says to the Ephesians, *bring them up in the training and admonition of the Lord* (Ephesians 6:4).

The fifth commandment is the first that ascribes authority to man, and defines parental authority as second to the authority of God. Honoring authority must be taught to children so that their inclination will be to submit to all earthly authority that is place over them, because all authority comes from God (Romans 13:1). Implicit in obedience is life, and specific to the fifth commandment is the promise of life. Jesus also promised eternal life to those that were obedient to Him and the commandments. Life on earth and eternal life are the blessings of obedience and respect for authority, which are rooted in the fifth commandment.

1. What is a Christian family?

A Christian family begins with marriage, the union of a man and a woman equally submitted to Jesus Christ. Marriage under the authority of Christ is the fundamental beginning of family.

Children are a gift from God, a blessing the Bible calls a reward (Psalm 127:3). With the addition of children to a marriage, the family becomes a *nuclear family*, which means a husband, a wife, and children. The Hebrew and Greek words in the Bible that describe family are often translated as household, which is similar in meaning to nuclear family (Genesis 12:1; Exodus 1:1 and Matthew 10:36). Family, or household, is a central element in Biblical teaching. In the Old Testament, family ties were what perpetuated the tribe and nation.

Family then is where authority is defined and practiced. The husband and wife are in submission to the authority of Jesus. Parents are in authority over their children. Authority under Christ is exemplified by Christian parents and taught to children. Each person in the family has a role and responsibility to be submissive to their respective authority.

2. What are the roles of husband and wife in a marriage?

The husband and the wife each have their God-ordained roles in a marriage, but as Christians, they are equal before the Lord. A marriage is entered into by mutual consent of a Christian man and Christian woman after a time of courtship, neither being forced to marry the other. In doing so, they are following the directive of Ephesians 5:21, which advises, *"Submit to one another out of reverence for Christ."* The context here is general, not speaking of marriage specifically, but it is the statement that leads into Paul's discussion of the roles of a Christian husband and wife.

Paul continues his thought in Ephesians 5:22 instructing wives to submit to their husbands as to the Lord. Submission here is no different than Paul's prior reference, willingly, not coerced, and out of reverence for Christ. This does not define a relationship of subjugation. A wife is to be her husband's *help meet* (Genesis 2:18). The meaning of this is that a true help meet is a husband's counterpart. Biblical doctrine shows the wife as a competent manager able to conduct the affairs of her husband if needed.

Psalm 127:3 NASB
Behold, children are a gift of the LORD, The fruit of the womb is a reward.

Genesis 12:1
The LORD had said to Abram, "Leave your country, your people and your father's household and go to the land I will show you

Exodus 1:1
Now these are the names of the children of Israel, which came into Egypt; every man and his household came with Jacob

Matthew 10:36
And a man's foes shall be they of his own household.

Ephesians 5:21-25 NIV
Submit to one another out of reverence for Christ. Wives, submit to your husbands as to the Lord. For the husband is the head of the wife as Christ is the head of the church, his body, of which he is the Savior. Now as the church submits to Christ, so also wives should submit to their husbands in everything. Husbands, love your wives, just as Christ loved the church and gave himself up for her

Genesis 2:18
And the LORD God said, It is not good that the man should be alone; I will make him an help meet for him.

The husband has a greater responsibility. He is the spiritual head of the wife, as Christ is head of the church; and He is the Savior of the Church. A husband is admonished to love his wife as Christ loved the Church and gave Himself up for her. As leader in the household, God has made the husband responsible. The husband is responsible for the protection of his wife and children. He is responsible for providing for the needs of his family. He is responsible for the spiritual leadership in the home. Husbands are to lead with consideration, kindness, and self-denial.

A married couple no longer has exclusive rights to their own bodies. They have become *one flesh*, and are instructed by God to yield to one another in sexual relations. Again this is willing submission, an expression of love for one another, but God does allow times of mutually agreed abstinence so that a husband and wife can build their relationships with Christ (1 Corinthians 11:11-12 and Galatians 3:28; see also 1 Peter 3:7 and 1 Corinthians 7:3-5).

As God sees fit to bless the union of husband and wife with the fruit of children, the children are to submit to their parents as the fifth commandment instructs.

3. What is the fifth commandment?

> *Exodus 20:12*
> *Honour thy father and thy mother: that thy days may be long upon the land which the LORD thy God giveth thee.*

4. What is the purpose of the fifth commandment?

The fifth commandment pertains to family, continuing generations of family, and to authority. In the commandments from first to fifth there is an implicit hierarchy of authority. The first four commandments share a common theme of worship, honoring God and His authority alone. The fifth commandment deals with authority bestowed upon mankind by God, beginning with parental authority, thereby identifying a proper line of authority. The authority of God is primary, above all, and shown in commandments one through four. Secondary authority is parental, established and given by God. In fact, God gives all authority and all in authority are beholden to Him (Romans 13:1).

1 Corinthians 11:11-12 NASB
However, in the Lord, neither is woman independent of man, nor is man independent of woman. For as the woman originates from the man, so also the man has his birth through the woman; and all things originate from God.

Galatians 3:28
There is neither Jew nor Greek, there is neither bond nor free, there is neither male nor female: for ye are all one in Christ Jesus.

Romans 13:1
For there is no authority except from God, and those which exist are established by God.

Deuteronomy 5:16
Honour thy father and thy mother, as the LORD thy God hath commanded thee; that thy days may be prolonged, and that it may go well with thee, in the land which the LORD thy God giveth thee.

Deuteronomy 5:33
Ye shall walk in all the ways which the LORD your God hath commanded you, that ye may live, and that it may be well with you, and that ye may prolong your days in the land which ye shall possess.

Ephesians 6:1
Children, obey your parents in the Lord: for this is right.

Colossians 3:20
Children, obey your parents in all things: for this is well pleasing unto the Lord"

Luke 2:51 NCV
Jesus went with [Joseph and Mary] to Nazareth and was obedient to them. But his mother kept in her mind all that had happened.

Matthew 15:3-6 NLT
Jesus replied, "And why do you, by your traditions, violate the direct commandments of God? For instance, God says, 'Honor your father and mother,' and 'Anyone who speaks evil of father or mother must be put to death.' But you say, 'You don't need to honor your parents by caring for their needs if you give the money to God instead.' And so, by your own tradition, you nullify the direct commandment of God.

Romans 13:1-6 NIV
Everyone must submit himself to the governing authorities, for there is no authority except that which God has established. The authorities that exist have been established by God. Consequently, he who rebels against the authority is rebelling against what God has instituted, and those who do so will bring judgment on themselves. For rulers hold no terror for those who do right, but for those who do wrong. Do you want to be free from fear of the one in authority? Then do what is right and he will commend you. For he is God's servant to do you good. But if you do wrong, be afraid, for he does not bear the sword for nothing. He is God's servant, an agent of wrath to bring punishment on the wrongdoer. Therefore, it is necessary to submit to the authorities... This is also why you pay taxes, for the authorities are God's servants, who give their full time to governing.

Family is a central element in Biblical teaching. In the Old Testament, family ties were what perpetuated tribe and nation. God underscores this fact when He states the promise, *that thy days may be long upon the land which the LORD thy God giveth thee*. The promise here is not to an individual but to a people who honored family; their days would be long in the land. This command indicates that proper family relationships based on respect lead to a strong nation and a long posterity in the land. (There are many examples in the Old Testament books of Samuel, Kings, and Chronicles of disobedient and disrespectful children affecting priests, kings, and the nation; for an example see 1 Samuel 2:22-31.) Hence, the fifth commandment gives the next line of authority under God, and defines how to preserve family from generation to generation (Deuteronomy 5:16 and Deuteronomy 5:33).

5. What does it mean to honor our father and mother?

Honor means showing respect or esteem to one who is in authority or of superior standing. In a family the relationship of parent to child changes as a child grows and matures into an adult. The apostle Paul said, *When I was a child, I spoke as a child, I understood as a child, I thought as a child; but when I became a man, I put away childish things* (1 Corinthians 13:11). As a child, honor is obedience, and it is the duty of a child to be obedient. Jesus is our example, as He was obedient to His earthly parents as a lad. As a child grows, honor translates into respect and obedience, and finally as an adult honor is kindness and respect (Ephesians 6:1; Colossians 3:20; Luke 2:51 and Matthew 15:3-6).

6. Does honor extend to others in authority?

When a child is born he is completely dependent on his parents. Parents stand in the place of God, experiencing every "first" with their child: A parent is the first provider, first educator, first disciplinarian, first coach, first Sunday school teacher, etc. As the child grows, obedience and respect are learned attributes taught by diligent parents. These lessons are not for parents only, as honor and respect is to be extended to all those in authority, *for there is no authority except from God, and those which exist are established by God,* (Romans 13:1). Hence it is consistent with the fifth commandment to honor all those in authority over us (Romans 13:1-6).

7. Must I obey my parents now that I am an adult?

"The marriage covenant is one of life-long *inter*dependence (mutual dependence for a lifetime), whereas the parent/child relationship has as its goal the eventual *in*dependence of the child. A parents' goal, then, is to 'raise up' the child so the child becomes a complete adult, fully responsible for his/her own life and welfare."[1] Obedience to parents is the requirement of a child living in the home under parental authority.

When a child comes of age and establishes his own home, God is the authority to be obeyed and parents are to be honored (Acts 5:29). It gives honor to parents when their offspring obey God and those in authority, and live a lifestyle that honors God. When an adult child honors God, he is also honoring his parents. In this way parents can be honored even if they are (or were) ungodly.

8. Do parents have a responsibility in this commandment?

Parents are responsible for raising their children, to *bring them up in the discipline and instruction of the Lord* (Ephesians 6:4 NASB). Paul prefaced this statement saying, *"Children, obey your parents in the Lord..., fathers, do not provoke your children to anger..."* (Ephesians 6:1, 4 NASB). The responsibility for the parents is to be in the Lord, treating and teaching their children according to the Word of God, not provoking them to anger.

This New Testament directive to teach children in the Lord was not new, but confirmed early Old Testament teaching. When Moses received the law from God, he also received much in the way of instruction for godly families and in raising and training children. God's directives were specific and sobering. The parents' responsibility was to teach their children His law as if their life and their posterity depended on it (Deuteronomy 32:46-47; Deuteronomy 11:18-21 and Proverbs 22:6).

Male children were made a part of the Old Testament covenant by being circumcised on the eighth day; girls were part of the covenant under the covering of their father. In all cases where parents enter into covenant with God, they bring their children with them. Parents act on behalf of their children to bring them under obligation and secure the benefits of the covenant. Responsible, believing, covenant parents honor God by making a public commitment to dedicate their children to Him, promising to raise their children in a Christian environment within a local church.

---

[1] *The Grace of Law*, Scott Sauls, 2004

Acts 5:29 NKJV
But Peter and the *other* apostles answered and said: "We ought to obey God rather than men.

Deuteronomy 32:46-47 NKJV
[Moses] said to them: "Set your hearts on all the words which I testify among you today, which you shall command your children to be careful to observe—all the words of this law. For it is not a futile thing for you, because it is your life, and by this word you shall prolong *your* days in the land which you cross over the Jordan to possess."

Deuteronomy 11:18-21
"You shall therefore impress these words of mine on your heart and on your soul; and you shall bind them as a sign on your hand, and they shall be as frontals on your forehead. "You shall teach them to your sons, talking of them when you sit in your house and when you walk along the road and when you lie down and when you rise up. "You shall write them on the doorposts of your house and on your gates, so that your days and the days of your sons may be multiplied on the land which the LORD swore to your fathers to give them, as long as the heavens remain above the earth.

Proverbs 22:6
Train up a child in the way he should go: and when he is old, he will not depart from it.

Luke 2:27-28, 33-34

And he came in the Spirit into the temple; and when the parents brought in the child Jesus, to carry out for Him the custom of the Law, then he took Him into his arms, and blessed God... And His father and mother were amazed at the things which were being said about Him. And Simeon blessed them...

Deuteronomy 4:40 NASB

So you shall keep His statutes and His commandments which I am giving you today, that it may go well with you and with your children after you, and that you may live long on the land which the LORD your God is giving you for all time."

Deuteronomy 5:29

O that there were such an heart in them, that they would fear me, and keep all my commandments always, that it might be well with them, and with their children for ever!

Lamentations 3:25-27

The LORD is wonderfully good to those who wait for him and seek him. So it is good to wait quietly for salvation from the LORD. And it is good for the young to submit to the yoke of his discipline.

Deuteronomy 5:16

Honour thy father and thy mother, as the LORD thy God hath commanded thee; that thy days may be prolonged, and that it may go well with thee, in the land which the LORD thy God giveth thee.

Deuteronomy 5:33

Ye shall walk in all the ways which the LORD your God hath commanded you, that ye may live, and that it may be well with you, and that ye may prolong your days in the land which ye shall possess. .

Matthew 19:17 NCV

Jesus answered, "...if you want to have life forever, obey the commands."

John 3:36 NCV

Those who believe in the Son have eternal life, but those who do not obey the Son will never have life.

9. What is dedication of children?

Dedication of children is a Christian sacrament where children are brought under the blessing of the New Covenant. By the outward act of the laying on of hands of local church elders, a child is blessed and sanctified (set apart) to be raised as a New Covenant Christian. Since infants and toddlers cannot exercise faith and make a public profession of faith, dedication is a way for parents to publicly commit to raise their children *in the discipline and instruction of the Lord* (Ephesians 6:4 NASB). Jesus was circumcised on the eighth day as a Jewish infant, but also blessed by the righteous man Simeon (Luke 2:27-34).

10. How should we keep the fifth commandment?

The fifth commandment is kept, as a child, by submitting to and being obedient to parents. As adults the commandment is kept by continuing to respect and revere parents, and being responsible as parents. Keeping the fifth commandment is the initial acknowledgment of being under authority ordained by God, and in keeping this command, submission to all lawful authority follows (Deuteronomy 4:40; Deuteronomy 5:29; Lamentations 3:25-27).

11. Is there a blessing in keeping the fifth commandment?

The blessing in keeping the fifth commandment is life in a New Covenant family, and the promise of the continuation of life, a legacy, and posterity. Implicit in obedience is life, and specific to the fifth commandment is the promise of life. Jesus also promised eternal life to those that were obedient to Him and the commandments. Life on earth and eternal life are blessings of obedience, which is rooted in the fifth commandment (Deuteronomy 5:16; Deuteronomy 5:33; Matthew 19:17; John 3:36).

Study Questions

1. Read Deuteronomy 5:16, 29-33. Explain the promise of the fifth commandment. _____

_____

_____

_____

_____

_____

2. Is obedience at all times required by the fifth commandment? _____

_____

_____

_____

_____

3. Read Deuteronomy 11:18-21 and Ephesians 6:1-4. Describe the responsibility of parents to raise and train their children. _____

_____

_____

_____

_____

_____

Lesson Journal

Use this section to record your thoughts on the topics in this lesson.

_____

_____

_____

_____

_____

_____

_____

Lesson 16
Marriage and Divorce

Scripture Reading

- Exodus 20:14 and Deuteronomy 5:18 (the seventh commandment)

- Leviticus chapter 18 (sexual sin)

- Matthew 5:27-32 and Matthew 19:3-12 (lust, marriage, and divorce)

- 1 Corinthians chapter 7 and Ephesians 5:23-33 (marriage)

Introduction

This lesson is focused on Christian marriage and what it means to keep a marriage pure, using the seventh commandment as the cornerstone of staying pure and faithful. Christian marriage is a sacrament and the Bible teaches that a man and woman become one flesh, emphasizing the importance of keeping sexual relationships within a marriage. The apostle Paul taught that becoming one flesh was a mystery, and he compared it with the relationship that Christ has with His Church. Marriages are meant to be lifelong, but divorce is reality, and a reality that is covered in the Bible. A look at what Jesus said about divorce is also given in this lesson.

The seventh commandment is God's emphatic directive to remain clean and pure by keeping from adultery and all sexual immorality. The command bans adultery, and Jesus couples the command with the thoughts and intents of the heart. The command then is not only for the physical, but pertains to intense sexual desires, i.e., lust. Following God's command keeps one pure in thought, protects marriage and family, and gives a nation strength with strong family units.

Keeping the commandments results in blessings. The seventh commandment has at its core the protection of marriage and family. Keeping this commandment results in a strong nation as family is the basic building block of a nation. If the family is strong and sound, the nation is strong and sound. Following God's law a nation will be blessed as the core unit, the family, is honored and protected.

Mark 10:9 NIV
[Jesus said], "Therefore what God has joined together, let man not separate."

2 Corinthians 6:14-15 NIV
Do not be yoked together with unbelievers. For what do righteousness and wickedness have in common? Or what fellowship can light have with darkness? [15]What harmony is there between Christ and Belial[? What does a believer have in common with an unbeliever?

Galatians 3:28 NIV
There is neither Jew nor Greek, slave nor free, male nor female, for you are all one in Christ Jesus.

Matthew 19:4-6
Have you not read that he who created them from the beginning made them male and female, and said, "For this reason a man shall leave his father and mother and be joined to his wife, and the two shall become one flesh?" so they are no longer two, but one flesh. What therefore God has joined together, let no man separate.

Ephesians 5:21 NIV
Submit to one another out of reverence for Christ.

Ephesians 5:31-33 NASB
For this reason a man shall leave his father and mother and shall be joined to his wife, and the two shall become one flesh. This mystery is great; but I am speaking with reference to Christ and the church. Nevertheless, each individual among you also is to love his own wife even as himself, and the wife must see to it that she respects her husband.

Ephesians 5:25
Husbands, love your wives, just as Christ also loved the church and gave Himself up for her

Mark 10:7-8
For this reason a man will leave his father and mother and be united to his wife, and the two will become one flesh. So they are no longer two, but one.

1. What is marriage?

Christian marriage is a sacrament, where a man and woman enter into a spiritual and physical union. Marriage is a God-ordained lifelong covenant union of one man and one woman. This union is entered into publicly, with mutual consent and vows of faithfulness and fidelity. There is no room in the definition of marriage to support transsexual or same sex unions. The Bible is very clear that any union other than man and woman within the bounds of marriage is sin.

2. What are the parameters of a Christian marriage?

The Bible gives clear guidelines for a Christian marriage:

• **Equality**

Jesus taught that a married man and woman are joined together by God (Mark 10:9). In his second letter to the Corinthians, Paul explained that a Christian should not be joined together (yoked) with an unbeliever (2 Corinthians 6:14-15). When a man and woman are planning to be married both should be Christians. As Christians, the man and the woman are equal before the Lord (Galatians 3:28). Each then is to submit to Jesus as Lord, and to one another (Ephesians 5:21).

• **Unity**

When a man and woman are joined together in marriage, they become united. The Bible teaches that a man and woman become one flesh, emphasizing unity and the importance of keeping sexual relationships within a marriage. The apostle Paul taught that becoming one flesh was a mystery, and he compared it with the relationship that Christ has with His Church (Matthew 19:4-6; Ephesians 5:31-33 and Ephesians 5:25).

Unity also requires moving beyond previous family bonds. A man and woman no longer submit to their parents, but to one another (Mark 10:7-8). This unity is essential to the beginning of a new family under the leadership of Jesus Christ.

- **Purity**

  Throughout Scripture, marriage is used as an example of the Covenant relationship God desires with His creation. In the Old Testament, God said He was Israel's husband (Jeremiah 31:32 and Isaiah 54:5). In the New Testament, Jesus said He was going to come back for His bride, the Church, a Church without spot or wrinkle or any such thing. This presents an example of purity in marriage, and marriage should reflect the purity that is pictured by the bride of Christ (Ephesians 5:25, 27 and Revelation 21:2).

  Two people who plan to be married should be pure physically and spiritually. In his writings on marriage, Paul taught that sexual immorality had no part in a marriage (Ephesians 5:3).

3. Is sex before marriage a sin?

Sex does not define marriage; rather it is marriage that gives two people the right and privilege to have sexual relations. Those that are "living together" or "committed" without making a public declaration of their fidelity are not married, and sexual relationships of this kind are a sin.

Couples may rationalize a need to determine their "compatibility." Thousands of years of history testify to the fact that a man and woman are physically compatible, and it cheapens both to submit to a "test." Dating should be used as a time to get to know a person, who they are, their likes and dislikes etc., and more importantly, getting to know their faith. Paul advised that believers should marry other believers (Ephesians 5:3; Hebrews 13:4; 1 Corinthians 6:16; 1 Thessalonians 4:3-4 and 2 Corinthians 6:14).

God requires fidelity and purity in sexual relations, forbidding sexual immorality, whether in married or in single life. Sexual relations outside of marriage are a sin against one's own body, and go against the direct command of God given in the seventh commandment.

Jeremiah 31:32 NIV
"...they broke my covenant, though I was a husband to them," declares the LORD

Isaiah 54:5 NASB
For your husband is your Maker, Whose name is the LORD of hosts; And your Redeemer is the Holy One of Israel, Who is called the God of all the earth.

Ephesians 5:25, 27
Husbands, love your wives, even as Christ also loved the church, and gave himself for it... That he might present it to himself a glorious church, not having spot, or wrinkle, or any such thing; but that it should be holy and without blemish.

Revelation 21:2
And I John saw the holy city, new Jerusalem, coming down from God out of heaven, prepared as a bride adorned for her husband.

Ephesians 5:3
But fornication and impurity of any kind, or greed, must not even be mentioned among you, as is proper among saints.

Hebrews 13:4 NASB
Let marriage be held in honor by all, and let the marriage bed be kept undefiled; for God will judge fornicators and adulterers.

1 Corinthians 6:16
Do you not know that he who unites himself with a prostitute is one with her in body? For it is said, "The two will become one flesh."

1 Thessalonians 4:3-4
For this is the will of God, your sanctification: that you abstain from fornication; that each one of you know how to control your own body in holiness and honor.

2 Corinthians 6:14 NIV
Do not be yoked together with unbelievers. For what do righteousness and wickedness have in common? Or what fellowship can light have with darkness?

4. What is the seventh commandment?

Exodus 20:14
Thou shalt not commit adultery.

5. What is the purpose of the seventh commandment?

The seventh commandment continues with God's directives regarding earthly relationships. In this commandment, the physical relationship between man and woman is addressed, and God's directive is to keep this relationship pure. In so doing, the primary purpose is the protection of marriage and the family.

When Jesus talked of sexual relationships He addressed the intentions of the heart. Jesus taught about the intention of the heart with respect to adultery, saying, *"You have heard that it was said, 'Do not commit adultery.' But I tell you that anyone who looks at a woman lustfully has already committed adultery with her in his heart."* (Matthew 5:27-28 NIV) It is evident Jesus connects lust with the seventh commandment. *"But those things which proceed out of the mouth come forth from the heart; and they defile the man. For out of the heart proceed evil thoughts, murders, adulteries, fornications…"* (Matthew 15:18-19 NIV).

The commandment protects marriage and the family by banning adultery, and Jesus couples adultery and fornication with the thoughts and intentions of the heart. The purpose of the commandment from a Christian perspective is not just the outlawing of adultery, but also a directive to eliminate lustful desires of the heart (Deuteronomy 5:18; Leviticus 18:20 and Genesis 2:18, 24).

6. What is adultery?

Adultery is extramarital sex that willfully and maliciously interferes with marriage relations, or more simply, having sexual relations with someone other than one's husband or wife. Adultery is defined within the context of a marriage; hence it results in the breaking of a covenant between a man and a woman (even when done secretly, one party has broken their covenant promise). Adultery discovered devastates the marriage partner, destroys trust, and often results in destruction of the marriage by divorce, breaking a family apart. God used adultery as an object lesson in unfaithfulness, identifying Israel's breaking of their covenant with God as "adultery," for example God said, *"And with their idols have they committed adultery,"*(Ezekiel 23:37). Their unfaithfulness destroyed their covenant relationship with God.

Deuteronomy 5:18 NIV
You shall not commit adultery.

Leviticus 18:20
Thou shalt not lie carnally with thy neighbour's wife, to defile thyself with her.

Genesis 2:18, 24
Then the LORD God said, "It is not good that the man should be alone... Therefore a man leaves his father and his mother and cleaves to his wife, and they become one flesh."

The law given to Moses placed marriage and family in the highest regard, as witnessed by the fifth commandment (honor thy father and mother), the seventh (thou shall not commit adultery), and the tenth (thou shall not covet thy neighbor's wife). The weight given the seventh commandment was on par with the sixth, as the penalty for breaking apart a marriage by adultery was the same as murder. In other words, adultery was a capital crime. The New Testament is no less severe, stating, *"Marriage is to be held in honor among all, and the marriage bed is to be undefiled; for fornicators and adulterers God will judge,"* (Hebrews 13:4 NASB).

In the New Testament, the Greek word *moicheia* is rendered adultery. There are other Greek words that are used for sexual sin, but *moicheia* is more narrowly defined, having to do with a marriage covenant (Deuteronomy 5:18; Proverbs 6:32 and Jeremiah 5:7).

7. Isn't adultery and fornication the same thing?

Fornication has a broader definition than adultery. While adultery is fornication, fornication is not always adultery. A dictionary definition says fornication is "consensual sexual intercourse between two persons not married to each other."[1] Biblically the definition, stemming from the Greek word *porneia* is broader, including every form of unchastity,[2] and all sinful sexual activity.[3]

Fornication therefore includes premarital sex, adultery and:

- **Rape and seduction** (forced and coerced sexual relations)

  Deuteronomy 22:23-29 and Exodus 22:16-17

- **Homosexuality** (sexual relations with the same gender)

  Leviticus 18:22 and Leviticus 20:12; see also Romans 1:26-27

- **Incest** (sexual relations between close family)

  Deuteronomy 27:20-23; see also Leviticus 18:7-17

- **Transvestitism** (Cross dressing)

  Deuteronomy 22:5

- **Bestiality** (sexual relations with animals)

  Leviticus 18:23-30; see also Deuteronomy 27:21

- **Pornography** (lust)

  James 1:14-15

---

[1] *Merriam-Webster's Collegiate Dictionary, Eleventh Edition*, Merriam-Webster, Inc., 2004.

[2] Orr, James, *International Standard Bible Encyclopedia*, Parsons Technology, Inc., Cedar Rapids, Iowa, 1998.

[3] Butler, Trent C., et. al, *Holman Bible Dictionary*, Holman Bible Publishers, 1991.

Deuteronomy 5:18
Neither shalt thou commit adultery.

Proverbs 6:32
But whoso committeth adultery with a woman lacketh understanding: he that doeth it destroyeth his own soul.

Jeremiah 5:7
How shall I pardon [Jerusalem] for this? Thy children have forsaken me, and sworn by them that are no gods: when I had fed them to the full, they then committed adultery...

Deuteronomy 22:23-29
But if a man find [her] in the field, and... force her, then the man only... shall die.

Exodus 22:16-17 NIV
If a man seduces a virgin who is not pledged to be married and sleeps with her, he must pay the bride-price, and she shall be his wife. If her father absolutely refuses to give her to him, he must still pay the bride-price for virgins.

Leviticus 18:22 NIV
Do not lie with a man as one lies with a woman; that is detestable.

Leviticus 20:12
If a man lie with mankind, as he lieth with a woman, both of them have committed an abomination: they shall surely be put to death; their blood shall be upon them.

Deuteronomy 27:20-23 NIV
Cursed is the man who sleeps with his father's wife, for he dishonors his father's bed...Cursed is the man who sleeps with his sister, the daughter of his father or the daughter of his mother... Cursed is the man who sleeps with his mother-in-law.

Deuteronomy 22:5
The woman shall not wear that which pertaineth unto a man, neither shall a man put on a woman's garment; for all that do so are abomination unto the LORD thy God.

Leviticus 18:23-30
Do not have sexual relations with an animal and defile yourself with it. A woman must not present herself to an animal to have sexual relations with it; that is a perversion.

James 1:14-15 NASB
But each one is tempted when he is carried away and enticed by his own lust. Then when lust has conceived, it gives birth to sin; and when sin is accomplished, it brings forth death,"

Matthew 5:27-28 NIV
You have heard that it was said, "Do not commit adultery." But I tell you that anyone who looks at a woman lustfully has already committed adultery with her in his hear.

1 Corinthians 6:18
Flee fornication.

2 Timothy 2:22
Now flee from youthful lusts and pursue righteousness.

Matthew 19:9 NIV
And I say unto you, Whosoever shall put away his wife, except it be for fornication, and shall marry another, committeth adultery: and whoso marrieth her which is put away doth commit adultery.

Matthew 5:31-32
It hath been said, Whosoever shall put away his wife, let him give her a writing of divorcement: But I say unto you, That whosoever shall put away his wife, saving for the cause of fornication [porneia], causeth her to commit adultery: and whosoever shall marry her that is divorced committeth adultery.

1 Corinthians 7:15 NASB
Yet if the unbelieving one leaves, let him leave; the brother or the sister is not under bondage in such cases, but God has called us to peace.

1 Corinthians 6:18-20 NASB
Flee immorality. Every other sin that a man commits is outside the body, but the immoral man sins against his own body. Or do you not know that your body is a temple of the Holy Spirit who is in you, whom you have from God, and that you are not your own? For you have been bought with a price: therefore glorify God in your body.

Exodus 19:5-6
Now then, if you will indeed obey My voice and keep My covenant, then you shall be My own possession among all the peoples, for all the earth is Mine; and you shall be to Me a kingdom of priests and a holy nation.

8. How can lust be avoided?

Jesus' teachings emphasized the intentions of the heart. To look is not a sin, but to lust, Jesus cautioned, was equal to adultery (Matthew 5:27-28). Lust is intense desire, often sexual in nature. James teaches that lustful desires lead to death, warning, *"But each one is tempted when he is carried away and enticed by his own lust. Then when lust has conceived, it gives birth to sin; and when sin is accomplished, it brings forth death,"* (James 1:14-15 NASB). Jesus said lust had to be dealt with seriously, advising to pluck out an eye that leads to sin. In other words, do whatever is necessary to avoid desires that lead to sin. Paul put it plainly; he advised to flee immorality, fornication, and lusts (1 Corinthians 6:18 and 2 Timothy 2:22).

9. Is adultery the only reason a Christian can be divorced?

Jesus taught that a divorce was allowed for *porneia* the Greek word rendered *fornication*, (Matthew 19:8-9 and Matthew 5:31-32) and Paul added another legitimate reason for divorce—the willful desertion of a Christian by a non-Christian spouse (those coming to Christ after marriage, in 1 Corinthians 7:15).

10. How should we keep the seventh commandment?

To follow the seventh commandment, keep sexual relationships within the bounds of a marriage covenant, and flee from lustful desires. A single Christian is to practice sexual abstinence, living a clean lifestyle: in thoughts, desires, and deeds. Married Christians follow God's instruction to honor their union of one flesh, and God's ordained roles for husband and wife (1 Corinthians 6:18-20 and 2 Timothy 2:22).

11. Is there a blessing in keeping the seventh commandment?

Protection of and respect for marriage and family are blessings that result from the keeping of the seventh commandment. The family is a very important institution, not of the will of man, but of God. It is the basic building block of a nation. If the family is strong and sound, the nation is strong and sound. Following God's law a nation will be blessed as the core unit, the family, is honored and protected (Exodus 19:5-6).

Study Questions

1. Read Matthew 5:27-30 and James 1:14-15. Explain the motivation for adultery._____

_____

_____

_____

_____

_____

2. "The Bible says 'don't commit adultery.' I'm not married, so I'm not sinning." Explain adultery and fornication, and why the previous statement is false. _____

_____

_____

_____

_____

_____

_____

3. A friend is considering marriage and wants your advice. What can you tell this friend about the biblical guidelines for marriage? Recommend some scriptures to support your advice. _____

_____

_____

_____

_____

_____

_____

Lesson Journal

Use this section to record your thoughts on the topics in this lesson.

_____

_____

_____

_____

_____

_____

_____

Lesson 17
Getting Along With Others

Scripture Reading

- Exodus 20:13 and Deuteronomy 5:17 (the sixth commandment)

- Matthew 5:21-26 and Matthew 18:15-17 (murder and reconciliation with a brother)

- Leviticus 19:17-18; Mark 12:29-31; Romans 13:9-10 and Galatians 5:13-14 (the sum of the law)

- Luke 10:30-37 (the parable of the Good Samaritan)

Introduction

Jesus advised clearing up disputes quickly, before animosity festers into bitterness. Jesus gave guidelines for dealing with offenses, emphasizing doing so in humility and a willingness to forgive. He reiterated the sum of the law, to love your neighbor as yourself, taking a proactive approach instead of looking at the law as a list of *don'ts*. Jesus used the illustration of the Good Samaritan, where a man whose culture taught he should hate someone different, instead cared for another regardless of his differences. This is the love that Jesus wants all to show, and by doing so life is protected and respected, which is a blessing that comes from keeping the sixth commandment.

The sixth commandment is direct, given in four short words: *Thou shalt not kill*. Although brief, the command is not short on depth or application. It is better understood in English to be *You shall not murder*, a statement that speaks directly to the unlawful taking of a life. It is in the definition of murder where the depth of this command is felt. The Bible speaks of mitigating circumstances and the intention of the heart when defining the unlawful taking of a life, or murder. Jesus related it to anger. Anger can lead to hate toward another that is in essence equal to murder. This is so because it is an attitude of contempt toward another life. Jesus' teaching about reconciliation and forgiveness requires offended people to lay anger aside and seek to be reconciled with their fellow Christians.

1. What is anger?

Anger is a human emotion that can be properly directed or sinful. The apostle Paul said, *"Be angry, and yet do not sin;"* (Ephesians 4:26 NASB). The apostle James described the source of sinful anger: *"What causes fights and quarrels among you? Don't they come from your desires that battle within you? You want something but don't get it. You kill and covet, but you cannot have what you want. You quarrel and fight,"* (James 4:1-2 NIV). Sinful anger stems from not getting one's own way. Sinful anger leads to quarrels and fights, and can even lead to murder, which goes against the sixth commandment.

2. What is the sixth commandment?

> *Exodus 20:13*
> *Thou shalt not kill.*

3. What is the purpose of the sixth commandment?

Deuteronomy 5:17 NIV
You shall not murder.

With the sixth commandment God begins a series of very direct commandments. The four short words of this commandment are better understood translated in English as, *You shall not murder.* In such a direct statement it is understood that a primary purpose is the condemnation and banning of murder, that is the unlawful taking of a life. Considering this command from a positive viewpoint, its objective is to protect life as it outlaws murder.

Jesus taught about the intention of the heart with respect to murder, saying, *"You have heard that it was said to the people long ago, 'Do not murder, and anyone who murders will be subject to judgment.' But I tell you that anyone who is angry with his brother will be subject to judgment. Again, anyone who says to his brother, 'Raca,' [a term of contempt] is answerable to the Sanhedrin. But anyone who says, 'You fool!' will be in danger of the fire of hell,"* (Matthew 5:21-22 NIV). Jesus connects contemptuous anger toward another with the sixth commandment. *"The things that come out of the mouth come from the heart, and these make a man 'unclean.' For out of the heart come evil thoughts, murder…"*(Matthew 15:18-19 NIV).

The commandment protects life by banning murder, but Jesus couples murder with the thoughts and intentions of the heart. The purpose of the commandment from a Christian perspective is not just the outlawing of murder, but also a directive to control anger and contempt toward others (Deuteronomy 5:17 NIV).

4. If I am angry with someone am I a murderer?

When Jesus spoke of anger toward another in Matthew chapter 5, He spoke of a hateful anger with contempt. Harboring anger toward another can lead to an attitude of contempt. In the first murder recorded in the Bible, the attitude of Cain toward Abel was one of contempt, which grew out of Cain's anger toward his brother (Genesis 4:5-6, 8). This is the anger that Jesus compared to murder, an attitude that must be remedied.

Jesus taught that offenses between one another should be rectified quickly, so that bitterness does not take root (Matthew 5:23-25). His view of the law was one of being proactive instead of reactive. Instead of looking at the law and the commandments as a list of *don'ts*, Jesus recommended considering the *do's*. Jesus said that the law hung on two commandments: Love the Lord with all of your heart, soul, strength, and mind; and love your neighbor as yourself (Mark 12:29-31). Loving your neighbor as yourself excludes hateful anger (Galatians 5:22-23).

5. What does it mean to love my neighbor?

After Jesus stated love your neighbor as yourself, a lawyer responded by asking, "Who is my neighbor?" Jesus answered this question with a parable commonly known as the story of the Good Samaritan (see Luke 10:30-37). In this story Jesus described a Jew who was traveling down the road from Jerusalem to Jericho, and was ambushed by robbers, beaten, and left for dead. Two of his own kinsmen passed him by, but a third, the Samaritan, saw the beaten man and felt compassion, tended to his wounds, and took him to an inn where he paid for the injured man's stay and care. When Jesus asked who the beaten man's neighbor was, the lawyer answered correctly by identifying the Samaritan, the one who had shown compassion.

In Jesus' story, the Samaritan overcame a hate and bitterness that existed between the Jews and the Samaritans. The Samaritans were a mixed origin of people comprised of Jews and the Gentiles who had conquered the Jews in the 8th century BC. The Samaritans followed a religion that was a mixture of Judaism and pagan idolatry. The anger between Jews and Samaritans began when the Jews refused to allow the Samaritans to assist in the rebuilding of the Jerusalem temple in the 6th century BC. The anger festered into hate, and "the bitter enmity between the Jews and Samaritans continued in the time of our Lord: the Jews had no dealings with the Samaritans."[1]

Genesis 4:5-6, 8
So Cain became very angry and his countenance fell. Then the LORD said to Cain, "Why are you angry? ...And it came about when they were in the field, that Cain rose up against Abel his brother and killed him.

Matthew 5:23-25
Therefore if you are presenting your offering at the altar, and there remember that your brother has something against you, leave your offering there before the altar and go; first be reconciled to your brother, and then come and present your offering. "Make friends quickly with your opponent at law while you are with him on the way, so that your opponent may not hand you over to the judge, and the judge to the officer, and you be thrown into prison.

Mark 12:29-31 NASB
And Jesus answered him, The first of all the commandments is, Hear, O Israel; The Lord our God is one Lord: And thou shalt love the Lord thy God with all thy heart, and with all thy soul, and with all thy mind, and with all thy strength: this is the first commandment. And the second is like, namely this, Thou shalt love thy neighbour as thyself. There is none other commandment greater than these.

Galatians 5:22-23 NIV
But the fruit of the Spirit is love, joy, peace, patience, kindness, goodness, faithfulness, gentleness and selfcontrol. Against such things there is no law.

[1] Easton, M. G., *Easton's Bible Dictionary*, Ellis Enterprises Inc., 1993.

1 John 3:15
Everyone who hates his brother is a murderer. And you know that no murderer has eternal life abiding in him.

1 John 4:20-21 NASB
If someone says, "I love God," and hates his brother, he is a liar; for the one who does not love his brother whom he has seen, cannot love God whom he has not seen. And this commandment we have from Him, that the one who loves God should love his brother also.

Matthew 18:15-17 NIV
If your brother sins against you, go and show him his fault, just between the two of you. If he listens to you, you have won your brother over. But if he will not listen, take one or two others along, so that "every matter may be established by the testimony of two or three witnesses." If he refuses to listen to them, tell it to the church; and if he refuses to listen even to the church, treat him as you would a pagan or a tax collector.

Matthew 18:21-22 NIV
Then Peter came to Jesus and asked, "Lord, how many times shall I forgive my brother when he sins against me? Up to seven times?" Jesus answered, "I tell you, not seven times, but seventy-seven times."

Ephesians 4:15 NIV
Instead, speaking the truth in love, we will in all things grow up into him who is the Head, that is, Christ.

Deuteronomy 19:15 NIV
One witness is not enough to convict a man accused of any crime or offense he may have committed. A matter must be established by the testimony of two or three witnesses.

Jesus used this parable to show that hate, rooted in anger, must be dealt with in order to love your neighbor as yourself. His directive to the lawyer was clear. Jesus said, *"Go and do the same"* as the Samaritan (Luke 10:37). When Jesus said love your neighbor as yourself, He was not establishing a new concept, but reminding those He taught that God had declared this to Moses long ago when God said, *"You must not hate your fellow citizen in your heart. If your neighbor does something wrong, tell him about it, or you will be partly to blame. Forget about the wrong things people do to you, and do not try to get even. Love your neighbor as you love yourself. I am the LORD,"* (Leviticus 19:17-18). The parable of the Good Samaritan put "love your neighbor" in terms that the lawyer and others could understand (1 John 3:15 and 1 John 4:20-21).

6. How should Christians reconcile their differences?

In Matthew 18:15-17, Jesus gave guidelines for reconciling two people. Jesus presented a four-step process:

1. The offended person is to go privately to the one that has caused an offense. This requires humility and love (the context of Matthew 18 is humility, based on the opening verses describing Jesus' disciples asking Him who is the greatest in the kingdom of heaven). Approaching someone that has been offensive requires laying aside anger, a willingness to forgive the offense (Matthew 18:21-22), and speaking the truth in love (Ephesians 4:15).

2. If the offending person refuses to receive the first attempt at reconciliation, the offended party is to bring two or three witnesses. Jesus bases this guideline on the principle of Deuteronomy 19:15, which required the testimony of two or three witnesses before an accused person could be convicted of a crime.

3. Should the second attempt fail to result in reconciliation, the matter is to be brought before the local church for the church leaders (pastor) to judge.

4. If all these attempts fail at reconciliation, then the offended party should not have any dealings with the offender.

7. Doesn't the death penalty go against the sixth commandment?

Although direct in its statement, the sixth commandment has had varied applications, mainly due to the interpretation and definition of murder. Some have taken the commandment to mean that no killing is justified, including that of man and animal, while others have considered it to apply only to man. Questions arise, having to do with warfare, capital punishment, self-defense, accidents, etc. To answer these questions it is best to look to the Bible.

The sixth commandment is short and to the point, but it is supported by *case* law. That is, individual cases or circumstances outlined by God that deal with such things as an accidental killing, the mauling of a man by an animal, etc. Exodus 21 and Deuteronomy 19 cover such case laws. From these passages we learn that not all killing is considered a violation of the sixth commandment.

Lawful killing is allowed because God demands the death penalty for murder. The authority to carry out the capital punishment is granted by God. However, intention is central to a verdict that requires the death penalty, as capital punishment is not to be meted out *"when he kills his friend unintentionally, not hating him previously,"* (Deuteronomy 19:4). Moreover, Deuteronomy 19:15 states that a matter must be confirmed *"on the evidence of two or three witnesses."* In other words, the death penalty is not to be applied indiscriminately or on the evidence of a single witness (Numbers 35:30-31; Romans 13:1, 3-4).

8. What about abortion, is it murder?

God created all people, and each person existed from the time of conception. There is ample scriptural support for this (Job 12:9-10; Psalm 139:13-14; Ecclesiastes 11:5; Isaiah 44:2). God is the giver of life, and He alone has the authority to take life. He has established the governing authorities and allows these authorities to exact justice, fight wars, and extend liberty to individuals to defend themselves. However, God does not give the authority to an individual to take the life of an unborn child. The ancient Hippocratic Oath, in its original form, was an oath to pagan gods, yet Hippocrates vows, "I will not give to a woman a pessary to cause abortion."[2] Even those who worshiped idols recognized abortion as murder (see also Isaiah 44:24; Isaiah 49:5; Jeremiah 1:5 and Acts 17:25).

---

[2] Durant, Will., *The Story of Civilization: 2 The Life of Greece*, Simon and Schuster, New York, 1939, pg. 347.

Numbers 35:30-31 NASB
If anyone kills a person, the murderer shall be put to death at the evidence of witnesses, but no person shall be put to death on the testimony of one witness. Moreover, you shall not take ransom for the life of a murderer who is guilty of death, but he shall surely be put to death.

Romans 13:1, 3-4 NIV
Everyone must submit himself to the governing authorities, for there is no authority except that which God has established. The authorities that exist have been established by God... Do you want to be free from fear of the one in authority? Then do what is right and he will commend you. For he is God's servant to do you good. But if you do wrong, be afraid, for he does not bear the sword for nothing. He is God's servant, an agent of wrath to bring punishment on the wrongdoer.

Job 12:9-10 NASB
"Who among all these does not know That the hand of the LORD has done this, In whose hand is the life of every living thing, And the breath of all mankind?

Psalm 139:13-14
For thou hast possessed my reins: thou hast covered me in my mother's womb. I will praise thee; for I am fearfully and wonderfully made:

Ecclesiastes 11:5 NASB
Just as you do not know the path of the wind and how bones are formed in the womb of the pregnant woman, so you do not know the activity of God who makes all things.

Isaiah 44:2
Thus saith the LORD that made thee, and formed thee from the womb, which will help thee...

Leviticus 19:17-18 NCV

"You must not hate your fellow citizen in your heart. If your neighbor does something wrong, tell him about it, or you will be partly to blame. Forget about the wrong things people do to you, and do not try to get even. Love your neighbor as you love yourself. I am the LORD."

Romans 13:9-10

Thou shalt love thy neighbour as thyself. Love worketh no ill to his neighbour: therefore love is the fulfilling of the law.

Galatians 5:13-14 NASB

For you were called to freedom, brethren; only do not turn your freedom into an opportunity for the flesh, but through love serve one another. For the whole Law is fulfilled in one word, in the statement, "You shall love your neighbor as yourself."

9. How should we keep the sixth commandment?

The sixth commandment is kept by protecting life and maintaining an attitude of self-control. In so doing, anger, which is so often the root of hate, will not be allowed to fester into bitterness. The sum of it all is following the teaching of Leviticus 19, reiterated by Jesus, and that is to love your neighbor as yourself (Leviticus 19:17-18 and Romans 13:9-10).

10. Is there a blessing in keeping the sixth commandment?

Protection of and respect for life are blessings that result from keeping the sixth commandment. By keeping this command as Christ taught, needless anger, hate, and bitterness toward others will be avoided as you love your neighbor as yourself (Galatians 5:13-14).

Study Questions

1. There is more to the purpose of the sixth commandment than just "not killing." Explain the purpose and a better English translation of *thou shalt not kill*. _____

    _____

    _____

    _____

    _____

    _____

    _____

2. Read Matthew 5:21-26. When can anger be equated with murder? _____

    _____

    _____

    _____

    _____

    _____

3. Read Luke 10:30-37. What are some guidelines for getting along with others that are illustrated in this parable? _____

    _____

    _____

    _____

    _____

    _____

    _____

Lesson Journal

Use this section to record your thoughts on the topics in this lesson.

_____

_____

_____

_____

_____

Lesson 18
Biblical Finance

Scripture Reading

- Exodus 20:15 and Deuteronomy 5:19 (the eighth commandment)

- Leviticus 19:9-15, 33-37; Deuteronomy 22:1-7, 25:13-16 and Amos 8:4-8 (stealing)

- Malachi 3:8-12 (robbing God, tithes and offerings)

- Mark 12:41-44; Matthew 6:1-4, 23:23-24 and Acts 11:27-30 (giving)

- Luke 18:8-9 and Ezekiel 33:15-16 (restitution)

- Ephesians 4:28 (stop stealing)

Introduction

The eighth commandment is another that is short and to the point, however it is supported by much case law and example throughout the Old and New Testaments. The commandment has at its core the approval of private property, with the goal of protecting property and the right of ownership. Stealing appears very straightforward on the surface, but the Bible points to many forms of theft that some would not consider to fall under the category of *thou shalt not steal*. Examples include extortion, bribery, dishonest scales, taking advantage of workers, not returning found property, and many more. Greed is often the motivator behind stealing, and Jesus cautioned to guard the heart against greed.

One notable form of theft is the robbery of God. The prophet Malachi posed the question, "How does a man rob God?" Although the tone is rhetorical Malachi gives the answer: By not giving God tithes and offerings. Malachi identified withholding from God as a form of theft. He also noted that blessings are missed when giving is withheld. Jesus spoke of the tithe and instructed that it should not be neglected, and He reiterated that blessing follows giving.

This lesson discusses improper taking by stealing, and proper giving of tithes and offerings. In the end, one who keeps the eighth commandment will be a cheerful giver who has heeded the instruction of Jesus to guard against greed, by remembering His words: It is better to give than to receive.

Matthew 16:26
What good will it be for a man if he gains the whole world, yet forfeits his soul? Or what can a man give in exchange for his soul?

Luke 12:27-28
Consider the lilies, how they grow: they neither toil nor spin; and yet I say to you, even Solomon in all his glory was not arrayed like one of these. If then God so clothes the grass, which today is in the field and tomorrow is thrown into the oven, how much more will He clothe you, O you of little faith?

Proverbs 10:4 NIV
Poor is he who works with a negligent hand,But the hand of the diligent makes rich.

Proverbs 21:25 NIV
The desire of the sluggard puts him to death, For his hands refuse to work

Psalm 24:1 NIV
The earth is the Lord's, and everything in it, the world, and all who live in it.

Colossians 1:16 NASB
For by Him all things were created, both in the heavens and on earth, visible and invisible, whether thrones or dominions or rulers or authorities--all things have been created by Him and for Him.

1. What is a steward?

The Bible refers to a steward as one who takes care of what belongs to another. A steward must work diligently to acquire and maintain all that comes under his stewardship. Jesus taught that a good steward was one who took the responsibility of stewardship seriously but with balance. He cautioned against seeking ownership of too much of the material in the world (Matthew 16:26 and Luke 12:27-28). Jesus said a good steward is one that focuses on following God and doing His business because that steward would be prepared to meet God. Jesus put it this way, *"Who then is that faithful and wise steward, whom his master will make ruler over his household, to give them their portion of food in due season? Blessed is that servant whom his master will find so doing when he comes. Truly, I say to you that he will make him ruler over all that he has,"* (Luke 12:42-44 NKJV).

2. If we are stewards of what belongs to God, can we own property?

From the very beginning God gave man dominion over the earth, a mandate to own property. To own property is to rightfully hold and be distinguished as the possessor of the property, which is confirmed by the eighth commandment. Becoming an owner does not happen automatically, it requires effort, work that is necessary to develop a respect for the value of property (Proverbs 10:4 and Proverbs 21:25).

Working to obtain and gain title of property does not change the fact that God is the source of everything. Everything belongs to Him and He is the true owner (Psalm 24:1; Colossians 1:16). Ownership of earthly possessions then is the privilege to be a steward of what really belongs to God.

3. What is the eighth commandment?

Exodus 20:15
Thou shalt not steal.

4. What is the purpose of the eighth commandment?

The eighth commandment is one in a series of God's commands having to do with respect: respect for parents (5th), respect for life (6th), and respect for marriage and the family (7th). The eighth commandment orders respect for what belongs to others. Implicit in the command is the right of ownership, as something cannot be stolen if it is not first of all owned. The command therefore has as its primary purpose the goal of protecting property and the right to own property (Deuteronomy 5:19 and Leviticus 19:11).

5. What is stealing?

A concise definition of stealing is the taking of the property of another without right or without detection. Stealing includes theft, robbery, burglary, embezzlement, and the like, where another's property is clearly identified. However, stealing encompasses much more, as seen in these Biblical examples:

- **Unjust gain**

  Using unjust or unfair means to gain an advantage in a contract or to obtain property is a form of theft. Examples include purchasing stolen property, unfair labor practices, not working a full day, using "insider" information to take advantage of another, etc. These behaviors are all theft (Proverbs 10:2; Leviticus 19:13 and 1 Timothy 5:18).

- **Negligence**

  Neglecting to return lost or stolen property to the rightful owner is theft. Not participating in the act of robbery itself does not eliminate the responsibility of returning lost or stolen property to its owner (Deuteronomy 22:1-4 and 1 John 3:17). In the New Testament, the apostle Paul advises against negligence in paying debts, to individuals or the government, whether money or respect (Romans 13:7).

- **Fraud**

  Obtaining property or making a gain by way of deceit is fraud, and it is theft. Fraud includes making false statements, false advertisement, hiding defects in property, embezzlement, or obtaining anything by way of false pretense. The Bible gives the example of a merchant using a dishonest scale and other forms of dishonest measuring (Leviticus 19:35-36 and Proverbs 11:1; see also Deuteronomy 25:13-16).

Deuteronomy 5:19
Neither shalt thou steal.

Leviticus 19:11 NKJV
You shall not steal, nor deal falsely, nor lie to one another.

Proverbs 10:2 NASB
Ill-gotten gains do not profit, But righteousness delivers from death.

Leviticus 19:13 NKJV
You shall not cheat your neighbor, nor rob him. The wages of him who is hired shall not remain with you all night until morning.

1 Timothy 5:18 NASB
For the Scripture says, "You shall not muzzle the ox while he is threshing," and "The laborer is worthy of his wages."

Deuteronomy 22:1-4 NIV
If you see your brother's ox or sheep straying, do not ignore it but be sure to take it back to him. If the brother does not live near you or if you do not know who he is, take it home with you and keep it until he comes looking for it. Then give it back to him. Do the same if you find your brother's donkey or his cloak or anything he loses. Do not ignore it. If you see your brother's donkey or his ox fallen on the road, do not ignore it. Help him get it to its feet.

1 John 3:17 NIV
If anyone has material possessions and sees his brother in need but has no pity on him, how can the love of God be in him? Dear children, let us not love with words or tongue but with actions and in truth.

Romans 13:7 NASB
Render to all what is due them: tax to whom tax is due; custom to whom custom; fear to whom fear; honor to whom honor.

Leviticus 19:35-36 NIV
Do not use dishonest standards when measuring length, weight or quantity. Use honest scales and honest weights, an honest ephah and an honest hin. I am the LORD your God, who brought you out of Egypt.

Proverbs 11:1 NIV
The LORD abhors dishonest scales, but accurate weights are his delight.

Ezekiel 22:29 NASB
The people of the land have practiced oppression and committed robbery, and they have wronged the poor and needy and have oppressed the sojourner without justice.

Amos 8:4-8 NASB
Hear this, you who trample the needy, to do away with the humble of the land, saying, "When will the new moon be over, So that we may sell grain, And the sabbath, that we may open the wheat market, To make the bushel smaller and the shekel bigger, And to cheat with dishonest scales, So as to buy the helpless for money And the needy for a pair of sandals, And that we may sell the refuse of the wheat?" The LORD has sworn by the pride of Jacob, "Indeed, I will never forget any of their deeds.

Proverbs 2:22
Do not rob the poor because he is poor...

Exodus 21:16
And he that stealeth a man, and selleth him, or if he be found in his hand, he shall surely be put to death

Deuteronomy 24:7
If a man be found stealing any of his brethren of the children of Israel, and maketh merchandise of him, or selleth him; then that thief shall die; and thou shalt put evil away from among you.

Malachi 3:8-9 NIV
"Will a man rob God? Yet you rob me. But you ask, "How do we rob you?" In tithes and offerings. You are under a curse-the whole nation of you-because you are robbing me.

Ephesians 5:3
But immorality or any impurity or greed must not even be named among you, as is proper among saints...

- **Exploitation**

  Taking advantage of another's ignorance, state of mind, physical condition, age, gender, etc., to make a gain is exploitation. To exploit another person in order to profit is theft (Ezekiel 22:29; Amos 8:4-8 and Proverbs 2:22).

- **Kidnapping and slavery**

  In the King James Version of the Bible there are references to stealing a man, i.e., kidnapping. Although modern English versions of the Bible use the word *kidnap*, the King James Version is insightful in its choice of words. Stealing a man is outlawed as is making *merchandise* of him, or treating him as property. Not only is kidnapping a form of theft, but also slavery as it robs a man of his freedom (Exodus 21:16 and Deuteronomy 24:7).

  Note: The Bible made allowances for one to be an indentured servant to pay a debt, but this agreement had limits, it was not permanent. A man could also voluntarily become a slave. Slaves became part of a family having rights within the household, and could choose to leave without being forced to return.

- **Robbing God**

  How can a man rob God? The prophet Malachi posed the question and also gave us the answer. A man robs God when he withholds his giving. It is a form of theft, as man seeks to keep what God has blessed him with, and build up earthly treasure (Malachi 3:8-9).

A common theme in all the forms of theft given above, and all others not mentioned, is a desire to have something for nothing, to obtain without work. There is an element of greed inherent in stealing, and Jesus taught to be on guard against greed, saying, *"Beware, and be on your guard against every form of greed; for not even when one has an abundance does his life consist of his possessions,"* (Luke 12:15 NASB). Paul reinforced this concept in Ephesians 5:3 and in his first letter to Timothy, with a reminder that *"the love of money is a root of all kinds of evil, for which some have strayed from the faith in their greediness, and pierced themselves through with many sorrows,"* (1 Timothy 6:10 NKJV).

6. What is a tithe?

A tithe is a tenth, ten percent. A tithe is a giving principle established throughout the Bible as a way of proportional giving to God. No one is expected to give more because of his prosperity or less because of his poverty. Abraham and Jacob exemplified tithing before God established formal tithing in the law with Moses.

Abraham tithed to the priest Melchizedek. *"This Melchizedek was king of Salem and priest of God Most High. He met Abraham returning from the defeat of the kings and blessed him, and Abraham gave him a tenth of everything,"* (Hebrews 7:1-2 NIV). Jacob made a vow to God to tithe to Him after having a dream where he saw heaven open up. Jacob ended his vow, saying, *"and this stone that I have set up as a pillar will be God's house, and of all that you give me I will give you a tenth,"* (Genesis 28:22 NIV).

The prophet Malachi said the tithe should be brought into the storehouse, i.e., God's house. At that time, the nation of Israel was neglecting their tithing, and Malachi equated this with robbery of God. He commanded the people to tithe and added two interesting points: Malachi said to the nation that God would provide blessings from heaven that they would not have room enough to hold and they could test God in this (Malachi 3:8-12 and Proverbs 3:9-10).

7. What is an offering?

In the Old Testament there were several types of offerings. Some offerings were required, some were for ritual, and others were voluntary as an act of worship to God. Voluntary offerings go above and beyond the tithe, and are called in the Bible freewill offerings. Freewill offerings are noted in both the Old and New Testaments.

Old Testament examples include the freewill offerings collected for the building of the tabernacle under Moses (see Exodus 25:1-9, 35:4-38:7), the building of the temple under David and Solomon (1 Chronicles 29:1-20), and the rebuilding of the temple under Joshua and Zerubbabel (Ezra 1:4; see also Nehemiah 7:70-72).

New Testament offerings are noted when the believers in Antioch collected offerings for the church at Jerusalem (see Acts 11:27-30). The apostle Paul also accepted offerings that the church at Philippi collected for his needs, and reminded them that blessings were associated with their giving (Philippians 4:15). Paul also encouraged giving to support the church in Jerusalem (see 1 Corinthians 16:1-4 and 2 Corinthians 8:1-7) and Jesus noted the impoverished widow who gave all that she had (Mark 12:41-44).

Malachi 3:8-12
"Will a man rob God? Yet you rob me. But you ask, 'How do we rob you?' In tithes and offerings. You are under a curse-the whole nation of you-because you are robbing me. Bring the whole tithe into the storehouse, that there may be food in my house. Test me in this," says the LORD Almighty, "and see if I will not throw open the floodgates of heaven and pour out so much blessing that you will not have room enough for it. I will prevent pests from devouring your crops, and the vines in your fields will not cast their fruit," says the LORD Almighty. "Then all the nations will call you blessed, for yours will be a delightful land," says the LORD Almighty.

Proverbs 3:9-10
Honor the Lord with your possession, And with the firstfruits of all your increase; So your barns will be filled with plenty, And your vats will overflow with new wine.

1 Chronicles 29:6-7
Then the chief of the fathers and princes of the tribes of Israel, and the captains of thousands and of hundreds, with the rulers of the king's work, offered willingly, And gave for the service of the house of God...

Ezra 1:4 NIV
And whoever is left in any place where he dwells, let the men of his place help him with silver and gold, with goods and livestock, besides the freewill offerings for the house of God which is in Jerusalem.

Philippians 4:15 NIV
Moreover, as you Philippians know, in the early days of your acquaintance with the gospel, when I set out from Macedonia, not one church shared with me in the matter of giving and receiving, except you only;

Mark 12:41-44 NIV
Jesus sat down opposite the place where the offerings were put and watched the crowd putting their money into the temple treasury. Many rich people threw in large amounts. But a poor widow came and put in two very small copper coins, worth only a fraction of a penny. Calling his disciples to him, Jesus said, "I tell you the truth, this poor widow has put more into the treasury than all the others. They all gave out of their wealth; but she, out of her poverty, put in everything–all she had to live on."

8. What did Jesus teach about giving?

Jesus was a law keeper. He followed the law of Moses and put it into practice perfectly. Many times He referenced the law and also referred to tithing. Jesus often pointed out the religious leaders' failures to follow the law although they were educated experts. His frequent admonishment was that the leaders followed the letter of the law, but neglected the spirit of the law. Jesus made such a statement when speaking of tithing, saying, *"Woe to you, scribes and Pharisees, hypocrites! For you pay tithe of mint and anise and cummin, and have neglected the weightier matters of the law: justice and mercy and faith. These you ought to have done, without leaving the others undone,"* (Matthew 23:23). Jesus' point was that giving a tithe was not enough; one must also exercise compassion.

Jesus also taught that giving should be done privately. He stated, *"Be careful not to do your 'acts of righteousness' before men, to be seen by them. If you do, you will have no reward from your Father in heaven. So when you give to the needy, do not announce it with trumpets, as the hypocrites do in the synagogues and on the streets, to be honored by men. I tell you the truth, they have received their reward in full. But when you give to the needy, do not let your left hand know what your right hand is doing, so that your giving may be in secret. Then your Father, who sees what is done in secret, will reward you,"* (Matthew 6:1-4 NIV).

Blessings are associated with giving, Jesus said, *"Give, and it will be given to you: good measure, pressed down, shaken together, and running over will be put into your bosom. For with the same measure that you use, it will be measured back to you,"* (Luke 6:38).

Jesus also said, *"...give to Caesar what is Caesar's and to God what is God's,"* (Luke 20:25 NIV).

9. How should we keep the eighth commandment?

This command is kept by following the instruction of Jesus and Paul. Guard against greed in the heart, and instead of stealing, work in order to earn the ownership of property (2 Thessalonians 3:6-10; Acts 20:35; Ephesians 4:28 and Hebrews 13:5).

10. Is there a blessing in keeping the eighth commandment?

By keeping the eighth commandment the right to own property is upheld and protected. One who keeps this command also affirms that God owns everything, and has taken seriously the privilege to be His steward through work. A good steward gives back to God the first tenth of his increase, as well as offerings, and is further blessed both corporately and individually (Acts 20:35).

2 Thessalonians 3:6-10 NIV
In the name of the Lord Jesus Christ, we command you, brothers, to keep away from every brother who is idle and does not live according to the teaching you received from us. For you yourselves know how you ought to follow our example. We were not idle when we were with you, nor did we eat anyone's food without paying for it. On the contrary, we worked night and day, laboring and toiling so that we would not be a burden to any of you. We did this, not because we do not have the right to such help, but in order to make ourselves a model for you to follow. For even when we were with you, we gave you this rule: "If a man will not work, he shall not eat"

Acts 20:35
In everything I showed you that by working hard in this manner you must help the weak...

Ephesians 4:28
He who steals must steal no longer; but rather he must labor, performing with his own hands what is good, so that he will have *something* to share with one who has need.

Hebrews 13:5
Keep your lives free from the love of money and be content with what you have, because God has said, "Never will I leave you; never will I forsake you.

Study Questions

1. Explain the purpose of the eighth commandment. _____

_____

_____

_____

_____

2. Describe some different types of stealing and give scripture references as examples. Do you think some people rationalize what the Bible considers stealing? Explain. _____

_____

_____

_____

_____

_____

3. Read Malachi 3:8-12 and Matthew 23:23. How is giving related to stealing? _____

_____

_____

_____

_____

Lesson Journal

Use this section to record your thoughts on the topics in this lesson.

_____

_____

_____

_____

_____

_____

_____

Lesson 19
Living Honestly

Scripture Reading

- Exodus 20:16-17 and Deuteronomy 5:20-21 (the ninth and tenth commandments)

- Zechariah 8:16-17 and Proverbs 19:9, 15-16 (perjury, presumption, lying, gossip, and slander)

- Matthew 26:69-74 (denying Jesus)

- Joshua 2:1-14 (the lie of Rahab)

- Proverbs 22:1 (having a good name, a good reputation)

- Colossians 3:5 (covetousness and idolatry)

- 1 Timothy 6:10-11; Philippians 4:11-13 and Hebrews 13:5 (contentment instead of covetousness)

Introduction

The ninth and tenth commandments continue to emphasize behavior as a reflection of the intent of the heart. The ninth commandment, *thou shalt not bear false witness against thy neighbor*, deals with living honestly, dealing honestly with every neighbor, seeking to uphold our own and our neighbor's reputation. False witness encompasses all forms of lying, such as gossip and slander. Purposing to be a Christian while practicing the sin of being a false witness, such as a gossip, makes one a false witness of Jesus Christ and harms the reputation of Christianity. The commandment is not a directive to be truthful in all things at all times. Though the focus of the command is honesty, being truthful must be weighed against the outcome, perhaps sinful, of being honest. Hence the lesson discusses the question: Is it ever okay to lie? A good reputation is a blessing that follows keeping the ninth commandment, as is upholding the good reputation of our neighbor.

The tenth commandment abbreviated is *thou shalt not covet*. The word *covet* does not have a moral connotation; it can be good or evil. We are encouraged to covet good things, but this commandment is focused on the elimination of evil desires. It specifies not coveting anything that belongs to another, from spouse to home. This command aims at the root of commands six through nine by condemning the wrongful desire that leads to murder, adultery and fornication, theft, and dishonesty. The essence of keeping this command is contentment, being satisfied regardless of our circumstance. The apostle Paul advised that he had learned to be content with little and content with much. It is through keeping this command that one is blessed with contentment.

1. Can my neighbor affect my goals and ambitions?

Goals and ambitions can be healthy desires, objectives set with a purpose and end in mind. Jesus taught that what we set out to gain should be eternally focused. He said, *"Do not store up for your-selves treasures on earth, where moth and rust destroy, and where thieves break in and steal. But store up for yourselves treasures in heaven, where neither moth nor rust destroys, and where thieves do not break in or steal; for where your treasure is, there your heart will be also,"* (Matthew 6:19-21 NASB). Too often though, the aspirations of one's heart are focused on worldly possessions and are a result of the influence of others.

A person can be motivated and influenced by his neighbor's possessions or station in life, without his neighbor ever knowing. When one cannot attain the same level as his neighbor, the result can be destructive talk against the neighbor or an over-zealous desire to have all that the neighbor owns. A neighbor's influence can be so strong that God gave Moses the ninth and tenth commandments to sum up how we are to regard our neighbor, and act as a curb against misguided desires.

2. What is the ninth commandment?

> *Exodus 20:16*
> *Thou shalt not bear false witness against thy neighbor.*

3. What is the purpose of the ninth commandment?

This is a commandment that must be considered with reference to the other commands of God. Telling the truth is required, but not when it results in murder, theft, adultery, or any other sin (more on this in Question 5). Also central to this command is one's neighbor, where not bearing false witness is respecting the good name of a neighbor. The ninth commandment then has as its purpose the maintaining and promoting of honest communication, and of our own and our neighbor's reputation.

As with the previous commandments the ninth commandment continues in a series of God's commands having to do with respect, It follows respect for parents (5th), respect for life (6th), and respect for marriage and the family (7th) respect for what belongs to others (8th) and in the ninth respect of another's name and reputation (Deuteronomy 5:20).

Deuteronomy 5:20
Neither shalt thou bear false witness against thy neighbour.

4. What is bearing false witness?

Bearing false witness stated simply is lying. But there are various forms of lying, from knowingly making false statements to speaking without full knowledge of the truth. False witness includes:

- **Lying**

  Lying is the making of an untrue statement with intent to deceive another. It is the broadest form of false witness, and leads to destruction (Proverbs 19:9). However lying is not always wrong (more on this in Question 5).

- **Perjury**

  Perjury is lying after making an oath or swearing by God, or not fulfilling an obligation that was promised by an oath. Most often, perjury is associated with lying in a court of law. Perjury is sin and offensive to God (Zechariah 8:16-17).

- **Gossip and slander**

  Gossip and slander is talk that hurts the reputation of another. Gossip is based on rumor and is talk about another person without that person's knowledge or consent. Gossip can also involve repeating information that was to be held in confidence.

  Slander is knowingly making false statements or false charges that defame and harm another's reputation. The Word of God condemns gossip and slander (Proverbs 25:23; Proverbs 11:13; Proverbs 10:18 and Leviticus 19:16).

- **Presumption and arrogance**

  Presumption is deliberately making judgments or statements about another without complete knowledge of the truth, and God hates it (Zechariah 8:16-17). Presumption is often accompanied by arrogance, an attitude of superiority. The Pharisees who frequently questioned Jesus were presumptuous and arrogant, and said such things as, *"No wonder he can cast out demons. He gets his power from Satan, the prince of demons,"* (Matthew 12:24 NLT).

Proverbs 19:9
A false witness shall not be unpunished, and he that speaketh lies shall perish.

Zechariah 8:16-17 NASB
"These are the things which you should do: speak the truth to one another; judge with truth and judgment for peace in your gates. Also let none of you devise evil in your heart against another, and do not love perjury; for all these are what I hate," declares the LORD."

Proverbs 25:23
As surely as a wind from the north brings rain, so a gossiping tongue causes anger!

Proverbs 11:13 NASB
He who goes about as a talebearer reveals secrets, But he who is trustworthy conceals a matter.

Proverbs 10:18
He that hideth hatred *with* lying lips, and he that uttereth a slander, *is* a fool.

Leviticus 19:16 NASB
You shall not go about as a slanderer among your people, and you are not to act against the life of your neighbor; I am the Lord.

Zechariah 8:16-17
Speak ye every man the truth to his neighbour; execute the judgment of truth and peace in your gates: And let none of you imagine evil in your hearts against his neighbour; and love no false oath: for all these are things that I hate, saith the LORD.

Matthew 26:69-74 NKJV
Now Peter sat outside in the courtyard. And a servant girl came to him, saying, "You also were with Jesus of Galilee." But he denied it before them all, saying, "I do not know what you are saying." And when he had gone out to the gateway, another girl saw him and said to those who were there, "This fellow also was with Jesus of Nazareth." But again he denied with an oath, "I do not know the Man!" And a little later those who stood by came up and said to Peter, "Surely you also are one of them, for your speech betrays you." Then he began to curse and swear, saying, "I do not know the Man!" Immediately a rooster crowed.

Joshua 2:4-5 NKJV
Then (Rahab) took the two men and hid them. So she said, "Yes, the men came to me, but I did not know where they were from. And it happened as the gate was being shut, when it was dark, that the men went out. Where the men went I do not know; pursue them quickly, for you may overtake them.

James 2:25
In the same way, was not Rahab the harlot also justified by works when she received the messengers and sent them out by another way?

Exodus 1:18-20
"And the king of Egypt called for the midwives, and said unto them, Why have ye done this thing, and have saved the men-children alive? And the midwives said unto Pharaoh, Because the Hebrew women are not as the Egyptian women; for they are lively, and are delivered ere the midwives come in unto them. Therefore God dealt well with the midwives."

James 1:26 NASB
If anyone thinks himself to be religious, and yet does not bridle his tongue but deceives his own heart, this man's religion is worthless.

Proverbs 22:1
A good name is rather to be chosen than great riches, and loving favour rather than silver and gold.

- **False witness of Christ**

  A person that professes to be a Christian but lives a lifestyle contrary to the teachings of Jesus is a false witness of Christ. Such a person is really not a Christian at all, but is giving the name of Jesus a bad reputation. Jesus said, *"No servant can serve two masters: for either he will hate the one, and love the other; or else he will hold to the one, and despise the other,"* (Luke 16:13).

  After having come to know Him, openly denying Jesus is also bearing false witness. Peter the apostle denied Jesus three times (Matthew 26:69-74), but he repented and was brought back into fellowship with Jesus.

5. Is it ever okay to lie?

The ninth commandment "has been widely misinterpreted to mean that 'Thou shalt at all times and under all circumstances tell the truth to all men who ask anything of you.'"[1] The Bible gives instances where the truth was not told, yet the "liar" was blessed. One example is that of Rahab the harlot, who lied to the King of Jericho to save the lives of Hebrew spies. Rahab is mentioned as an ancestor of Christ, and commended in the New Testament. Hebrew midwives also lied to the Pharaoh of Egypt in order to save the lives of innocent infants.

The common theme in the examples given is that lies were told to save innocent lives. Life took precedence over telling the absolute truth. Had Rahab not lied, she would have been an accomplice to murder (Joshua 2:4-5; James 2:25 and Exodus 1:18-20).

6. How should we keep the ninth commandment?

We keep the ninth commandment by being honest in our dealings with our neighbor and when we are required to be truthful. Falling to temptation to speak falsely of another does harm to Christianity. When in doubt, it is better to bridle the tongue and not say anything at all rather than take part in what might be gossip, any form of false witness, or what may result in sin (James 1:26).

7. Is there a blessing in keeping the ninth commandment?

The blessing in keeping the ninth commandment is the good reputation that is built on being honest in all communication and dealing with others. Our neighbor is also blessed with a good reputation that is not torn down by false witness, and others see a positive witness of Jesus Christ (Proverbs 22:1).

[1] Rushdoony, R. J., *The Institutes of Biblical Law, Volume 1*, The Craig Press, 1973, pg. 542

8. What is the tenth commandment?

Exodus 20:17

Thou shalt not covet thy neighbour's house, thou shalt not covet thy neighbour's wife, nor his manservant, nor his maidservant, nor his ox, nor his ass, nor any thing that is thy neighbour's.

9. What is the purpose of the tenth commandment?

The purpose of the tenth commandment is to provide a summation of commandments six through nine acting as a guard against breaking any form of these commands by taking aim at their root.

The tenth commandment outlaws coveting all that belongs to another, including spouse and home, and all other belongings. Therefore, all forms of obtaining a neighbor's property, the specifics of murder, adultery and fornication, theft, and dishonesty are included in the tenth, as is the intention to commit such acts (Deuteronomy 5:21 and Ephesians 5:3).

10. What does it mean to covet?

The Hebrew word *chamad* rendered covet means to desire greatly. It can grow to an excessive desire, a desire that goes beyond reasonable limits. In some scripture passages it is clear that the excessive desire of covetousness results in taking what is desired (for example: Joshua 7:21 and Micah 2:2). Hence to covet is not only to desire, but also can include an act. The acts of murder, adultery, theft, and lying are clearly forbidden in commandments 6 through 9, and reiterated by *thou shalt not covet*.

Covet is most often associated with desire. It is an internal matter, having to do with the intent of the heart. However, *covet* is not a moral word, as it can be associated with good or evil. 1 Corinthians 12:31 mentions a good form of coveting: to covet the gifts of the Spirit. The commandment, however, deals with evil coveting; a desire that grows so strong it results in discontentment.[2] Covetousness can be so strong it leads to resentment of a neighbor's possessions, social status, job, position, etc. The apostle Paul equated covetousness with idolatry (Colossians 3:5). The discontentment for one's situation and obsession to have what belongs to another makes the object of desire a god. Covetousness can also be characterized by lust, envy, and greed (1 Corinthians 12:31).

Deuteronomy 5:21 NASB
You shall not covet your neighbor's wife, and you shall not desire your neighbor's house, his field or his male servant or his female servant, his ox or his donkey or anything that belongs to your neighbor.

Ephesians 5:3
But fornication, and all uncleanness, or covetousness, let it not be once named among you…

Joshua 7:21 NIV
When I saw in the plunder a beautiful robe from Babylonia, two hundred shekels of silver and a wedge of gold weighing fifty shekels, I coveted them and took them. They are hidden in the ground inside my tent, with the silver underneath."

Micah 2:2 NIV
They covet fields and seize them, and houses, and take them. They defraud a man of his home, a fellowman of his inheritance.

Colossians 3:5
Therefore put to death your members which are on the earth: fornication, uncleanness, passion, evil desire, and covetousness, which is idolatry.

1 Corinthians 12:31
But covet earnestly the best gifts…

---

[2] *The Westminster Larger Catechism*, public domain, q148

1 Timothy 6:9-11
If we have food and covering, with these we shall be content. But those who want to get rich fall into temptation and a snare and many foolish and harmful desires which plunge men into ruin and destruction. For the love of money is a root of all sorts of evil, and some by longing for it have wandered away from the faith and pierced themselves with many griefs. But flee from these things, you man of God, and pursue righteousness, godliness, faith, love, perseverance and gentleness.

11. What are the results of coveting?

Coveting leads to action, sin that leads to destruction. Paul said coveting leads one to fall into temptation, being ruined and destroyed, and ultimately falling away from the faith, becoming full of grief (1 Timothy 6:9-11). There are many examples in modern society of the results of covetousness, a few are:

- **Excessive debt**

  "In 2001, the typical U.S. household carried an average credit card balance of $7,500 up from less than $3,000 in 1990."[3] But the United States is not the only country with upward spiraling credit card debt. "UK personal debt broke through the 1 trillion pound barrier in July 2004 and is likely to break through the 1.1 trillion pound barrier in the middle of 2005. Britain's personal debt is increasing by 1 million pounds every four minutes."[4] These two examples show how many people desire to live beyond their means.

- **Fraud**

  "Credit and charge card fraud costs cardholders and issuers hundreds of millions of dollars each year."[5] And credit card fraud is only one method of theft to satisfy a covetous desire. Many other forms of fraud exist as the result of acting on covetousness.

- **Gambling**

  Although some consider gambling a form of entertainment, it is addictive and a method used to satisfy a covetous desire. It most often fails. In California, the California Conference on Problem Gambling reports the "average annual expenditure reported (among problem gamblers) amounted to $28,297. 63% indicated that they financed their gambling problem with credit cards. 55% indicated that their credit cards were 'maxed out' as a result of gambling problems."

  "(The dream world) is another common characteristic of compulsive gamblers. A lot of time is spent creating images of the great and wonderful things they are going to do as soon as they make the big win. They often see themselves as quite philanthropic and charming people. They may dream of providing families and friends with new cars, mink coats, and other luxuries... made possible by the huge sums of money they will accrue from their 'system.'"[6]

---

[3] Belsky, Gary, *Drowning in Debt*, My Generation (Sep-Oct 2001)
[4] Talbot, Richard, *Credit Action*, www.creditaction.org.uk, Lincoln, UK
[5] United States Federal Trade Commission, *Avoiding Credit and Charge Card Fraud*, August 1997
[6] *Questions and Answers About the Problem of Compulsive Gambling and the G.A. Recovery Program*, Gamblers Anonymous, www.gamblersanonymous.org.

12. How should we keep the tenth commandment?

Don't focus on what you do not have, but count yourself blessed for all that God has already given to you. Keeping the tenth commandment is accomplished by learning to be content regardless of our circumstance (Philippians 4:11-13).

13. Is there a blessing in keeping the tenth commandment?

The blessing in keeping the tenth commandment is contentment. To be content does not mean to be complacent. A content person lives within his means, and while focusing on Jesus Christ, can be ambitious, set goals and accomplish much (Hebrews 13:5).

Philippians 4:11-13 NASB
...for I have learned to be content in whatever circumstances I am. I know how to get along with humble means, and I also know how to live in prosperity; in any and every circumstance I have learned the secret of being filled and going hungry, both of having abundance and suffering need. I can do all things through Him who strengthens me.

Hebrews 13:5
Let your conversation be without covetousness; and be content with such things as ye have: for he hath said, I will never leave thee, nor forsake thee.

Study Questions

1. Zechariah 8:16-17; Proverbs 19:9, 15-16 and 22:1. What does the ninth commandment have to do with my reputation or my neighbor's reputation? _____

   _____

   _____

   _____

2. Read Exodus 20:16-17; Deuteronomy 5:20-21. The tenth commandment is in some ways a summary of commandments six through nine. How so? _____

   _____

   _____

   _____

   _____

3. Instead of coveting we should strive to be content. Explain how one might be content with very little.

   _____

   _____

   _____

   _____

Lesson Journal

Use this section to record your thoughts on the topics in this lesson.

_____

_____

_____

_____

_____

_____

_____

_____

Lesson 20
Leading and Serving

Scripture Reading

- Genesis 18:3-4; Genesis 43:24; 1 Samuel 25:41; 1 Timothy 5:10 and Luke 7:44-50 (foot washing in the Bible)

- Mark 10:35-45 (argument among disciples and Jesus' correction)

- Luke 22:24-27 (argument among disciples and Jesus' correction)

- John 13:1-17, 34-38 (Jesus' foot washing, prediction of Peter's denial)

Introduction

Jesus chose twelve men to be His closest disciples. These twelve traveled with Him as He ministered and they learned from Him. The Bible tells of their travels and of discussions that arose among the twelve as they tried to better understand the teachings of Jesus. On certain occasions their discussions grew into arguments and Jesus had to step in to mediate. On three of these occasions the twelve argued over which one of them was the greatest (the first in Luke 9:46 and Mark 9:34, the second in Matthew 20:24 and Mark 10:41, and the third in Luke 22:24 at the last supper). The first two arguments Jesus responded to by talking with the twelve, and teaching them the importance of not being the greatest but rather to be least, a servant of all.

On the third occasion of this argument, at the last supper, Jesus gave them more than words. This night Jesus knew was His last, but instead of focusing on His trials, He showed the twelve what He meant when He told them to be servant of all. Their Lord took a bowl of water and a towel and put Himself in the place of a servant, and began to wash His disciples' feet. The gospel of John says that Jesus was expressing the full extent of His love. This act changed the tone of the evening, and when Jesus was done He directed His disciples to do the same for one another.

In foot washing Jesus gave us an example of love, humility, and service to others. His example showed that the greatest should serve the least. To His disciples, the lesson was to set aside their feelings of superiority and pride and focus on serving another. This was a sobering lesson to the arguing disciples, a message that is explored deeper in this lesson.

John 13:1 NIV
Having loved his own who were in the world, he now showed them the full extent of his love.

Luke 22:26-27 NKJV
...he who is greatest among you, let him be as the younger, and he who governs as he who serves. For who is greater, he who sits at the table, or he who serves? Is it not he who sits at the table? Yet I am among you as the One who serves.

Genesis 18:3-4 NIV
(Abraham) said, "If I have found favor in your eyes, my lord, do not pass your servant by. Let a little water be brought, and then you may all wash your feet and rest under this tree.

Genesis 43:24 NIV
The steward took the men into Joseph's house, gave them water to wash their feet and provided fodder for their donkeys.

1 Samuel 25:41 NIV
She bowed down with her face to the ground and said, "Here is your maidservant, ready to serve you and wash the feet of my master's servants.

1 Timothy 5:10 NIV
(Care for a widow who) is well known for her good deeds, such as bringing up children, showing hospitality, washing the feet of the saints, helping those in trouble and devoting herself to all kinds of good deeds.

1. What is foot washing?

Foot washing is a sacrament instituted by Jesus Christ, having both an outward sign and an inward work of the Holy Spirit. In foot washing the outward sign is the act of washing another's feet as the Holy Spirit works in us repentance, humility, and love (John 13:1 and Luke 22:26-27).

2. Is foot washing in the Bible?

Washing feet is mentioned as early as the book of Genesis, and in several other Old Testament books. Foot washing was a necessary custom because travel was often on foot, and the land was dry and dusty. Biblical passages indicate that visitors were offered water to wash their feet upon entering a home, or servants would provide water and assist in washing feet. Foot washing was an act of hospitality and service to others. Biblical examples include:

- In Genesis 18, the Lord (a pre-incarnate form of Jesus), and two angels visited Abraham. When Abraham saw his visitors he hurried to them and bowed to the ground, and asked them to stay after offering water to be brought to wash their feet. Abraham's example is one of being hospitable and a humble servant (Genesis 18:3-4).

- When Joseph's brothers returned to Egypt from Canaan (their second trip, Genesis 43), they no doubt arrived with dirty feet. The brothers were brought into Joseph's house, and a servant gave them water to wash their feet (Genesis 43:24).

- David asked Abigail for her hand in marriage, and her reply was one of humility, offering even to wash the feet of David's servants (1 Samuel 25:41).

- As the apostle Paul gave instructions to Timothy about caring for widows, he described a worthy widow as one that was well known for good deeds, hospitality, and washing the feet of the saints (1 Timothy 5:10).

- The gospel of Luke describes an incident where a repentant woman washed the feet of Jesus with her tears and dried his feet with her hair. Although there is not a record of her confessing her sins, her act was one of repentance before Christ. Jesus told her directly, *"Your sins are forgiven… Your faith has saved you, go in peace,"* (Luke 7:47, 50).

- John 13 tells of Jesus washing the feet of His disciples.

3. What led to Jesus washing His disciples' feet?

Jesus washed His disciples' feet on the night of the last supper, the night He was betrayed. The four gospel writers give different details and perspectives of the events of Jesus' last night. John is the only writer that tells of the foot washing, but combining the gospel of John with the others, the following story unfolds of the events leading to the foot washing (Mark 10:35, 37-39, 41-45 and Luke 22:24):

Several days before the Passover celebration, Jesus was in Jericho, about 20 miles northeast of Jerusalem, with His disciples. As they began their walk to Jerusalem, the twelve apostles began to talk among themselves about which one of them was greatest. James and his brother John (the writer of the gospel) upset the other ten, as they were bold enough to approach Jesus and ask if one of them could be seated at his right hand and the other at his left hand in heaven. Jesus responded by saying, "You don't know what you are asking," and went on to explain that He had "not come to be served, but to serve," and they should behave likewise.

As Passover approached, Jesus and His twelve apostles gathered together in an upper room in Jerusalem to celebrate the feast. Once again the twelve argued about which one of them was the greatest. This time instead of telling them that He had not come to be served, but to serve, Jesus began to wash their feet.

4. What was the significance of Jesus washing feet?

The gospel of John gives several points of significance:

- **Love for others**

    First there is showing love for others through foot washing. Instead of giving details of the argument that took place in the upper room, John gives insight into the significance of Jesus' love for His disciples. He sets the stage of the foot washing with this preface:

    John 13:1-4 NIV

    It was just before the Passover Feast. Jesus knew that the time had come for him to leave this world and go to the Father. Having loved his own who were in the world, he now showed them the full extent of his love. The evening meal was being served, and the devil had already prompted Judas Iscariot, son of Simon, to betray Jesus. Jesus knew that the Father had put all things under his power, and that he had come from God and was returning to God; so he got up from the meal, took off his outer clothing, and wrapped a towel around his waist.

Mark 10:35, 37-39, 41-45 NKJV
Then James and John, the sons of Zebedee, came to Him... They said to Him, "Grant us that we may sit, one on Your right hand and the other on Your left, in Your glory." But Jesus said to them, "You do not know what you ask. Are you able to drink the cup that I drink, and be baptized with the baptism that I am baptized with?" They said to Him, "We are able..." And when the ten heard it, they began to be greatly displeased with James and John. But Jesus called them to Himself and said to them, "...whoever desires to become great among you shall be your servant. And whoever of you desires to be first shall be slave of all. For even the Son of Man did not come to be served, but to serve, and to give His life a ransom for many."

Luke 22:24 NKJV
Now there was also a dispute among them, as to which of them should be considered the greatest.

John 13:34-35 NIV
A new command I give you: Love one another. As I have loved you, so you must love one another. By this all men will know that you are my disciples, if you love one another."

John 13:14-16 NIV
Now that I, your Lord and Teacher, have washed your feet, you also should wash one another's feet. I have set you an example that you should do as I have done for you. I tell you the truth, no servant is greater than his master, nor is a messenger greater than the one who sent him.

Mark 10:44 NKJV
And whoever of you desires to be first shall be slave of all.

John 13:2, 10-11 NIV
The evening meal was being served, and the devil had already prompted Judas Iscariot, son of Simon, to betray Jesus... Jesus answered, "A person who has had a bath needs only to wash his feet; his whole body is clean. And you are clean, though not every one of you." For he knew who was going to betray him, and that was why he said not every one was clean.

John 13:38 NIV
I tell you the truth, before the rooster crows, you will disown me three times!

John 21:17 NKJV
He said to him the third time, "Simon, son of John, do you love Me?" Peter was grieved because He said to him the third time, "Do you love Me?" And he said to Him, "Lord, You know all things; You know that I love You." Jesus said to him, "Tend My sheep."

Jesus knew it was His last day, He knew the Father had granted all things to Him, yet He was going to show His disciples the full extent of His love by putting aside all that was taking place in His life on earth, and focusing instead on serving the twelve by washing their feet. After washing their feet, Jesus gave them a new command: To love one another as Jesus had loved them (John 13:34-35).

- **Serving others**

When Jesus finished washing His disciples' feet, He explained what He had done. He told them that He had set an example; as their Lord He had washed their feet and they should follow His example and wash one another's feet. Remember, this was a group of men that were quarrelling among themselves about who was the greatest, and the greatest among them had humbled Himself and washed their feet (John 13:14-16 and Mark 10:44).

- **Forgiveness and cleansing for sins after salvation**

Peter protested when Jesus tried to wash his feet, and said he would not allow it. Jesus explained to Peter that although he did not understand what Jesus was doing, he would understand later. Then Jesus began to speak spiritually. He said that if He did not wash Peter's feet, Peter would have no part with Him. He continued by saying that if a person had bathed, the feet may get dirty and be in need of cleaning, but not the entire body. Jesus emphasized that He was speaking spiritually by indicating that that one in their company was not clean, a reference to Judas, His betrayer (John 13:2, 10-11).

Jesus provided a picture of forgiveness. He was indicating that from time to time a clean person, a person who has repented of his sins and believes in Jesus, would sin and need to repent and be forgiven. This does not mean that one must keep repenting for salvation, but after salvation in a life dedicated to Christ sins are still committed for which repentance is required (see Romans 7).

Again it is Jesus and Peter that provide another example. After the foot washing, Jesus informed Peter that three times he would deny knowing Him before the new day dawned. Peter did not believe it, but this came to pass and he wept bitterly in repentance. Peter was a believer that fell short after his salvation. His forgiveness was assured when he was later given the opportunity to affirm his love for Jesus. After the resurrection, Jesus asked Peter three times, *"Do you love me?"* and He received three affirmative answers (John 13:38 and John 21:17).

5. Is foot washing practiced today?

Jesus said that His example should be followed, a directive that He gave to men who were arguing and thinking too highly of themselves. Foot washing provides an opportunity to put into practice the attitude that Jesus exemplified, one of humility and service to another, setting aside attitudes and thoughts of superiority. Washing another's feet, especially of a person with whom there is an offense, is a way to show true repentance, service, and love. Barriers can be overcome and hard feelings softened by taking on the attitude of Jesus, laying aside personal feelings and truly serving another in humility (John 13:14-15 and John 13:35).

6. How is foot washing conducted?

Foot washing is conducted as Jesus provided the example, serving others in humility by washing and drying another's feet (John 13:4-5). One who is washing should prepare by repenting of feelings and attitudes of superiority and any ill will toward the other, and focus on serving and blessing the other. If our feet are being washed, we should allow the other person as the disciples allowed Jesus, not protesting as Peter did. Jesus washed the feet of men. Christians should follow His lead, men should wash men's feet, and women should wash women's feet

7. Is there a blessing in foot washing?

There are spiritual and practical blessings that come from participating in a foot washing service through washing feet and having feet washed:

- **Love**
  We show the full extent of our love for others and receive their love, following the command of Christ to love one another.

- **Humility**
  We learn to humble ourselves before another, regardless of our standing socially, economically, spiritually, etc. with respect to the other. We learn to receive another's humble approach.

- **Service**
  We are reminded to be servants to others as we serve them through foot washing.

- **Repentance**
  Jesus used clean feet as a spiritual picture of forgiveness, received through repentance. We receive a clean conscience by repenting before God and when necessary to others we have offended.

- **Forgiveness**
  God forgives the truly repentant, and foot washing is a time for Christians to repent of any sins committed against Christ and receive His forgiveness (John 13:17).

John 13:14-15 NIV
Now that I, your Lord and Teacher, have washed your feet, you also should wash one another's feet. I have set you an example that you should do as I have done for you.

John 13:35 NIV
By this all men will know that you are my disciples, if you love one another.

John 13:4-5 NKJV
Jesus rose from supper and laid aside His garments, took a towel and girded Himself. After that, He poured water into a basin and began to wash the disciples' feet, and to wipe them with the towel with which He was girded.

John 13:17
Now that you know these things, you will be blessed if you do them.

Study Questions

1. Read John 13:1-17. What was Jesus' example in footwashing? _____

   _____

   _____

   _____

   _____

   _____

2. What might keep a Christian from practicing what Jesus taught regarding foot washing? Could you offer any advice to this fellow Christian regarding footwashing? _____

   _____

   _____

   _____

   _____

   _____

   _____

3. Can you think of occasions where you might not practice a literal foot washing, but need to serve another in a similar way? How can the attitude required for foot washing be maintained?_____

   _____

   _____

   _____

   _____

   _____

   _____

Lesson Journal

Use this section to record your thoughts on the topics in this lesson.

_____

_____

_____

_____

_____

_____

_____

Lesson 21
Where Do I Go When I Die?

Scripture Reading

- Luke 16:19-31 (the rich man and Lazarus, life after death)
- 1 Corinthians 3:13-15; Revelation 21:8 and 2 Corinthians 5:1-10 (resurrection and judgment)
- 1 Corinthians 15:35-57 (resurrection and the second coming of Christ)
- 1 Thessalonians 4:16-18 (second coming of Christ)
- 2 Corinthians 12:1-4 and Luke 23:43 (paradise)
- Revelation 20:15; 2 Thessalonians 1:5-10 and Matthew 25:30, 41 (hell and judgment)
- 2 Timothy 4:6-8; Matthew 24:46-47 and Luke 19:11-27 jJudgment and rewards)
- Psalm chapter 82 (corrupt judges)

Introduction

Where do I go when I die? It is an age-old question, one that was posed thousands of years ago by Job when he asked, *"If a man die, will he live again?"* (Job 14:14). Job seemed to grasp that the end of physical life was not the end of life, but something more was to come, as he immediately followed his question stating, *"I will wait for my renewal to come. You will call and I will answer you,"* (Job 14:14-15). Job begins to see things more clearly when he later says, *"I know that my Redeemer lives, and that He shall stand at the latter day upon the earth... Whom I shall see for myself, and my eye shall behold, and not another. How my heart yearns within me!"* (Job 19:25, 27).

We now know more than Job about what happens after physical death because Jesus and His apostles have given us more explanation. A Christian has victory over death, because his soul and spirit go on to be with the Lord when the body dies. Though the body is dead, at the second coming of Jesus the body will be raised, resurrected, and incorruptible. Jesus Christ is our example of resurrection, and Paul the apostle taught this reality often. Both Christians and unbelievers will experience a resurrection of the body, which will be followed by judgment before Jesus. Believers will be rewarded for their works done after their salvation, and the unrighteous will be cast into the lake of fire. Many non-Christians are skeptical of teachings such as the resurrection and a place called Hell. This lesson lends insight into what happens after death, and how a good God could send people to Hell.

Luke 23:42-43 NASB
And he was saying, "Jesus, remember me when You come in Your kingdom!" And He said to him, "Truly I say to you, today you shall be with Me in Paradise."

2 Corinthians 5:6-9 NIV
Therefore we are always confident and know that as long as we are at home in the body we are away from the Lord. We live by faith, not by sight. We are confident, I say, and would prefer to be away from the body and at home with the Lord. So we make it our goal to please him, whether we are at home in the body or away from it.

Luke 16:22-24 NASB
(Jesus said), "Now the poor man died and was carried away by the angels to Abraham's bosom; and the rich man also died and was buried. In Hades he lifted up his eyes, being in torment, and saw Abraham far away and Lazarus in his bosom. And he cried out and said, 'Father Abraham, have mercy on me, and send Lazarus so that he may dip the tip of his finger in water and cool off my tongue, for I am in agony in this flame.'"

1 Corinthians 15:35-38, 42
But someone will say, "How are the dead raised? And with what kind of body do they come?" You fool! That which you sow does not come to life unless it dies; and that which you sow, you do not sow the body which is to be, but a bare grain, perhaps of wheat or of something else. But God gives it a body just as He wished, and to each of the seeds a body of its own... So also is the resurrection of the dead. It is sown a perishable body, it is raised an imperishable body.

James 2:26 NIV
As the body without the spirit is dead, so faith without deeds is dead.

Mark 12:26-27 NASB
(Jesus said), "But regarding the fact that the dead rise again, have you not read in the book of Moses, in the passage about the burning bush, how God spoke to him, saying, 'I am the god of Abraham, and the god of Isaac, and the God of Jacob?' He is not the God of the dead, but of the living."

1. What happens when a Christian dies?

Man is a three part being: body, soul, and spirit (refer to Lesson 4, question 10), a parallel to God's tri-unity. The body is the physical portion of man that makes him conscious of the physical world. God breathed into man making him a "living soul" conscious of life. The soul then is the personality of an individual, the inward part of a person that is reflected through the actions of the body; it is the soul that makes one self-conscious. The spirit of a man is that portion which was created in the image and likeness of God.

When a Christian dies:

- The soul and the spirit depart to reside with God (Luke 23:42-43 and 2 Corinthians 5:6-9).

- The soul is conscious, able to discern other souls, and retains a memory of mortal life (the rich man and Lazarus, Luke 16:19-31).

- The body decays, but a seed of the body awaits resurrection. The apostle Paul likened the body to a seed that must die in the ground before new life can spring forth. The same is true of a dead body. A seed of the body remains and will come back to life at the time of the resurrection of the dead (1 Corinthians 15:35-38, 42; James 2:26 and Mark 12:26-27).

2. Where is a Christian's soul and spirit after death?

The soul and spirit of a believer depart the body and go on to be with God in Paradise. When Jesus was dying on the cross, one of the thieves hanging next to him acknowledged the just punishment he was receiving and said, "*Jesus, remember me when You come in Your kingdom!*" Jesus replied to the repentant thief, "*Truly I say to you, today you shall be with Me in Paradise,*" (Luke 23:42-43 NASB).

Jesus spoke of Paradise. It is a real place. Before Jesus died and was resurrected, Paradise was located in the center of the earth, which was referred to in the Bible as *Sheol-Hades* (*Sheol* (Hebrew) and *Hades* (Greek) mean "the place of departed souls"). At that time Sheol-Hades was comprised of two distinct areas separated by an impassable chasm. One side was the abode of the wicked dead, and the other side was called paradise and housed the righteous dead (Refer to story of the rich man and Lazarus in Luke 16:19-31).

After the resurrection of Jesus, Paradise was relocated in the "third heaven." The apostle Paul taught that Jesus had first descended to the lower parts of the earth then ascended leading "captive a host of captives." The righteous dead in Paradise were in a sense captive, and Jesus, having shed his blood and making a way for the righteous dead to be in the presence of God, led them as his liberated captives to a relocated Paradise (1 Corinthians 12:2-4 and Ephesians 4:8-10).

3. What happens when an unbeliever dies?

Like any other person, an unbeliever is a three part being: body, soul, and spirit. The difference between a believer and an unbeliever is the spirit. In the gospel of John, Jesus declared, "I tell you the truth, no one can see the kingdom of God unless he is born again… Flesh gives birth to flesh, but the Spirit gives birth to spirit," (John 3:3, 6). Being born again, or regenerate, has to do with the spirit, and it is a work that is done by the regeneration and renewing of the Holy Spirit (Titus 3:5).

An unregenerate spirit cannot enter the presence of God. Jesus told of a rich man that died and went to Sheol-Hades. The rich man was not a believer, and he discovered that after death his spirit went on to reside in a place of torment. Though he had no mortal body, the rich man was conscious and aware of pain. Sheol-Hades exists at the center of the earth and is the place where the soul and spirit of unbelievers exist and await the resurrection and judgment (Luke 16:22-24 and Titus 3:5-6).

4. Is Sheol-Hades Hell?

There is a difference between Hades and Hell. Sheol-Hades is a place that the Bible describes as located in the center of the earth where the wicked dead abide awaiting the resurrection of the dead and judgment. Hell is a final abode that is not yet populated. It is a place that has been prepared for the devil and his angels. Hell is a place of darkness and torment, and those that will reside there will forever be away from the presence of God (Matthew 25:41 and Matthew 25:30; see also 2 Thessalonians 1:9 and Revelation 20:15).

1 Corinthians 12:2-4
I know a man in Christ who fourteen years ago was caught up to the third heaven. Whether it was in the body or out of the body I do not know–God knows. And I know that this man... was caught up to paradise.

Ephesians 4:8-10 NASB
Therefore it says, "When He ascended on high, He led captive a host of captives, And He gave gifts to men." (Now this expression, "He ascended," what does it mean except that He also had descended into the lower parts of the earth? He who descended is Himself also He who ascended far above all the heavens, so that He might fill all things.)

Luke 16:22-24
... the rich man also died and was buried. In Hades he lifted up his eyes, being in torment, and saw Abraham far away and Lazarus in his bosom. And he cried out and said, "Father Abraham, have mercy on me, and send Lazarus so that he may dip the tip of his finger in water and cool off my tongue, for I am in agony in this flame."

Titus 3:5-6
He saved us, not on the basis of deeds which we have done in righteousness, but according to His mercy, by the washing of regeneration and renewing by the Holy Spirit, whom He poured out upon us richly through Jesus Christ our Savior...

Matthew 25:41 NIV
Then he will say to those on his left, "Depart from me, you who are cursed, into the eternal fire prepared for the devil and his angels."

Matthew 25:30 NIV
And throw that worthless servant outside, into the darkness, where there will be weeping and gnashing of teeth.

5. Is there a resurrection of the dead?

Job asked this question thousands of years ago, asking, *"If a man dies, will he live again?"* (Job 14:14). The answer is yes; the resurrection of the dead will take place at the return of Jesus Christ. The Bible teaches that Christ is going to return, the dead in Christ will be resurrected first, and then those who are alive in Christ will meet Him in the air (1 Thessalonians 4:16-18 and 1 Corinthians 15:52-53). The apostle Paul teaches that at the time of the resurrection this saying will come true: *"Death has been swallowed up in victory. Where, O death, is your victory Where, O death, is your sting?"* (1 Corinthians. 15:54-55). So a Christian need not fear death.

The wicked will also be raised from the dead to stand in judgment before Christ (John 5:28-29; see also Acts 24:15).

6. Is there going to be a judgment?

There is a judgment that will be carried out by Christ when He returns. All will stand before Christ to render an account of their actions on earth, whether they *be good or bad* (2 Corinthians 5:10). Believers who have been washed with a *washing of regeneration and renewing by the Holy Spirit* are justified to stand before Christ, their works after salvation being judged. The unregenerate will be judged for their sins (John 5:28-29; Hebrews 9:27 and 2 Corinthians 5:10; see also 2 Thessalonians 1:7-10).

7. What happens at the judgment?

Jesus Christ will judge both the righteous and the wicked based on their works on earth (Daniel 7:9-10 and Luke 12:42-46). Believers will be judged on their life after salvation and will receive everlasting life and rewards. Paul explained it this way; *(Each man's) work will be shown for what it is, because the Day will bring it to light. It will be revealed with fire, and the fire will test the quality of each man's work. If what he has built survives, he will receive his reward. If it is burned up, he will suffer loss; he himself will be saved, but only as one escaping through the flames,"* (1 Corinthians 3:13-15 NIV). So believers will be judged and rewarded according to their works, their expressions of true faith in Jesus Christ that come after salvation.

Those who have rejected Jesus will suffer the second death as described in Revelation 21:8 (NIV): *"But the cowardly, the unbelieving, the vile, the murderers, the sexually immoral, those who practice magic arts, the idolaters and all liars—their place will be in the fiery lake of burning sulfur. This is the second death."*

8. Would a good God send people to Hell?

Jesus Christ is a righteous judge, the only truly righteous judge (Romans 2:11, Proverbs 24:12). He is just. Psalm 82 says God granted men on earth the authority to judge earthly matters, but their judgment was wicked. God said that the authority He granted made these judges gods in the eyes of men, but they abused their power: *God presides in the great assembly; He gives judgment among the "gods": "How long will you defend the unjust and show partiality to the wicked... I said, 'You are "gods"; you are all sons of the Most High.' But you will die like mere men..."* (Psalm 82:1-2, 6-7 NIV).

When a crime is brought before an earthly judge, people expect justice; the criminal is to be punished. Psalm 82 shows this expectation is put on human judges who can be corrupt. If justice is expected from corrupt earthly judges, it should also be expected of Jesus Christ who is going to judge all who have broken His laws and remain unrepentant. Jesus cannot be corrupt like earthly judges who *defend the unjust and show partiality to the wicked*, (Psalm 82:2 NIV).

9. What are the rewards for the righteous?

The Bible speaks of rewards for believers based on their works after salvation. These are not works that earn salvation (Titus 3:5), but are actions expressed after salvation in concert with faith in Jesus Christ (Matthew 24:46-47 and Matthew 6:19-21).

Jesus said of believers who persevere through suffering because they believe in Him, *"great is your reward in heaven,"* (Matthew 5:12). Jesus also told several parables about receiving rewards after the judgment (see Luke 19:11-27 and Mark 12:1-12), and the apostle Paul spoke of receiving a crown of righteousness, not only for himself, but also for those who believe in Jesus (2 Timothy 4:6-8).

Romans 2:11 NIV
For God does not show favoritism.

Proverbs 24:12
Shall not he render to every man according to his works?

Titus 3:5
Not by works of righteousness which we have done, but according to his mercy he saved us, by the washing of regeneration, and renewing of the Holy Ghost.

Matthew 24:46-47
Blessed is that servant, whom his lord when he cometh shall find so doing. Verily I say unto you, That he shall make him ruler over all his goods.

Matthew 6:19-21 NIV
Do not store up for yourselves treasures on earth, where moth and rust destroy, and where thieves break in and steal. But store up for yourselves treasures in heaven, where moth and rust do not destroy, and where thieves do not break in and steal. For where your treasure is, there your heart will be also.

2 Timothy 4:6-8
For I am already being poured out as a drink offering, and the time of my departure has come. I have fought the good fight, I have finished the course, I have kept the faith; in the future there is laid up for me the crown of righteousness, which the Lord, the righteous Judge, will award to me on that day; and not only to me, but also to all who have loved His appearing.

Study Questions

1. A Christian friend has just died. What words of comfort from the scriptures in this lesson can you offer?_____

    _____

    _____

    _____

    _____

    _____

2. "When you're dead, you're dead—there is no afterlife." Give a few scriptures that counter this statement. _____

    _____

    _____

    _____

    _____

    _____

3. Describe the results of the judgment of believers and nonbelievers. _____

    _____

    _____

    _____

    _____

    _____

Lesson Journal

Use this section to record your thoughts on the topics in this lesson.

_____

_____

_____

_____

_____

_____

Lesson 22
Examine Yourself

Scripture Reading

- Luke 22:14-20; 1 Corinthians 10:15-17 and 1 Corinthians 11:17-34 (the Lord's Supper)

- Exodus 12:3-14 (Passover)

- John 1:29 and 1 Corinthians 5:7-8 (the Lamb of God)

- Hebrews 9:13-15 (Jesus the final sacrifice)

Introduction

On the night before Jesus died He instituted a sacrament with His disciples, the Lord's Supper. Jesus used broken bread and a cup of wine to signify His body would be broken and His blood shed as a final sacrifice for all. He instructed His disciples to continue the practice as a memorial. The memorial of the Lord's Supper, or Communion, is a fulfillment of the Old Testament Passover. As the Passover was an annual feast that celebrated the salvation of Israel from the bondage of Egypt by shedding the blood of a spotless lamb, Jesus gave His life and shed His blood at the time of Passover ending the need for sacrifice. His blood is sufficient to take away sin, and John the Baptist rightly referred to Him as the *"lamb of God who takes away the sin of the world,"* (John 1:29).

The Lord's Supper is an important aspect in the life of a Christian. Receiving Communion gives a believer an opportunity to reflect on and remember the sacrifice of Jesus, have hope in His resurrection, and look forward to His return. This sacrament reaffirms the new covenant ushered in by Jesus. It is a time for cleansing through self-examination, which the apostle Paul teaches is a way to steer free of judgment. This lesson takes a close look at Paul's Communion instructions, and the blessings that follow those who rightly partake of the Lord's Supper.

Luke 22:14-20 NKJV

When the hour had come, He sat down, and the twelve apostles with Him. Then He said to them, "With fervent desire I have desired to eat this Passover with you before I suffer; for I say to you, I will no longer eat of it until it is fulfilled in the kingdom of God." Then He took the cup, and gave thanks, and said, "Take this and divide it among yourselves; for I say to you, I will not drink of the fruit of the vine until the kingdom of God comes." And He took bread, gave thanks and broke it, and gave it to them, saying, "This is My body which is given for you; do this in remembrance of Me." Likewise He also took the cup after supper, saying, "This cup is the new covenant in My blood, which is shed for you.

1 Corinthians 5:7-8 NKJV

Purge out therefore the old leaven, that ye may be a new lump, as ye are unleavened. For even Christ our Passover is sacrificed for us: therefore let us keep the feast, not with old leaven, neither with the leaven of malice and wickedness; but with the unleavened bread of sincerity and truth.

John 1:29

The next day John saw Jesus coming toward him and said, "Look! There is the Lamb of God who takes away the sin of the world!

Hebrews 10:4

For it is impossible for the blood of bulls and goats to take away sins.

Hebrews 9:13-15 NASB

For if the blood of goats and bulls and the ashes of a heifer sprinkling those who have been defiled sanctify for the cleansing of the flesh, how much more will the blood of Christ, who through the eternal Spirit offered Himself without blemish to God, cleanse your conscience from dead works to serve the living God? For this reason He is the mediator of a new covenant, so that, since a death has taken place for the redemption of the transgressions that were committed under the first covenant, those who have been called may receive the promise of the eternal inheritance.

1. What is the Lord's Supper?

The Lord's Supper (see 1 Corinthians 11:20) or Communion, (see 1 Corinthians 10:16) is a sacrament established by Jesus Christ on the night before He died. As a sacrament, the Lord's Supper has both an outward part and an inward work of grace. The Lord's Supper uses bread and wine (or fruit of the vine, juice) as the outward sign. Those who receive in faith the bread receive by faith the benefits of Christ's body as broken for sin, and those who in faith receive the cup, receive by faith the new covenant of Jesus Christ.

2. What brought about the Lord's Supper?

On the last night of His life on earth, Jesus celebrated the Passover meal with His disciples. During the meal Jesus began to speak of His imminent suffering, and He took bread and broke it, saying it was His body. He also took a cup of wine and said it was His blood. Jesus used the bread and wine as symbols of His approaching suffering and death.

Jesus instituted the Lord's Supper on the night before He died as He celebrated the Passover (Luke 22:14-20). The next day He was crucified, becoming our Passover (1 Corinthians 5:7-8). This is why the Lord's Supper is sometimes called the Christian Passover.

3. How is Jesus our Passover?

- **Salvation by the blood of the Lamb**

    At the first Passover, God directed Moses to instruct each family to select a year old lamb without defect to be slaughtered. The blood of the lamb was to be wiped on the top and the sides of the doorframe of the family's house. The blood was to signify that the house was to be passed over, and the Lord would not strike down the firstborn as He was going to do to Egypt. The blood of the Passover sacrifice was used as a means of salvation for the Israelites.

    John the Baptist referred to Jesus as *"The Lamb of God, who takes away the sin of the world,"* (John 1:29). The apostle Paul in his first letter to the Corinthians said, *"Christ our Passover is sacrificed for us,"* (1 Corinthians 5:7). Paul's reference to Jesus as a Passover sacrifice indicates that there is a "Christian Passover." Jesus, by His sacrifice on the cross, became a Passover sacrifice. His sacrifice was superior to the sacrifice of animals, and did away with the need for animal sacrifice. No longer was the blood of animals necessary to cover sin, because the blood of Jesus is sufficient to take away sin (Hebrews 10:4 and Hebrews 9:13-15).

- **Passover is a remembrance**

  After the first Passover, God instituted the annual Passover feast to commemorate Israel's salvation from Egypt (Exodus 12:14). Jesus said that the Lord's Supper should be celebrated as a remembrance (Luke 22:12 and 1 Corinthians 11:24-25). In the Lord's Supper we remember our salvation bought by Jesus Christ when He submitted His own life to die on a cross.

4. What should we remember during the Lord's Supper?

The Lord's Supper is an opportunity to recall what Jesus has done, what He is doing, and what He is going to do. It is an opportunity to remember the past, consider the present, and look to the future.

- **Remembering the past**

  Communion is a reminder of what Jesus Christ has done by becoming a man and giving His life as a payment for sin. The broken bread is a sign of His broken body, and the cup a sign of His shed blood. Jesus said, *"This cup is the new covenant in My blood,"* (1 Corinthians 11:25). He was tortured, spit upon, humiliated, stripped, and nailed to a cross, and left to die a slow and painful death. The Lord's Supper is a time to recall all that Jesus did so that His sacrifice is never a fading memory, trivialized, taken for granted, or forgotten. It is an opportunity to remember and reaffirm the new covenant which allows anyone who believes to have a relationship with Him.

- **Consider the present**

  His Supper speaks to the here-and-now as a present reminder of salvation, an ongoing relationship with Him, and of fellowship in the Body of Christ. Paul said, *"Since there is one bread, we who are many are one body; for we all partake of the one bread,"* (1 Corinthians 10:17).

- **Look forward to the future**

  The Lord's Supper looks to the future. Paul advised that by partaking of the Lord's Supper we *"proclaim His death until He comes,"* (1 Corinthians 11:26). It is a reminder that Jesus did not die in vain, but was resurrected and promised to return.

Exodus 12:14
Now this day will be a memorial to you, and you shall celebrate it as a feast to the LORD; throughout your generations you are to celebrate it as a permanent ordinance.

Luke 22:12 NASB
And when He had taken some bread and given thanks, He broke it and gave it to them, saying, "This is My body which is given for you; do this in remembrance of Me."

1 Corinthians 11:24-25
Take, eat: this is my body, which is broken for you: this do in remembrance of me. After the same manner also he took the cup, when he had supped, saying, This cup is the new testament in my blood: this do ye, as oft as ye drink it, in remembrance of me.

1 Corinthians 11:16-30 NASB
But if one is inclined to be contentious, we have no other practice, nor have the churches of God. But in giving this instruction, I do not praise you, because you come together not for the better but for the worse. For, in the first place, when you come together as a church, I hear that divisions exist among you; and in part I believe it. For there must also be factions among you, so that those who are approved may become evident among you. Therefore when you come together in one place, it is not to eat the Lord's Supper. For in eating, each one takes his own supper ahead of others; and one is hungry and another is drunk. What! Do you not have houses to eat and drink in? Or do you despise the church of God and shame those who have nothing? What shall I say to you? Shall I praise you in this? I do not praise you. For I received from the Lord that which I also delivered to you: that the Lord Jesus on the same night in which He was betrayed took bread; and when He had given thanks, He broke it and said, "Take, eat; this is My body which is broken for you; do this in remembrance of Me." In the same manner He also took the cup after supper, saying, "This cup is the new covenant in My blood. This do, as often as you drink it, in remembrance of Me." For as often as you eat this bread and drink this cup, you proclaim the Lord's death till He comes. Therefore whoever eats this bread or drinks this cup of the Lord in an unworthy manner will be guilty of the body and blood of the Lord. But let a man examine himself, and so let him eat of the bread and drink of the cup. For he who eats and drinks in an unworthy manner eats and drinks judgment to himself, not discerning the Lord's body.

1 Corinthians 5:7-8 NKJV
Purge out therefore the old leaven, that ye may be a new lump, as ye are unleavened. For even Christ our Passover is sacrificed for us: therefore let us keep the feast, not with old leaven, neither with the leaven of malice and wickedness; but with the unleavened bread of sincerity and truth.

5. How should we take the Lord's Supper?

The apostle Paul in his first letter to the Corinthian church advised its members about properly partaking of the Lord's Supper. Their methods were disorderly, some eating a full meal, others getting drunk, yet others going hungry. Paul gave them instruction on proper conduct when partaking of the Lord's Supper (1 Corinthians 11:20-30).

6. What does it mean, a man must examine himself?

Paul was giving a warning against judgment. He continued his instruction by stating, *"For if we would judge ourselves, we would not be judged. But when we are judged, we are chastened by the Lord, that we may not be condemned with the world,"* (1 Corinthians 11:31-32). Self-examination is a time to repent of sin, and consider bad attitudes toward others (Paul had mentioned the Corinthians were disregarding each other). These sins hinder a relationship with Jesus.

Paul warns that to partake of the Lord's Supper without self-examination is to partake in an unworthy manner, not discerning the Lord's body. To be worthy does not have to do with works, but with being repentant and contrite. This is an inward grace that is part of the sacrament. Paul advised the judgment of eating and drinking in and unworthy manner was very serious when he said, *"For this reason many are weak and sick among you, and many sleep,"* (1 Corinthians 11:30).

7. What does "not discerning the Lord's body" mean?

To discern is to perceive or recognize, and can be akin to appreciate. Not discerning the Lord's body is not recognizing or appreciating all that Christ has done by giving His life. Professing to be a Christian yet living contrary, practicing sin, harboring unconfessed sin or going against any of the commands of Christ are all a failure to discern the Lord's body.

The context of Paul's instruction also has to do with the corporate Body of Christ, the body of believers. He preceded his instruction on Communion by reprimanding the Corinthians for divisions and factions in their church, and for despising the church and heaping shame on the poor believers (1 Corinthians 11:16-21). They were not a unified community of believers, and were neglecting the needy among them. Today one might describe their church as "cliquey," a behavior that does not appreciate or recognize the Body of Christ. It is not discerning, and the taking of communion is unto judgment (1 Corinthians 5:7-8).

Jesus taught a parable pointing out that neglecting others is a failure to recognize Him, and leads to judgment. This parable takes place on the day of judgment, where Jesus will tell some that they did not give Him a room, did not clothe Him, did not give Him food or drink, and refused to visit Him in prison. Then they will say, *"'Lord, when did we see You hungry or thirsty or a stranger or naked or sick or in prison, and did not minister to You?' Then He will answer them, saying, 'Assuredly, I say to you, inasmuch as you did not do it to one of the least of these, you did not do it to Me.' And these will go away into everlasting punishment, but the righteous into eternal life,"* (Matthew 25:44-46).

8. Are there blessings in taking the Lord's Supper?

Blessing comes from participating in the Lord's Supper (1 Corinthians 10:15-17). Paul describes the Communion cup as a *"cup of blessing which we bless."* From rightly taking part, there are these blessings:

- Repentance and forgiveness through confession

- We are not judged, as we have judged ourselves

- Believers are in unity properly discerning the Lord's body

- We remain mindful of the sacrifice of Jesus Christ

- Our covenant with Him is reaffirmed

1 Corinthians 10:15-17 NKJV
I speak as to wise men; judge for yourselves what I say. The cup of blessing which we bless, is it not the communion of the blood of Christ? The bread which we break, is it not the communion of the body of Christ? For we, though many, are one bread and one body; for we all partake of that one bread.

Study Questions

1. From your reading of 1 Corinthians 11, why is self-examination so important in the Lord's Supper?

_____

_____

_____

_____

_____

2. Can you give some examples of not discerning the Lord's body? _____

_____

_____

_____

_____

3. What do we miss if we don't participate in Communion? _____

_____

_____

_____

_____

Lesson Journal

Use this section to record your thoughts on the topics in this lesson.

_____

_____

_____

_____

_____

_____

_____

_____

Lesson 23

Prayer

Scripture Reading

- Matthew 6:9-13 (the Lord's Prayer)

- Philippians 4:6 and Psalm 100 (praise, thanksgiving and prayer)

- Matthew 6:5-7 (attitude in prayer)

- John 4:24; Jude 1:20; Ephesians 6:18 and Romans 8:26-27 (praying in the Holy Spirit)

- Isaiah 59:2; Proverbs 28:9; Matthew 6:15 and 1 Peter 3:7 (sin and prayer)

- Matthew 17:20 and James 1:6-7 (faith and prayer)

- Matthew 26:39-42 and James 4:3 (your will [motives] or God's will in prayer)

- Mark 6:12-23 and James 5:14-15 (prayer and anointing with oil)

Introduction

Prayer at its core is communication with God: Talking to Him, singing to Him, worshiping and sharing thoughts with Him. These are all forms of communicating and building a relationship with God. Examples of communication with God are throughout the Bible, starting in the very beginning with God and Adam. Prayer was encouraged throughout the Old Testament and Jesus and His apostles continued to teach and exemplify prayer in the New Testament.

Prayer can be both individual and with a group of others. Individual prayer is central to an ongoing and growing relationship with God, and as such can be very personal and intimate. Community prayer builds bonds of unity with others as the needs of the group or another individual are raised to God. There is much given in God's Word that addresses both individual and corporate prayer.

This lesson gives an overview of prayer while focusing on some key elements of prayer and common questions that are raised on the topic. The lesson is an introduction to prayer, as prayer is central to the life of a Christian with much more to learn as a relationship with God develops and deepens.

Galatians 4:6 NIV
Because you are *sons*, God sent the Spirit of his Son into our hearts, the Spirit who calls out "Abba, Father".

Ephesians 3:14 NIV
For this reason I kneel before the Father...

Psalm 100:1-2, 4
Make a joyful noise unto the LORD, all ye lands. Serve the LORD with gladness: come before his presence with singing... Enter into his gates with thanksgiving, and into his courts with praise: be thankful unto him, and bless his name.

Luke 17:21 KJV
...the kingdom of God is within you.

John 4:34 NIV
"My food", said Jesus, "is to do the will of him who sent me..."

Matthew 26:39,42 NIV
"...Yet not as I will, but as you will... May your will be done."

Proverbs 30:8 NIV
Keep falsehood and lies far from me; give me neither poverty or riches, but give me only my daily bread.

Luke 11:4 NASB
And forgive us our sins, for we ourselves also forgive everyone who is indebted to us.

Mark 11:25 NASB
Whenever you stand praying, forgive, if you have anything against anyone, so that your Father who is in heaven will also forgive you your transgressions.

Luke 22:40 NIV
...Pray so that you will not fall into temptation.

1 Chronicles 29:11 NIV
"Yours, O Lord, is the greatness and the power and the glory and the majesty and the splendor, for everything in heaven and earth is yours. Yours, O Lord, is the kingdom; you are exalted as head over all."

Psalm 145:10-13 NIV
All you have made will praise you, O Lord; your saints will extol you. They will tell of the glory of your kingdom and speak of your might, so that all men may know of your mighty acts and the glorious splendor of your kingdom. Your kingdom is an everlasting kingdom, and your dominion endures through all generations...

1. What is prayer?

Prayer is communicating with God by addressing Him with worship, adoration, thanksgiving, or supplication. Prayer can be audible, by thought, put in writing, or even in song. Prayer is part of an ongoing and growing relationship with God.

2. How should I pray?

Jesus' disciples had a similar request of Jesus. They said, "Lord, teach us to pray." Jesus responded with what is called the Lord's Prayer: *"After this manner therefore pray ye: Our Father which art in heaven, Hallowed be thy name. Thy kingdom come. Thy will be done in earth, as it is in heaven. Give us this day our daily bread. And forgive us our debts, as we forgive our debtors. And lead us not into temptation, but deliver us from evil: For thine is the kingdom, and the power, and the glory, for ever. Amen,"* (Matthew 6:9-13).

The Lord's Prayer serves as a model prayer. Breaking it down into separate phrases we can use it to learn how to pray:

- **Our Father which art in heaven, Hallowed be thy name**

  Prayer begins with worship. Acknowledge God as your Father in Heaven, and honor and praise His name (Galatians 4:6; Ephesians 3:14 and Psalm 100:1-2, 4).

- **Thy kingdom come. Thy will be done in earth, as it is in heaven**

  Be motivated by His will, not your own (Luke 17:21; John 4:34 and Matthew 26:39,42; see also Mark 3:35 and Ephesians 5:10,17).

- **Give us this day our daily bread**

  Pray for your needs (Proverbs 30:8; see also Philippians 4:6).

- **And forgive us our debts, as we forgive our debtors**

  Ask for forgiveness, and expect it if you forgive those that seek your forgiveness (Luke 11:4 and Mark 11:25; see also Matthew 6:14-15; Ephesians 4:32 and Colossians 3:13).

- **And lead us not into temptation, but deliver us from evil**

  Temptation itself is not a sin, but a trial or test that can lead to sin. We can pray to be kept from the test and delivered from evil (Luke 22:40; see also 2 Thessalonians 3:3 and 2 Timothy 4:18).

- **For thine is the kingdom, and the power, and the glory, for ever**

  The doxology—an expression of praise to God. The prayer is encompassed by praise, as it is opened and closed with praise to God (1 Chronicles 29:11 and Psalm 145:10-13).

3. Should I pray alone, or with others?

Prayer is both individual and corporate. As individuals, prayer is part of an intimate relationship with God through Jesus His son. Individual prayer to God is not something to be done for public recognition. Jesus frowned on such behavior, advising that individual prayer is a time between the Father and His child not done before men, but instead done in secret. It is a time for closeness with God, admitting faults and failures, asking forgiveness and seeking His direction, guidance, blessing of petitions, and a time to pray in the Holy Spirit. Jesus not only spoke of individual prayer, He was a living example as He often went off by Himself to pray to His Father (Matthew 6:6 and Matthew 14:23).

Corporate prayer is prayer that unites two or more Christian believers together before God. Both the Old and New Testament give many examples where believers united in prayer for a common goal. A key to group prayer is unity and agreement. Prayer in harmony and agreement with others builds bonds of unity as God is approached for needs of another or a shared purpose. Collective prayer also offers a time to learn about prayer while agreeing with others (Matthew 18:19-20; Acts 2:42 and Acts 1:14).

4. What is praying in the Holy Spirit?

Praying in the Holy Spirit encompasses the full spectrum of prayer, and does not mean exclusively "praying in tongues." Certainly praying in tongues is a way to "pray in the Spirit" but not the only way.

What then, does "praying in the Holy Spirit" mean? The proper way to understand this phrase is: "pray in the Spirit" as opposed to "pray in the flesh." A key is to consider the motivation for prayer. For example: the Pharisees were dedicated to prayer, but was the Holy Spirit "in them" and guiding them? The Pharisees were motivated by religious instinct, showing off, legalism, and carnality (their flesh). All such prayer is worthless, an expression of vanity—even if in "tongues." Instead, pray at the prompting of the Holy Spirit and by His leading in the way that is fit for the need, by His grace.

Don't let the idea of "praying in the Spirit" be a "tongues only" mode of prayer, for there are many ways to "pray in the Spirit" besides the gift of tongues. Let the Spirit lead you to pray with the type of prayer needed in the moment (Matthew 6:5; Jude 1:20; Ephesians 6:18 and John 3:8).

Matthew 6:6 NIV
But when you pray, go into your room, close the door and pray to your Father, who is unseen. Then your Father, who sees what is done in secret, will reward you.

Matthew 14:23
After he had dismissed them, he went up on a mountainside by himself to pray. When evening came, he was there alone...

Matthew 18:19-20
Again I say unto you, That if two of you shall agree on earth as touching any thing that they shall ask, it shall be done for them of my Father which is in heaven. For where two or three are gathered together in my name, there am I in the midst of them.

Acts 2:42 NIV
They devoted themselves to the apostles' teaching and to the fellowship, to the breaking of bread and to prayer.

Acts 1:14 NIV
They all joined together constantly in prayer...

Matthew 6:5 NIV
And when you pray, do not be like the hypocrites, for they love to pray standing in the synagogues and on the street corners to be seen by men. I tell you the truth, they have received their reward in full.

Jude 1:20 NIV
But you, dear friends, build yourselves up in your most holy faith and pray in the Holy Spirit.

Ephesians 6:18 NIV
And pray in the Spirit on all occasions with *all kinds* of prayers and requests...

John 3:8 NASB
The wind blows where it wishes, and you hear the sound of it, but do not know where it comes from and where it is going; so is *every one* who is born of the Spirit.

Romans 8:26-27
Likewise the Spirit also helpeth our infirmities: for we know not what we should pray for as we ought: but the Spirit itself maketh intercession for us with goanings which cannot be uttered. And he that searcheth the hearts knoweth what is the mind of the Spirit, because he maketh intercession for the saints according to the will of God.

John 4:24
God is a Spirit: and they that worship him must worship him in spirit and in truth.

Psalm 51:10, 15, 17
Create in me a clean heart, O God; and renew a right spirit within me... O Lord, open thou my lips; and my mouth shall show forth thy praise... The sacrifices of God are a broken spirit: a broken and a contrite heart, O God, thou wilt not despise.

Psalm 95:6 NIV
Come let us bow down in worship, let us kneel before the Lord our Maker.

Romans 14:11 NIV
Every knee will bow before me; every tongue will confess to God.

Acts 21:5 NIV
...and there on the beach we knelt to pray.

Psalm 123:1 NIV
I lift up my eyes to you, to you whose throne is in heaven.

John 11:41 NASB
...Jesus looked upward and said, "Father, I thank you for having heard me."

1 Timothy 2:1, 8 NIV
I urge, then, first of all, that requests, prayers, intercession and thanksgiving be made for everyone... I want men everywhere to lift up holy hands in prayer...

Luke 18:1, 7 NIV
Then Jesus told his disciples a parable to show them that they should always pray and not give up... will not God bring about justice for his chosen ones, who cry out to him day and night? Will he keep putting them off?

Matthew 6:5, 7 NIV
And when you pray, do not be like the hypocrites, for they love to pray standing in the synagogues and on the street corners to be seen by men. I tell you the truth, they have received their reward in full... And when you pray, do not keep on babbling like pagans, for they think they will be heard because of their many words.

5. When should I pray in tongues?

The apostle Paul taught that prayer with other believers should be understood. Does this mean that Paul preferred prayer with the understanding to praying in tongues? In the church, in the fellowship of other believers, the answer is yes, but in private prayer to God praying in tongues is a powerful prayer mode of which Paul approved. Paul said, *"For anyone who speaks in a tongue does not speak to men but to God. Indeed, no one understands him; he utters mysteries with his spirit... So what shall I do? I will pray with my spirit, but I will also pray with my mind; I will sing with my spirit, but I will also sing with my mind... I thank God that I speak in tongues more than all of you. But in the church I would rather speak five intelligible words to instruct others than ten thousand words in a tongue... do not forbid to speak in tongues,"* (1 Corinthians 14:2, 15, 18-19, 39 NIV).

Prayer in tongues is spiritual communication with God where the Holy Spirit makes intercession for a believer and he is edified (built up). When the right words to pray escape us, the Holy Spirit helps us to pray according to the will of God. Prayer in the Holy Spirit is a gift that should not be neglected (Romans 8:26-27 and John 4:24; see also Ephesians 6:18).

6. When I pray do I have to kneel?

The Bible does not teach a specific posture for prayer, but of a variety of ways to approach God that are fitting to a given situation. For example, repentant prayers are often in a position of humility such as laying face down or prostrate. Joyful prayers are sometimes with bowing down and sometimes with faces looking upward and hands held high. God does not require a special stance, but is concerned with the intentions of the heart (Psalm 51:10, 15, 17; Psalm 95:6; Romans 14:11; Acts 21:5; Psalm 123:1; John 11:41 and Timothy 2:1, 8; see also Psalm 134:2 and Psalm 63:4).

7. Can I pray the same prayer more than one time?

Jesus said don't pray like the pagans with many words, but did advise that prayer could be persistent. That is, if a prayer isn't answered, it can be prayed again. How does the idea that we should not use "many words" in prayer harmonize with the instruction and examples of persistent prayer? The key is to understand that there is no magic in repetition or in the form of words. Rather, the issue is relational: being faithful and determined in going to Him. God knows in advance what we need or desire, and He does not need to be lectured. Instead, go to Him consistently and persistently with simple humility to make requests known (Luke 18:1, 7 and Matthew 6:5, 7).

8. What if God doesn't answer my prayer?

The Bible speaks of three things that affect prayer: sin, faith, and will.

- **Sin**

    Sin hinders prayers. Sins such as harboring anger, mistreating another, selfishness, not heeding the Word of God, unforgiveness, or any other unrepented sin interferes in a relationship with God and affects prayer. If sin is the issue, make amends with others, repent before God, and ask for forgiveness (Isaiah 59:2; 1 Peter 3:7; Matthew 5:23-24; Matthew 6:15; Proverbs 28:9 and Psalm 66:18).

- **Faith**

    Throughout the Old Testament the prayers of the nation of Israel were not heard for lack of faith, or simply put, unbelief. Even after witnessing great miracles of God, the faith of Israel quickly waned. Moses contended with people who lost their faith in God after they had witnessed ten plagues against Egypt and were led across the Red Sea on dry ground.

    In the New Testament Jesus uses the phrases *"O ye of little faith,"* and *"Because of your unbelief,"* on several occasions to describe those that doubt His ability (Matthew 14:31; James 1:6-7 and Matthew 17:20; see also Matthew 16:8).

- **Will**

    Will has to do with the motivation behind praying (James 4:3)—is it according to our own motivation or the will of the Father? Praying according to the will of the Father is necessary, this is why praying in the Spirit is such a powerful gift.

    Jesus prayed the same prayer three times, but He prayed according to the will of the Father, saying each time, *"Yet not as I will, but as you will..."* (Matthew 26:39 NIV). The apostle Paul brought the same prayer to God three times regarding a "thorn in the flesh." Although Paul pleaded with God, the will of God was that Paul's flesh would not be healed. Paul explained it this way, *"Three times I pleaded with the Lord to take [the thorn in my flesh] away from me. But he said to me, 'My grace is sufficient for you, for my power is made perfect in weakness,'"* (2 Corinthians 12:8-9 NIV).

    In both the prayers of Jesus and Paul, God did not grant their request, and they each accepted the will of the Father.

Isaiah 59:2
But your iniquities have separated between you and your God, and your sins have hid his face from you, that he will not hear.

1 Peter 3:7
Likewise, ye husbands, dwell with them according to knowledge, giving honour unto the wife, as unto the weaker vessel, and as being heirs together of the grace of life; that your prayers be not hindered.

Matthew 5:23-24
Therefore if thou bring thy gift to the altar, and there rememberest that thy brother hath ought against thee; Leave there thy gift before the altar, and go thy way; first be reconciled to thy brother, and then come and offer thy gift.

Matthew 6:15
But if ye forgive not men their trespasses, neither will your Father forgive your trespasses.

Proverbs 28:9
He that turneth away his ear from hearing the law, even his prayer shall be abomination.

Psalm 66:18
If I regard iniquity in my heart, the Lord will not hear me:

Matthew 14:31 NIV
Immediately Jesus reached out his hand and caught him. "You of little faith," he said, "why did you doubt?"

James 1:6-7
But let him ask in faith, nothing wavering. For he that wavereth is like a wave of the sea driven with the wind and tossed. For let not that man think that he shall receive any thing of the Lord.

Matthew 17:20 NIV
He replied, "Because you have so little faith. I tell you the truth, if you have faith as small as a mustard seed, you can say to this mountain, 'Move from here to there' and it will move. Nothing will be impossible for you."

James 4:3 NIV
When you ask, you do not receive, because you ask with wrong motives, that you may spend what you get on your pleasures.

9. I'm sick; whom should I ask to pray for me?

When in need, ask other Christians and your church to pray (Galatians 6:2). If the need is specifically sickness, James advised to go to the elders of the church, giving this instruction, *"Is any sick among you? let him call for the elders of the church,"* (James 5:14 NIV). The elders of the church are charged with praying for the sick and anointing the sick with oil.

10. Why do the elders use oil?

Throughout the Old Testament oil was used for holy purposes. The priests were consecrated and ordained unto God as oil was poured upon their heads: *"Then shalt thou take the anointing oil, and pour it upon his head, and anoint him,"* (Exodus 29:7). During such ceremonies oil was used generously, as it ran down the priest's beard and clothing: *"It is like the precious ointment upon the head, that ran down upon the beard, even Aaron's beard: that went down to the skirts of his garments,"* (Psalm 133:2). The kings of Israel were also anointed with oil as they took up office.

In the New Testament oil was used to promote healing as the example of the Good Samaritan shows when Jesus said; *"he went to him and bandaged his wounds, pouring on oil and wine,"* (Luke 10:33). Jesus also taught His disciples to anoint the sick with oil and this practice continued in the New Testament church (Mark 6:12-13 and James 5:14-15).

Galatians 6:2 NIV
Carry each other's burdens, and in this way you will fulfill the law of Christ.

Mark 6:12-13
So they went out and preached that people should repent. And they cast out many demons, and anointed with oil many who were sick, and healed them.

James 5:14-15
Is any sick among you? let him call for the elders of the church; and let them pray over him, anointing him with oil in the name of the Lord: And the prayer of faith shall save the sick, and the Lord shall raise him up; and if he have committed sins, they shall be forgiven him.

Study Questions

1. Read Matthew 6:9-13. Does the example of Jesus give you a model for prayer? Could you use this to help a new Christian who does not know how to pray? _____

    _____

    _____

    _____

2. A Christian friend wonders why you are going to a prayer meeting when you can just as easily pray at home. Can you give an explanation with scripture references that will help your friend? _____

    _____

    _____

    _____

3. Read Matthew 6:5-7 and Luke 18:1-8. Is persistent prayer the same as using "many words?" Can you keep going to God with the same prayer? _____

    _____

    _____

    _____

4. A friend at church has been suffering with chronic back pain. Do you have any advice regarding prayer? Give a scripture reference._____

    _____

    _____

    _____

Lesson Journal

Use this section to record your thoughts on the topics in this lesson.

_____

_____

_____

_____

_____

_____

_____

_____

_____

Lesson 24
The Importance of Belonging

Scripture Reading

- Matthew 16:13-19 (the church established) Matthew 28:19-20 (the great commission)

- Romans 12:6-8; Ephesians 4:11-12 and 1 Timothy 4:14 (church ministries)

- Titus 1:5-9 (local church leadership)

- Hebrews 10:24-25 (gathering together)

- Acts 20:8 and Hebrews 13:17 (submit to leaders)

- Acts 14:22, 15:30-32; 1 Corinthians 1:1-6; Colossians 2:6-7 and 1 Timothy 4:14 (confirmation)

Introduction

When Jesus walked the earth He talked about belonging to a kingdom, a kingdom where entrance is gained through a relationship with Him. Jesus and His disciples used word pictures to give examples of what it means to belong: a member of a body, a sheep in a flock, the bride of a husband, and many others. These are illustrations of the Church of Jesus Christ, a universal body of believers. After Jesus resurrected, His Church grew as the apostles began preaching and teaching about Him. As believers were added, the apostles established regional or local bodies: the local church.

A local church is a community of believers structured and governed in accordance with New Testament principles and practices. It is a place where fellow believers meet regularly to worship and *"grow in the grace and knowledge of our Lord and Savior Jesus Christ,"* (2 Peter 3:18), and where new believers are established and strengthened, or confirmed. The New Testament speaks of the churches at Jerusalem, Corinth, Ephesus, Thessalonica, Antioch, Smyrna, Pergamum, Thyatira, Sardis, Philadelphia, Laodicea, and others, all examples of communities that formed local churches.

The apostle's writings gave instruction on the form of leadership these churches were to have, with ample evidence that local church leaders—pastors, elders and deacons—were to be recognized, challenged, trained, and publicly placed in areas of responsibility. Acts 20 speaks of their responsibilities as gatekeepers, feeding and guarding the flock, and establishing sound doctrine. As a Christian we have a place to belong. The Bible is clear on the benefits of belonging to a community of Christians, a local church: to learn and grow, worship, pray, fellowship, serve, while in submission to the leaders for spiritual guidance and discipline.

1. What is the Church?

The Church is people, a universal body of believers in Jesus Christ, comprised of many groups of believers (local churches) structured and governed in accordance with New Testament principles and practices. Jesus taught about the establishment of a Church when He said to Peter, *"I also say to you that you are Peter, and upon this rock I will build My church; and the gates of Hades will not overpower it,"* (Matthew 16:18).

The apostle Paul described the New Covenant Church as the Body of Christ, of which Jesus Christ is the head (Romans 12:5; 1 Corinthians 12:12; Ephesians 1:22-23 and Colossians 1:24). With this analogy Paul emphasizes both the unity of the body and the individuality of each particular member. That Jesus Christ is the Head of the body suggests that it is our Lord who directs and guides the body, and that its unity comes from the Head of the body, who coordinates and directs each individual part. It also stresses the connectedness of each individual part, with no isolated or disconnected members of a body.

There are other descriptions and analogies of what the Church is, including:

- **The Temple or House of God**

  1 Corinthians 3:16; Ephesians 2:19 and 1 Peter 2:5

- **The Bride of Christ**

  2 Corinthians 11:2; Ephesians 5:22 and Revelation 19:7, 22:17

- **The Flock of God**.

  John 10:1-18; Acts 20:28 and 1 Peter 5:2

All of these pictures, and others also in the New Testament, show that Jesus Christ is the head of the Church and has a relationship with the Church, as well as each individual believer.

The above illustrations show that believers are not to be isolated, but are part of a family and fellowship designed by God. Christians have been called out of sin and worldly ways to follow Jesus Christ in unity. In the New Testament, the word church comes from the Greek *ekklēsi*, literally *to call from out of*.[1] Depending on the context, church can refer to the whole body of believers throughout the earth, or a gathering of citizens called out from their homes into some public place to form an assembly (a local church).

---

[1] *Thayer's Greek Definitions*, Electronic Edition STEP Files, 1999, Findex.com, Inc.

Romans 12:5 NIV
...so in Christ we who are many form one body, and each member belongs to all the others.

1 Corinthians 12:12
For as the body is one, and hath many members, and all the members of that one body, being many, are one body: so also is Christ.

Ephesians 1:22-23 NIV
And God placed all things under (Jesus) feet and appointed him to be head over everything for the church, which is his body...

Colossians 1:24 NIV
...for the sake of his body, which is the church.

1 Corinthians 3:16
Know ye not that ye are the temple of God...

Ephesians 2:19
Now therefore ye are no more strangers and foreigners, but fellowcitizens with the saints, and of the household of God.

1 Peter 2:5 NIV
you also, like living stones, are being built into a spiritual house...

2 Corinthians 11:2 NIV
I promised you to one husband, to Christ...

Ephesians 5:22 NIV
For the husband is the head of the wife as Christ is the head of the church...

Revelation 19:7
for the marriage of the Lamb is come, and his wife hath made herself ready...

Revelation 22:17
And the Spirit and the bride say, Come.

John 10:14, 16 NIV
I am the good shepherd; I know my sheep and my sheep know me... They too will listen to my voice, and there shall be one flock and one shepherd.

Acts 20:28 NIV
Keep watch over yourselves and all the flock of which the Holy Spirit has made you overseers. Be shepherds of the church of God, which he bought with his own blood.

1 Peter 5:2
Feed the flock of God which is among you...

2. What is a local church?

A local church is a community of believers built up and governed according to the New Testament that regularly come together to worship and *"grow in the grace and knowledge of our Lord and Savior Jesus Christ,"* (2 Peter 3:18). The New Testament speaks of the churches at Jerusalem, Corinth, Ephesus, Thessalonica, Antioch, Smyrna, Pergamum, Thyatira, Sardis, Philadelphia, Laodicea, and others. These are examples of communities of believers that formed local churches (Ephesians 4:16).

Ephesians 4:16
...from whom the whole body, being fitted and held together by what every joint supplies, according to the proper working of each individual part, causes the growth of the body for the building up of itself in love.

3. What is the purpose of a local church?

The primary purpose of a local church is to add to the Body of Christ through effective witnessing, preaching, and teaching. As people come into a relationship with Jesus Christ the community of the local church grows, as does the universal Church. Each believer serves a purpose in the local church. As a believer grows in the grace and knowledge of our Lord Jesus Christ, his purpose will become evident and mature. Whether a new Christian or mature believer, each one can participate in an area of purpose:

- **Witness**: Jesus commissioned his disciples to witness to their community, the region and the world, and this remains a primary purpose of the local church (Acts 2:40-41 and Acts 13:30).

- **Make disciples**: Jesus instructed his followers to make disciples of those that heard and believed their witness of Him. Disciple and discipline come from the same Latin word *discipulus*, meaning pupil (student). A disciple is one who accepts and assists in spreading the doctrines of another.[2] To accept a doctrine, one must first be taught, or disciplined, as discipline means to train or develop by instruction and exercise.[3] A disciple of Christ then is one that accepts and is trained and developed in His doctrines. Every believer in a local church can contribute to the discipleship of others (Matthew 28:19-20).

- **Equip believers**: Learning about and growing in Jesus Christ is an ongoing lifelong process. Jesus established leadership functions in the church for preaching, teaching, and the ongoing equipping of believers (Ephesians 4:11-12).

Acts 2:40-41
With many other words [Peter] warned them; and he pleaded with them, "Save yourselves from this corrupt generation." Those who accepted his message were baptized, and about three thousand were added to their number that day.

Acts 13:30 NKJV
He was seen for many days by those who came up with Him from Galilee to Jerusalem, who are His witnesses to the people.

Matthew 28:19-20 NKJV
Go therefore and make disciples of all the nations, baptizing them in the name of the Father and of the Son and of the Holy Spirit, teaching them to observe all things that I have commanded you.

Ephesians 4:11-12 NKJV
And He Himself gave some to be apostles, some prophets, some evangelists, and some pastors and teachers, for the equipping of the saints for the work of ministry, for the edifying of the body of Christ.

---

[2] *Merriam-Webster's Collegiate Dictionary, Eleventh Edition*, Merriam-Webster, Inc., 2004.
[3] Ibid

Hebrews 13:15-16 NIV
Through Jesus, therefore, let us continually offer to God a sacrifice of praise–the fruit of lips that confess his name. And do not forget to do good and to share with others, for with such sacrifices God is pleased.

1 Timothy 2:1 NIV
I urge, then, first of all, that requests, prayers, intercession and thanksgiving be made for everyone.

Galatians 6:2 NIV
Carry each other's burdens, and in this way you will fulfill the law of Christ.

Hebrews 10:25 NIV
Let us not give up meeting together, as some are in the habit of doing, but let us encourage one another–and all the more as you see the Day approaching.

Philippians 4:3
And I urge you also, true companion, help these women who labored with me in the gospel, with Clement also, and the rest of my fellow workers, whose names are in the Book of Life.

Titus 2:15
These things speak, and exhort, and rebuke with all authority. Let no man despise thee.

- **Worship**: Worship is both personal and individual, and corporate as a community. A local church serves as a gathering place for Christians to come together to offer up their praise and thanksgiving to God in one accord (Hebrews 13:15-16).

- **Prayer**: Prayer like worship can be both personal and corporate. Jesus, in a discussion about disagreements brought before the church, said, *"I say unto you, That if two of you shall agree on earth as touching any thing that they shall ask, it shall be done for them of my Father which is in heaven. For where two or three are gathered together in my name, there am I in the midst of them,"* (Matthew 18:19-20). Jesus speaks of unity (agreement) in bringing petitions before God in Jesus' name. Being active in a local church means praying in concert with other believers, and lifting up the needs of others (1 Timothy 2:1 and Galatians 6:2; see also Acts 21:5 and 1 Thessalonians 5:25).

- **Fellowship**: Fellowship means community, and the local church serves as a place for people of all walks of life to be unified in their faith in Jesus building each other up (Hebrews 10:25).

- **Serve**: A local church provides a focal point for serving others within the community. Life situations are always changing, as are the needs within the group. As one needs, another serves. From visiting the sick and shut-ins, providing food, clothes, mentoring, etc., opportunities to serve are always present. Those being served learn to serve others. A local church also provides opportunity to grow and serve in areas of ministry from evangelizing the lost to teaching while under the direction of the church leadership (Philippians 4:3; see also Romans 12: 6-8).

- **Judge spiritual matters**: Judging spiritual matters and disputes among believers is the purpose of local church leaders (Titus 2:15).

4. Who's in charge of a local church?

The government of a local church varies, as there are various interpretations of God's Word on how to structure a local church. By examining the Bible and considering the early church set in place by the apostles as described in Acts 15, the following pattern for local church government emerges:

- Leadership of a presiding elder called a pastor (Greek *poimhvn* meaning shepherd) (Ephesians 4:11-12).

- Multiple supporting elders and deacons (a presbytery) who work as overseers in unity with their spiritual leader, the pastor (1 Timothy 4:14; Acts 20:17 and Acts 21:18; see also 1 Timothy 5:17 and Philippians 1:1).

- A community of Christians from all walks of life and with various spiritual maturity (a congregation) united in growing in the grace and knowledge of our Lord Jesus Christ (Acts 15:30).

5. How do pastors and elders get their authority?

God establishes local church authority. The Bible says that all power comes from God and this includes government on all levels. This includes local church authority. Jesus taught his apostles and disciples for three years and granted them authority to establish His Church. They in turn established local churches, ordaining proven leaders after prayer and the guidance of the Holy Spirit (Romans 12:6, 8; see also Romans 13:1-2 and Titus 2:15).

Leaders are put in place the same way today. 1 Timothy 3 and Titus 1 outline the qualifications for local church elders:

- **Spiritual**: An elder exhibits leadership qualities and behavior that is blameless, mature, and exemplary. They are full of the Holy Spirit, faith, wisdom, and sound judgment.

- **Character**: An elder displays the fruit of the Spirit, being above reproach, self-controlled, not given to any addictive behaviors, not self-willed or quick-tempered, and honest in all dealings.

- **Domestic**: The home life of an elder is to be an example to the local church community. A married elder is to maintain an exemplary marriage and all minor children are to be kept under parental authority.

- **Ministerial**: Elders are to be able to teach and gather people into the Kingdom of God. They are not new Christians, but faithful believers that have proven their devotion to Christ and know the Scriptures (Titus 1:5-9).

Ephesians 4:11-12 NKJV
And He Himself gave some to be apostles, some prophets, some evangelists, and some pastors and teachers, for the equipping of the saints for the work of ministry, for the edifying of the body of Christ.

1 Timothy 4:14 NASB
Do not neglect the spiritual gift within you, which was bestowed on you through prophetic utterance with the laying on of hands by the presbytery.

Acts 20:17
And from Miletus he sent to Ephesus, and called the elders of the church.

Acts 21:18
And the day following Paul went in with us unto James; and all the elders were present.

Acts 15:30 NASB
So when they were sent away, they went down to Antioch; and having gathered the congregation together, they delivered the letter.

Romans 12:6,8 NIV
We have different gifts, according to the grace given us... if it is leadership, let him govern diligently.

Titus 1:5-9 NIV
The reason I left you in Crete was that you might straighten out what was left unfinished and appoint elders in every town, as I directed you. An elder must be blameless, the husband of but one wife, a man whose children believe and are not open to the charge of being wild and disobedient. Since an overseer is entrusted with God's work, he must be blameless–not overbearing, not quicktempered, not given to drunkenness, not violent, not pursuing dishonest gain. Rather he must be hospitable, one who loves what is good, who is selfcontrolled, upright, holy and disciplined. He must hold firmly to the trustworthy message as it has been taught, so that he can encourage others by sound doctrine and refute those who oppose it.

6. What is the job of local church leaders?

The New Testament gives ample evidence that in each local church, leaders were to be recognized, trained, challenged and publicly placed in areas of responsibility. Acts 20 relates that in the local church at Ephesus the leaders, called elders, were recognized as the guardians of the church with clear knowledge of their responsibility to take the oversight, feed the flock (congregation), guard the flock against false teaching and establish sound doctrine.

Church leaders must judge spiritual matters. In Matthew 18 Jesus gives instruction on how to take care of a dispute with another Christian. His instruction is to speak one-on-one, then if necessary with witnesses, and finally if required bring the matter to the church. The leaders of a local church must also judge the teaching and prophecies brought before the congregation to guard against deviation from sound doctrine and the Word of God.

The pastor and church leaders are responsible to God to care for the spiritual well being of all those who have submitted to their authority (Acts 20:28; Hebrews 13:17 and 1 Timothy 5:20; see also 1 Peter 5:2 and 2 Timothy 4:2).

7. What does it mean to submit to a local church?

A primary meaning of submit is to yield to governance or authority. Churches vary in their methods of acknowledging people as members of their flock, but it most often requires a voluntary act of submission, such as requesting to be recognized as part of the fold.

Submission to a local church is voluntary, but the act of submitting grants to the pastor and overseers the authority to be the Christian's spiritual guide. Hence it is not something to be taken lightly. As part of a local church a member is to follow the direction of the Pastor and the overseers, and follow the Biblical instructions for dealing with any matters that may require the counsel of the church leaders.

If a member desires to move to another congregation, the courtesy of a meeting with the current pastor should be scheduled. A pastor concerned for the congregation will want to be informed when a member moves on, and have the opportunity to pray with and bless the departing member (Hebrews 13:17 and 1 Timothy 5:19).

Acts 20:28
Take heed therefore unto yourselves, and to all the flock, over the which the Holy Ghost hath made you overseers, to feed the church of God, which he hath purchased with his own blood.

Hebrews 13:17 NIV
Obey your leaders and submit to their authority. They keep watch over you as men who must give an account.

1 Timothy 5:20 NIV
Those [elders] who sin are to be rebuked publicly, so that the others may take warning.

1 Timothy 5:19 NIV
Do not entertain an accusation against an elder unless it is brought by two or three witnesses.

8. I like my "TV church," must I belong to a local church?

Television, radio, and internet ministries serve a purpose, but they are not a local church. A television or radio audience cannot fellowship with one another; there is no real belonging. Messaging via the internet as part of a "virtual" church misses personal one-on-one Christian relationships. These types of ministries can be wonderful evangelism and teaching tools, but there is no oversight of the audience by the ministry.

The Bible is clear on the benefits of belonging to a community of Christians: to learn and grow, worship, pray, fellowship, serve, while in submission to the leaders for spiritual guidance and discipline (Hebrews 10:24-25). It is under the guidance of local church leaders that one is trained and confirmed in the faith.

Hebrews 10:24-25 NIV
And let us consider how we may spur one another on toward love and good deeds. Let us not give up meeting together, as some are in the habit of doing, but let us encourage one another–and all the more as you see the Day approaching.

9. What does it mean to be confirmed in the faith?

To be confirmed, or confirmation, is a sacrament administered by a local church elder to establish and strengthen the spiritual life of a growing Christian. The Greek words *episterizo* and *bebaioo*, which are translated confirmation and confirm, are synonyms which mean to establish, strengthen, and render more firm.

The sacrament of confirmation has both an outward sign and an inward work of grace. The outward sign is the laying on of hands of an elder while praying for the inward spiritual establishment and firming of a Christian believer.

10. Who should be confirmed?

Christian believers are to be confirmed. Biblical references note that believers---*the brethren, disciples, them that are sanctified in Christ Jesus, saints*—were confirmed (Acts 14:22; Acts 15:30-32 and 1 Corinthians 1:2-6).

Acts 14:22
...confirming the souls of the disciples...

Acts 15:30-32
So when they were dismissed, they came to Antioch: and when they had gathered the multitude together, they delivered the epistle: Which when they had read, they rejoiced for the consolation. And Judas and Silas, being prophets also themselves, exhorted the brethren with many words, and confirmed them.

1 Corinthians 1:2, 4, 6
Unto the church of God which is at Corinth, to them that are sanctified in Christ Jesus, called to be saints... I thank my God... Even as the testimony of Christ was confirmed in you.

11. When should one be confirmed?

Confirmation was first conducted by the apostles after the early churches outside of Jerusalem were established. In Acts 14 the evangelistic ministry of the apostles Barnabas and Paul is recorded. Following their initial church planting they returned to the new churches, *"confirming the souls of the disciples, and exhorting them to continue in the faith, and that we must, through much tribulation, enter into the kingdom of God,"* (Acts 14:22).

So confirmation follows after a Christian has had a time of learning and growing in Jesus Christ (Colossians 2:6-7). The Corinthian church that Paul visited is a good example of the process of coming to Christ, believing, being taught, and then confirmed. When Paul visited Corinth, *"many of the Corinthians when they heard were believing and being baptized… And Paul settled there a year and six months, teaching the word of God among them,"* (Acts 18:8, 11). The Corinthians believed in Jesus, were taught by Paul for over a year, and then were confirmed. When Paul wrote his first letter to the Corinthians he reminded them of their confirmation, saying, *"I thank my God always concerning you for the grace of God which was given you in Christ Jesus, that in everything you were enriched in Him, in all speech and all knowledge, even as the testimony concerning Christ was confirmed in you,"* (1 Corinthians 1:4-6 NASB).

12. How is confirmation administered?

Confirmation is accomplished through the laying on of hands of an elder or minister of the local church. The Bible refers to these church leaders as the presbytery (1 Timothy 4:14). It is through the laying on of hands and a prayer of faith that the inward work of strengthening and establishing of a believer is imparted by the Holy Spirit.

Colossians 2:6-7 NIV
So then, just as you received Christ Jesus as Lord, continue to live in him, rooted and built up in him, strengthened in the faith as you were taught, and overflowing with thankfulness.

1 Timothy 4:4
Neglect not the gift that is in thee, which was given thee by prophecy, with the laying on of the hands of the presbytery.

Study Questions

1. Your friend says, "I believe in God and Jesus, so I don't need to go to church." Can you give some Scripture to help this friend understand the local church? _____

   _____

   _____

   _____

   _____

   _____

2. "Why should I go to church when I can watch Christian TV?" asks a new Christian. Show this person why he needs to belong to a local church. _____

   _____

   _____

   _____

   _____

   _____

3. Read 1 Corinthians 1:1-6 and Colossians 2:6-7. Explain what should precede confirmation and the benefits of being confirmed. _____

   _____

   _____

   _____

   _____

   _____

Lesson Journal

Use this section to record your thoughts on the topics in this lesson.

_____

_____

_____

_____

_____

_____

Index

A

abortion 153
Abraham 56
    covenant 56
    covenant sign 57
adultery 144
anesthesia 5
angels 22
    appearance 24
    purpose 23
anger 150
    murder 151
anointing with oil 204
ark
    animals 50
    time to build 50
arrogance 167
ascension 102
authority 136, 211
    parental 137

B

baptism 95, 96
    Holy Spirit 106, 107
    infants 98
    water 95, 96
Bible 2
    anesthesia 5
    cannon 7
    dead sea scrolls 3, 10
    evaporation 4
    global earth 4
    inspired 4
    mesha stele 3
    moabite stone 3
    new testament 7
    old testament 6
    organization 5
    relevance 10
    rosetta stone 3
    testament 6
Bibles
    different 10
    english 10
body 184

C

cannon 7
children
    dedication 138
christian 124, 134
    false witness of 168
    family 134
    marriage 142
church
    local 209
    universal 208
circumcision 57, 96
    of heart 96
commandments
    first 115
communion 192, 193
    blessings 195
confirmation 213
covenant 43, 45
    Abraham 56
    Abraham sign 57
    blood 57
    David 60
    Moses 58
    new 86
    Noah 51
    Noah sign 51
covet 169
creation 30
    animals 33
    man 33
    order 31
    purpose 30
    time 31
    woman 33
credit card 170

D

David 60
    covenant 60
    throne 61
dead sea scrolls 3, 10
death
    christian 184
    unbeliever 185

debt.. 170
dedication of children............................ 138
disobedience 40
divorce 146

E

eighth commandment............................. 158
   blessing 162
   keeping 162
   purpose 159
elders.. 204
evaporation 4
evil 25
   influence in world 26
   satan 26

F

faith 203
fall of man 40
   consequences 41
false witness 167, 168
family 134
father
   honor 136
   responsibility...................................... 137
fellowship 210
fifth commandment 135
   blessing 138
   keeping 138
   purpose 135
first commandment
   blessing 116
   keeping 116
   purpose 115
flood 49
   global.. 50
   length 50
footwashing 176
   blessing 179
   Jesus... 177
   today 179
forgiveness 89, 94
fourth commandment.............................. 126
   blessing 129
   keeping 129
   purpose 126
fraud... 159, 170

G

gambling... 170
giving... 162
God 14
   attributes 15
   creation.. 30
   existence 16
   jealous.. 117
   names of 17
   revealed 16
   triune 14
   will.. 203
godhead 14
gossip 167

H

hades 185
hell 79, 185, 187
Holy Spirit 15, 30, 103, 108, 201
   baptism..................................... 106, 107
   coming 104
   pentecost 104
   prayer 201
   purpose 109
husband 134

I

idols... 18, 118
iniquity... 25, 117
Israel 57, 58, 59, 60, 61

J

Jesus............................... 15, 30, 43, 66, 67
   alive 84
   arrest 74
   ascension.. 102
   birth 68
   charges 75
   false witness of.................................... 168
   giving.. 162
   Holy Spirit 103
   in hell.. 79
   king 70
   ministry 69
   murder 151
   place of birth.. 67
   purpose 69
   redemption 43, 69

rest..128
resurrection...79, 84
sentance..78
significance...85
sinless...74
upbringing...68
virgin birth..67
judgement
rewards...187
judges 59
judgment 186
self..194
spiritual..210

K

kidnapping 160
kill 151

L

language..56
law...58, 59
laying on of hands 108, 138, 213, 214
local church
leaders 212
membership 212, 213
serving 210
Lord's supper 192
blessings...195
love 151
Lucifer 24
satan..25
lust 146
lying..165, 167, 168

M

man
body soul spirit 34
image of God 34
purpose...34
marriage..134, 142
mesha stele..3
moabite stone 3
Moses..58
covenant 58
mother
honor...136
responsibility 137
murder..151, 153

N

negligence 159
neighbor 151, 166
new covenant...86
new testament..7
organization 7
ninth commandment 166
blessing..168
keeping 168
purpose 166
Noah 49
covenant sign 51

O

obedience..137
offering 161
old testament 6
organization 6
ownership 158

P

passover...75, 192
pentecost 104
perjury 167
prayer...200, 210
alone 201
anointing with oil 204
answers 203
Holy Spirit 201
how..200
posture 202
repetitive..202
tongues 202
presumption 167
property..158

R

reconciliation 152
redemption...69
repentance 86, 88, 94
necessity 87
resurrection 79, 80, 186
rewards 187
rosetta stone 3

S

sabbath	127
sacrament	94
confirmation	213
dedication of children	138
footwashing	176
Lord's supper	192
marriage	141, 142
water baptism	95
satan	25
saturday	127
second commandment	116
blessing	118
keeping	118
purpose	116
serving	210
seventh commandment	144
blessing	146
keeping	146
sex	143
adultery	144
sheol-hades	185
sin	24, 40, 44, 48, 59, 60, 74, 78, 84, 102, 143, 203
fall of man	41
fogiven	89
nature	96
sixth commandment	150
blessing	154
keeping	154
purpose	150
slander	167
slavery	160
soul	184
spirit	184
steal	159
stealing	
from God	160
steward	158
sunday	128

T

ten commandments	114
eighth	158
fifth	135
first	114
fourth	126
ninth	166
second	116
seventh	144
sixth	150
tenth	169
third	124
worship	114
tenth commandment	169
blessing	171
keeping	171
purpose	169
testament	6
third commandment	124
blessing	126
purpose	124
tithe	160, 161
tongues	104, 106
pray	202
tower of Babel	52
trinity	14

U

unjust gain	159

W

wife	134
will of God	203
woman	
body soul spirit	34
image of God	34
purpose	34
worship	114, 115, 118, 128, 210

Index of Scripture

Genesis

Genesis 1:1 30
Genesis 1:1-3 31
Genesis 1:2 .... 15, 30
Genesis 1:3 31
Genesis 1:6 31
Genesis 1:7 32
Genesis 1:9 31
Genesis 1:9, 11 32
Genesis 1:11 31
Genesis 1:14, 16 32
Genesis 1:20 31
Genesis 1:20, 22 32
Genesis 1:24 31
Genesis 1:24, 26-27 32
Genesis 1:24-28 33
Genesis 1:26 31
Genesis 1:27, 31 40
Genesis 1:28-29 34
Genesis 2:2 32
Genesis 2:7 35
Genesis 2:8-9 40
Genesis 2:15-17 33
Genesis 2:16-17 .... 34, 40
Genesis 2:18 134
Genesis 2:18, 24 144
Genesis 2:20-23 33
Genesis 2:21 .... 5, 29
Genesis 2:23-24 33
Genesis 3:2-3 35
Genesis 3:5 126
Genesis 3:6 40
Genesis 3:7-19 41
Genesis 3:8-10 35
Genesis 3:14-15 67
Genesis 3:15 .... 43, 96
Genesis 3:20 33
Genesis 3:21 41
Genesis 3:24 23
Genesis 4:3-5, 8 48
Genesis 4:4 50
Genesis 4:5-6, 8 151
Genesis 4:25-26 48
Genesis 4:26 126
Genesis 6:5, 11-12 48

Genesis 6:5, 12 25
Genesis 6:6-7 49
Genesis 6:8-9, 22 49
Genesis 6:15-16 50
Genesis 7:6 50
Genesis 7:11 51
Genesis 7:18-20 50
Genesis 8:13-16 50
Genesis 8:20 50
Genesis 9:3 51
Genesis 9:5-6 51
Genesis 9:8-11 51
Genesis 9:14-15 51
Genesis 11:1-2, 4 51
Genesis 11:4 52
Genesis 11:7-8 52
Genesis 12:1 134
Genesis 12:1-3 56
Genesis 12:6-7 56
Genesis 15:5 56
Genesis 15:9-10, 17-18 56
Genesis 16:7 23
Genesis 17:1 15
Genesis 17:5 56
Genesis 17:10-14 57
Genesis 17:11-12 97
Genesis 18:3-4 176
Genesis 21:4 97
Genesis 22:18 .... 57, 67
Genesis 28:22 161
Genesis 43:24 176
Genesis 44:16 25

Exodus

Exodus 1:1 134
Exodus 1:18-20 168
Exodus 3:2 16
Exodus 3:14-15 18
Exodus 6:2 18
Exodus 12:14 193
Exodus 13:21 16
Exodus 19:5-6 .... 58, 146
Exodus 20:1-2 114
Exodus 20:3 115
Exodus 20:4 116
Exodus 20:7 126

Exodus 20:8-11 126
Exodus 20:11 31
Exodus 20:12 135
Exodus 20:13 150
Exodus 20:14 144
Exodus 20:15 158
Exodus 20:16 166
Exodus 20:17 169
Exodus 21:16 160
Exodus 22:16-17 145
Exodus 23:16 102
Exodus 23:23 23
Exodus 25:18 118
Exodus 26:31 118
Exodus 29:7 204
Exodus 31:3 35
Exodus 31:3-5 118
Exodus 34:7 59
Exodus 35:2 129
Exodus 40:34 17

Leviticus

Leviticus 12:7-8 68
Leviticus 18:20 144
Leviticus 18:22 145
Leviticus 18:23-30 145
Leviticus 19:11 159
Leviticus 19:13 159
Leviticus 19:16 167
Leviticus 19:17-18 ...... 152, 154
Leviticus 19:26 117
Leviticus 19:35-36 159
Leviticus 20:12 145
Leviticus 23:3-7 127
Leviticus 23:15-16 102
Leviticus 25:55 58
Leviticus 26:3, 12 58
Leviticus 26:12 55

Numbers

Numbers 11:17 35
Numbers 14:11 58
Numbers 35:30-31 153

Deuteronomy

Deuteronomy 4:40 138
Deuteronomy 5:15 127
Deuteronomy 5:16 ...... 136, 138

Deuteronomy 5:17 150
Deuteronomy 5:18 ...... 144, 145
Deuteronomy 5:19 159
Deuteronomy 5:20 166
Deuteronomy 5:21 169
Deuteronomy 5:29 138
Deuteronomy 5:33 ...... 136, 138
Deuteronomy 6:4 18
Deuteronomy 6:13-14 ...... 118, 125
Deuteronomy 10:12-16 97
Deuteronomy 11:13-16 115
Deuteronomy 11:18-21 137
Deuteronomy 18:14 117
Deuteronomy 19:4 153
Deuteronomy 19:15 ...... 152, 153
Deuteronomy 22:1-4 159
Deuteronomy 22:5 145
Deuteronomy 22:23-29 145
Deuteronomy 24:7 160
Deuteronomy 24:16 42
Deuteronomy 27:15 118
Deuteronomy 27:20-23 145
Deuteronomy 30:16 97
Deuteronomy 32:46-47 137

Joshua

Joshua 2:4-5 168
Joshua 7:21 169
Joshua 22:17 25
Joshua 24:2 56

Judges

Judges 6:11 23
Judges 7:15 119
Judges 8:22-23 59
Judges 21:25 59

1 Samuel

1 Samuel 3:14 25
1 Samuel 8:5-7 59
1 Samuel 10:1 59
1 Samuel 13:14 59
1 Samuel 25:41 176

1 Kings

1 Kings 6:21, 28 118
1 Kings 8:7 24
1 Kings 8:11 17

2 Kings

2 Kings 19:35 23

1 Chronicles

1 Chronicles 17:7-15 60
1 Chronicles 29:6-7 161
1 Chronicles 29:10 15
1 Chronicles 29:11 200

2 Chronicles

2 Chronicles 7:14 86
2 Chronicles 20:18 119
2 Chronicles 20:26 119

Ezra

Ezra 1:4 161
Ezra 9:6 25

Job

Job 1:7 26
Job 2:2 26
Job 12:9-10 153
Job 14:14 186
Job 14:14-15 183
Job 19:25, 27 183
Job 26:7 29
Job 32:8 35
Job 33:4 .... 15, 30, 103
Job 36:27-28 4
Job 38:1 30
Job 38:4-7 .... 22, 30
Job 42:1-6 88

Psalms

Psalm 14:1 87
Psalm 19:1 16
Psalm 22:1 66
Psalm 22:3 119
Psalm 22:7-8 66
Psalm 22:14 66
Psalm 22:16 66
Psalm 22:17 66
Psalm 22:18 66
Psalm 24:1 158
Psalm 31:5 66
Psalm 34:20 66
Psalm 35:11 66
Psalm 38:11 66

Psalm 40:12 87
Psalm 41:9 66
Psalm 47:10 120
Psalm 51:1-4, 10 88
Psalm 51:3-4 86
Psalm 51:10, 15 202
Psalm 51:12 15
Psalm 51:17 .... 115, 202
Psalm 66:18 203
Psalm 69:4 66
Psalm 69:21 66
Psalm 69:21 66
Psalm 78:21-22 58
Psalm 82:1-2, 6-7 187
Psalm 89:26 15
Psalm 90:2 15
Psalm 95:6 202
Psalm 96:8-9 120
Psalm 98:4-6 120
Psalm 100:1-2, 4 200
Psalm 100:4 119
Psalm 103:20-21 23
Psalm 109:8 102
Psalm 109:24 66
Psalm 109:25 66
Psalm 115:4-8 18
Psalm 119:11 .... 10, 26
Psalm 123:1 202
Psalm 127:3 134
Psalm 133:2 204
Psalm 134:2 119
Psalm 139:7-10 15
Psalm 139:13-14 153
Psalm 145:10-13 200
Psalm 148:2 23
Psalm 150 120

Proverbs

Proverbs 2:22 160
Proverbs 3:9-10 161
Proverbs 6:32 145
Proverbs 10:2 159
Proverbs 10:4 158
Proverbs 10:18 167
Proverbs 11:1 159
Proverbs 11:13 167
Proverbs 17:27 35
Proverbs 19:9 167
Proverbs 21:25 158

Proverbs 22:1 168
Proverbs 22:6 137
Proverbs 24:12 187
Proverbs 25:23 167
Proverbs 28:9 203
Proverbs 30:4 17
Proverbs 30:8 200

Ecclesiastes

Ecclesiastes 11:5 153

Song of Solomon

Song of Solomon 2:4 15

Isaiah

Isaiah 6:2 .... 22, 24
Isaiah 6:2-3 119
Isaiah 7:14 67
Isaiah 9:6-7 .... 61, 70
Isaiah 14:12 .... 25, 26
Isaiah 14:12-15 24
Isaiah 29:13 115
Isaiah 40:8 10
Isaiah 40:22 4
Isaiah 42:1, 6, 9 85
Isaiah 44:2 153
Isaiah 45:21 115
Isaiah 50:6 66
Isaiah 53:3 66
Isaiah 53:5 66
Isaiah 53:7 66
Isaiah 53:9 66
Isaiah 53:12 66
Isaiah 54:5 143
Isaiah 55:3 85
Isaiah 55:3-4 4
Isaiah 55:11 10
Isaiah 55:12 120
Isaiah 59:2 203
Isaiah 59:21 .... 15, 103
Isaiah 64:8 .... 15, 30
Isaiah 66:2 115
Isaiah 66:22-23 129

Jeremiah

Jeremiah 4:4 97
Jeremiah 5:7 145
Jeremiah 10:10-11 14

Jeremiah 13:10 14
Jeremiah 31:29-30 42
Jeremiah 31:31 4
Jeremiah 31:31-32 85
Jeremiah 31:31-34 43
Jeremiah 31:32 143
Jeremiah 31:34 .... 65, 67

Lamentations

Lamentations 3:25-27 138
Lamentations 4:13 25

Ezekiel

Ezekiel 10:20-21 22
Ezekiel 16:59-60 85
Ezekiel 18:20 42
Ezekiel 20:16 127
Ezekiel 22:29 160
Ezekiel 23:37 144
Ezekiel 28:12-17 24
Ezekiel 28:15, 18 25
Ezekiel 28:17 25

Daniel

Daniel 2:3 35
Daniel 5:12 35
Daniel 5:14 15
Daniel 6:22 23
Daniel 7:9-10 186
Daniel 10:6 24

Amos

Amos 8:4-8 160
Amos 8:9 66

Micah

Micah 2:2 169
Micah 5:1 66
Micah 5:1-2 15
Micah 5:2 67
Micah 6:8 115

Habakkuk

Habakkuk 2:4 88
Habakkuk 2:18-19 118

Zechariah

Zechariah 8:16-17 167

Zechariah 11:12 66
Zechariah 11:13 66
Zechariah 12:1 35
Zechariah 12:10 66
Zechariah 13:7 66

Malachi

Malachi 2:10 ....15, 30
Malachi 3:6 15
Malachi 3:8-12 161
Malachi 3:8-9 160
Malachi 3:16-18 126
Malachi 4:6 9

Matthew

Matthew 1:21 15
Matthew 1:22 67
Matthew 2:1-2 68
Matthew 2:2 74
Matthew 2:5-6 67
Matthew 2:13 23
Matthew 2:16 ....68, 74
Matthew 3:8 86
Matthew 4:11 23
Matthew 4:17 86
Matthew 4:4 10
Matthew 5:12 187
Matthew 5:17-18 114
Matthew 5:21-22 150
Matthew 5:23-24 203
Matthew 5:23-25 151
Matthew 5:27-28 144,146
Matthew 5:31-32 146
Matthew 5:37 125
Matthew 5:45 ....15, 30
Matthew 6:1-4 162
Matthew 6:5 201
Matthew 6:5, 7 202
Matthew 6:6 201
Matthew 6:9 ....15, 125
Matthew 6:9-13 200
Matthew 6:15 203
Matthew 6:19-21 ....166, 187
Matthew 8:22 42
Matthew 9:2 89
Matthew 10:4 66
Matthew 10:36 134
Matthew 11:28-30 128
Matthew 12:14 74

Matthew 12:24 167
Matthew 13:55 68
Matthew 14:23 201
Matthew 14:31 203
Matthew 15:3-6 136
Matthew 15:3-9 124
Matthew 15:18-19 ....144, 150
Matthew 16:18 208
Matthew 16:26 158
Matthew 17:20 203
Matthew 18:10 23
Matthew 18:15-17 152
Matthew 18:19-20 ....201, 210
Matthew 18:21-22 152
Matthew 19:4-6 142
Matthew 19:9 146
Matthew 19:17 138
Matthew 20:24 175
Matthew 20:28 44
Matthew 21:6-13 75
Matthew 23:23 162
Matthew 24:37-39 48
Matthew 24:46-47 187
Matthew 25:30 185
Matthew 25:31 22
Matthew 25:41 185
Matthew 25:44-45 87
Matthew 25:44-46 195
Matthew 26:15 66
Matthew 26:39 203
Matthew 26:39, 42 200
Matthew 26:57, 59-61, 63-66 76
Matthew 26:59-61 66
Matthew 26:67 66
Matthew 26:69-74 168
Matthew 27:5 66
Matthew 27:7 66
Matthew 27:12-19 66
Matthew 27:26 66
Matthew 27-30 69
Matthew 27:31 66
Matthew 27:34 66
Matthew 27:38 66
Matthew 27:39 66
Matthew 27:45 66
Matthew 27:46 66
Matthew 27:57-60 66
Matthew 27:65-66 79
Matthew 28:11-13 79

Matthew 28:3...24
Matthew 28:18...15
Matthew 28:18-20 95
Matthew 28:19...14
Matthew 28:19-20 ....69, 93, 209
Matthew 28:20...15

Mark

Mark 1:14-18..69
Mark 2:27-28..128
Mark 6:12-13..204
Mark 9:34..175
Mark 10:7-8..142
Mark 10:9..142
Mark 10:35, 37-39, 41-45 177
Mark 10:41...175
Mark 10:44...178
Mark 10:45..44
Mark 11:25...200
Mark 12:26-27...184
Mark 12:29-31...151
Mark 12:30...116
Mark 12:41-44...161
Mark 14:50..66
Mark 15:1-5...76
Mark 15:6-14..77
Mark 15:33-39...78
Mark 16:4-6...79
Mark 16:19..84

Luke

Luke 1:19..22
Luke 1:26-27..68
Luke 1:34-35..67
Luke 1:47..35
Luke 2:10-14..68
Luke 2:22, 24...68
Luke 2:27-28, 33-34.......................................138
Luke 2:28-30..68
Luke 2:51..136
Luke 2:52..68
Luke 3:7-8, 10-14...95
Luke 4:4...60
Luke 4:18-19..69
Luke 4:21..69
Luke 4:28-30..74
Luke 6:38...162
Luke 7: 44, 48, 50..88
Luke 7:47, 50..176

Luke 7:50..89
Luke 9:46...175
Luke 10:33..204
Luke 10:37..152
Luke 11:4...200
Luke 11:13..108
Luke 12:15..160
Luke 12:27-28...158
Luke 12:42-44...158
Luke 12:42-46...186
Luke 16:13...117, 168
Luke 16:19-31...184
Luke 16:22-24...184, 185
Luke 17:21..200
Luke 18:1, 7..202
Luke 19:8-10...88
Luke 20:25..162
Luke 22:12..193
Luke 22:14-20...192
Luke 22:24...175, 177
Luke 22:26-27...176
Luke 22:40..200
Luke 22:43...23
Luke 22:66-71...76
Luke 22:70...76
Luke 23:2..76
Luke 23:6-12...77
Luke 23:26...66
Luke 23:33...66, 69
Luke 23:34...66
Luke 23:35...66
Luke 23:42-43...184
Luke 23:46...66
Luke 23:49...66
Luke 24:49..109

John

John 1:1...15
John 1:1-3...30
John 1:3...15, 30
John 1:4-5...15
John 1:10, 14..66
John 1:14..17
John 1:18..16
John 1:29..191, 192
John 1:30, 33...103
John 1:32..17
John 1:33...107
John 3:3, 6-7..42
John 3:8..201

John 3:16 44
John 3:36 138
John 4:23-24 119
John 4:24 ....16, 34, 202
John 4:34 200
John 5:7 15
John 5:24 43
John 5:28-29 186
John 6:44 16
John 7:5, 48 66
John 8:12 15
John 8:58-59 74
John 10:10 26
John 10:11 44
John 10:14, 16 208
John 11:25-26 80
John 11:41 202
John 11:41-48, 53 74
John 11:50 74
John 11:57 74
John 13:1 176
John 13:1-4 177
John 13:2, 10-11 178
John 13:4-5 179
John 13:14-15 179
John 13:14-16 178
John 13:17 179
John 13:34-35 178
John 13:35 179
John 13:38 178
John 14:16 103
John 14:26 103
John 15:25 66
John 15:26 103
John 16:7 103
John 16:23 84
John 16:30 15
John 18:12-14, 19-24 75
John 18:36 70
John 19:1-3, 19-22 77
John 19:12, 15 77
John 19:16-18 78
John 19:17 66
John 19:23-24 66
John 19:28 66
John 19:33 66
John 19:34 66
John 19:38-42 78
John 21:17 178

Acts

Acts 1:3-6, 8-9 84
Acts 1:4-5 106
Acts 1:5, 8 103
Acts 1:8 109
Acts 1:14 201
Acts 2:1-4, 14-18 102
Acts 2:1-4, 38 104
Acts 2:3-4 .... 17, 104
Acts 2:6 104
Acts 2:16-18 .... 104, 107
Acts 2:24, 41 79
Acts 2:25-36 61
Acts 2:30 70
Acts 2:37 94
Acts 2:37-38 86
Acts 2:37-39 95
Acts 2:38-39 .... 94, 107
Acts 2:39 104
Acts 2:40-41 209
Acts 2:41 94
Acts 2:42 201
Acts 5:3-4 .... 15, 103
Acts 5:29 137
Acts 7:8 97
Acts 8:14-16 .... 107, 108
Acts 8:14-17 105
Acts 8:14-18 104
Acts 9:17-18 .... 105, 107, 108
Acts 9:17-19 104
Acts 10:44-46 .... 105, 107
Acts 10:44-48 104
Acts 11:15-16 107
Acts 11:15-17 105
Acts 13:22-23 61
Acts 13:30 209
Acts 14:22 .... 213, 214
Acts 15:30 211
Acts 15:30-32 213
Acts 18:8 106
Acts 18:8, 11 214
Acts 18:8-11 104
Acts 19:1-7 .... 98, 104
Acts 19:4 95
Acts 19:5-6 106
Acts 19:1–5 108
Acts 19:19 117

Acts 20:7...128
Acts 20:17...211
Acts 20:28...208, 212
Acts 20:35...162
Acts 21:5...202
Acts 21:18...211

Romans

Romans 1:3..70
Romans 1:3-4...80
Romans 1:17...88
Romans 1:20...16
Romans 1:21-23..14
Romans 2:11..187
Romans 3:20-24..59
Romans 3:23...24, 42, 87
Romans 3:28...88
Romans 4:15...40
Romans 4:20-21..116
Romans 4:22-25..80
Romans 5:1-2..88
Romans 5:6-8..44
Romans 5:12..40, 42
Romans 5:15, 18-19..42
Romans 5:15-17..43
Romans 6:1-8..96
Romans 6:3-8..95
Romans 6:4..80
Romans 6:23..129
Romans 8:4..59
Romans 8:4-6..129
Romans 8:7..96
Romans 8:11...80
Romans 8:26-27..202
Romans 12:1...120, 125
Romans 12:5..208
Romans 12:6, 8..211
Romans 13:1.................................133, 135, 136
Romans 13:1, 3-4..153
Romans 13:1-6..136
Romans 13:7..159
Romans 13:9-10..154
Romans 14:11..202
Romans 14:23..88
Romans 15:19..15
Romans 15:30..15

1 Corinthians

1 Corinthians 1:2, 4, 6...213
1 Corinthians 1:4-6..214
1 Corinthians 1:7, 2:4..................................104, 106
1 Corinthians 2:11...15, 35
1 Corinthians 3:13-15..186
1 Corinthians 3:16..208
1 Corinthians 5:7-8..192, 194
1 Corinthians 6:16..143
1 Corinthians 6:18-20..146
1 Corinthians 6:19..119
1 Corinthians 7:15..146
1 Corinthians 8:4..18
1 Corinthians 8:4-6..14
1 Corinthians 10:13-14...26
1 Corinthians 10:15-17...195
1 Corinthians 10:17..193
1 Corinthians 11:11-12...135
1 Corinthians 11:16-30...194
1 Corinthians 11:24-25...193
1 Corinthians 11:25..85
1 Corinthians 11:31-32...194
1 Corinthians 12:2-4...185
1 Corinthians 12:7..108
1 Corinthians 12:12..35, 208
1 Corinthians 12:12-14...96
1 Corinthians 12:13..108
1 Corinthians 12:31..169
1 Corinthians 13:11..136
1 Corinthians 14:2, 15...................................108, 202
1 Corinthians 14:18-19...202
1 Corinthians 14:15, 26...120
1 Corinthians 14:39.......................................106, 202
1 Corinthians 15:3-6...79
1 Corinthians 15:6..84
1 Corinthians 15:14..79
1 Corinthians 15:35-38, 42.......................................184
1 Corinthians 15:52-53...186
1 Corinthians 15:54-55...186
1 Corinthians 11:26..193
1 Corinthians 11:30..194

2 Corinthians

2 Corinthians 3:6, 14...6
2 Corinthians 5:6-9..184
2 Corinthians 5:10..186
2 Corinthians 5:20..124
2 Corinthians 5:21..68
2 Corinthians 6:14..143

2 Corinthians 6:14-15 142
2 Corinthians 11:2 208
2 Corinthians 12:7 26
2 Corinthians 12:8-9 203

Galatians

Galatians 3:3 109
Galatians 3:11 88
Galatians 3:16 67
Galatians 3:24 10
Galatians 3:26-27 124
Galatians 3:28 ....135, 142
Galatians 4:6 200
Galatians 5:13-14 154
Galatians 5:16 109
Galatians 5:19-21 87
Galatians 5:22-23 ....101, 109, 151
Galatians 6:2 ....204, 210
Galatians 6:8 ....15, 103

Ephesians

Ephesians 1:22-23 208
Ephesians 2:1 43
Ephesians 2:1-3 42
Ephesians 2:19 208
Ephesians 2:19-22 119
Ephesians 3:14 200
Ephesians 4:6 15
Ephesians 4:8-10 ....79, 185
Ephesians 4:11-12 ....209, 211
Ephesians 4:15 152
Ephesians 4:16 209
Ephesians 4:26 150
Ephesians 4:28 162
Ephesians 5:3 ....143, 160, 169
Ephesians 5:3-5 87
Ephesians 5:5 115
Ephesians 5:19 120
Ephesians 5:21 142
Ephesians 5:21-25 134
Ephesians 5:25 ....15, 142
Ephesians 5:25, 27 143
Ephesians 5:31-33 142
Ephesians 6:1 ....136, 137
Ephesians 6:4 ....133, 137, 138
Ephesians 6:11, 13-18 26
Ephesians 6:12 26
Ephesians 6:18 ....108, 201

Philippians

Philippians 1:2 15
Philippians 2:4-7 66
Philippians 2:7-8 44
Philippians 2:12-13 30
Philippians 3:10-11 80
Philippians 4:3 210
Philippians 4:11-13 171
Philippians 4:15 161
Philippians 4:18 120

Colossians

Colossians 1:15 16
Colossians 1:15-16 22
Colossians 1:16 ....15, 30, 158
Colossians 1:24 208
Colossians 2:6-7 214
Colossians 2:9 ....14, 15
Colossians 2:11-12 97
Colossians 2:16-17 ....128, 129
Colossians 3:5 ....115, 169
Colossians 3:8-11 ....96, 97
Colossians 3:16 120
Colossians 3:17 126
Colossians 3:20 136

1 Thessalonians

1 Thessalonians 4:3-4 143
1 Thessalonians 4:14 80
1 Thessalonians 4:16-18 186
1 Thessalonians 5:23 34

2 Thessalonians

2 Thessalonians 2:13 15
2 Thessalonians 3:6-10 162

1 Timothy

1 Timothy 1:17 16
1 Timothy 2:1 210
1 Timothy 2:1, 8 202
1 Timothy 2:8 119
1 Timothy 2:14 40
1 Timothy 3:16 14
1 Timothy 4:4 214
1 Timothy 4:14 211
1 Timothy 5:10 176
1 Timothy 5:18 159
1 Timothy 5:19 212

1 Timothy 5:20 212
1 Timothy 6:9-11 170
1 Timothy 6:10 160

2 Timothy

2 Timothy 2:10 15
2 Timothy 2:19 .... 124, 125
2 Timothy 2:22 146
2 Timothy 3:2-5 117
2 Timothy 3:16 10
2 Timothy 4:6-8 187

Titus

Titus 1:5-9 211
Titus 2:11, 13-14 69
Titus 2:15 210
Titus 3:5 .... 42, 187
Titus 3:5-6 185

Hebrews

Hebrews 1:14 .... 22, 23
Hebrews 2:6-7 22
Hebrews 3:7-11 128
Hebrews 3:13, 4:7 128
Hebrews 3:16-19 58
Hebrews 4:3, 10-11 .... 123, 128
Hebrews 4:12 10
Hebrews 4:15 95
Hebrews 7:1 16
Hebrews 7:1-2 161
Hebrews 7:20 6
Hebrews 7:25 84
Hebrews 8:6, 10-11 85
Hebrews 8:12 89
Hebrews 9:12, 15-16 85
Hebrews 9:13-15 192
Hebrews 9:15-18 6
Hebrews 9:27 186
Hebrews 10:4 192
Hebrews 10:10-12 59
Hebrews 10:16-18 43
Hebrews 10:17 .... 65, 67
Hebrews 10:23-25 128
Hebrews 10:24-25 213
Hebrews 10:25 .... 119, 210
Hebrews 11:3 31
Hebrews 11:4 48
Hebrews 11:6 16

Hebrews 11:7 49
Hebrews 11:8-9 57
Hebrews 11:27-29 58
Hebrews 13:4 .... 87, 143, 145
Hebrews 13:5 .... 162, 171
Hebrews 13:8 15
Hebrews 13:15 119
Hebrews 13:15-16 210
Hebrews 13:17 212

James

James 1:6-7 203
James 1:14-15 145
James 1:14-15 146
James 1:15 .... 24, 87
James 1:26 168
James 1:26-27 125
James 2:25 168
James 2:26 184
James 4:1-2 150
James 4:3 203
James 4:4 96
James 4:7 26
James 4:17 .... 24, 87
James 5:14-15 204

1 Peter

1 Peter 1:18-19 69
1 Peter 2:2 10
1 Peter 2:5 208
1 Peter 3:7 203
1 Peter 3:20 49
1 Peter 3:22 22
1 Peter 4:6 42
1 Peter 5:2 208
1 Peter 5:8 26

2 Peter

2 Peter 2:5 .... 48, 49, 50
2 Peter 3:9 16
2 Peter 3:18 .... 207, 209

1 John

1 John 1:5 15
1 John 1:9 89
1 John 3:4 .... 24, 40, 87
1 John 3:11-12 48
1 John 3:15 .... 87, 152

1 John 3:16..44
1 John 3:17...159
1 John 3:20..15
1 John 3:24...114
1 John 4:7-8, 16..15
1 John 4:20-21...152
1 John 5:7...15, 30

2 John

2 John 1:3...15

Jude

Jude 1:6...22
Jude 1:9...22
Jude 1:20...201

Revelation

Revelation 1:8... 15
Revelation 1:18... 84
Revelation 3:8... 124
Revelation 4:11.. 30
Revelation 12:4, 9.. 26
Revelation 12:9.. 41
Revelation 14:19.. 23
Revelation 19:7... 208
Revelation 19:10... 118
Revelation 21:2... 143
Revelation 21:8... 186
Revelation 22:9... 118
Revelation 22:17... 208
Revelation 22:21.. 9

CPSIA information can be obtained
at www.ICGtesting.com
Printed in the USA
LVHW060030220220
647895LV00034B/774